DAVID NIVEN
The Man Behind
the Balloon

DAVID NIVEN

The Man Behind the Balloon

by Michael Munn

BOOKS

This book is for Coralie who watched her father
and David Niven play cricket.

First published in Great Britain in 2009 by
JR Books, 10 Greenland Street, London NW1 0ND

ISBN 978-1-906779-16-0

1 3 5 7 9 10 8 6 4 2

Printed by MPG Books, Bodmin, Cornwall

Contents

A Brief Foreword

All, like me, who enjoyed *The Moon's a Balloon* and *Bring on the Empty Horses* can still enjoy them as the most entertaining memoirs any actor – any *celebrity* – ever wrote. I think more than his films, those books are the main legacy David Niven left us. They are treasures and through them, so is he.

This is a very personal biography and so reveals more about myself than I would normally do – but only as much as you need to know or might care about. I can't be an objective author writing from a distance with this biography because I am a part of it. I couldn't write it any other way. It may not seem apparent from the outset, but David Niven would approve. It was, after all, his request that I write it.

CHAPTER I

—

In the Flesh

David Niven's appearance was diminished. He was 72 and looked 10 years older. But then, he was a dying man. Motor Neurone Disease was slowly wasting and taking him.

It was July 1982 and he'd come to London from his home on the Côte d'Azur to stay with Leslie and Eve Bricusse to watch Wimbledon on TV. I'd spoken to him earlier that day by telephone – his voice had sounded very slurred over the phone from the disease that was killing him – and he had said, 'I need to see you, Mike. And bring a tape recorder.'

So, of course, I went straight to London, found his Mayfair flat and was greeted by him more warmly than ever before. I had difficulty understanding some of what he said, but he was patient with me, showing that I had to be patient with him, and he took his time saying what he felt needed to be said. He told me he wouldn't speak a great deal because it frustrated him that he couldn't enunciate properly any more, but typical of him, he went on to talk as much as he ever did.

He said he had to refrain from laughing because he had lost control over his facial muscles and laughing simply made him hysterical with tears running down his face. 'My face becomes so contorted that I look like someone dying of laughter and crying in agony, so please, promise you won't make me laugh,' he said. Of course I promised him, and he proceeded to tell me about the bizarre treatments carried out by quacks on him that were so hilarious that we were soon both laughing. I saw what he meant by his face being contorted and how the tears flowed.

When he gained control of himself, he said, 'I'm sorry but I still have the need to laugh and make people laugh. I have had little talent as an actor, not much more as a writer, but I can tell a funny story, and I don't want to lose that single talent.'

He finally got around to the reason he had wanted to see me. He said, 'You're exactly what I need – a friend, an author and a priest.'

I was glad he thought of me as a friend. I was honoured that he thought of me, with just one book published, as an author. I was surprised that he should suddenly think of me as a priest. I was, at that time, an Elder in the Mormon Church. I had been for two years. I no longer believe what I did back then – and that's all that needs to be said about that. But my faith was important to him.

I asked him what I could do for him, and he said, 'I don't know how long I have to live. Maybe only months. I don't feel I want to meet my maker without having got a few things off my chest.'

I told him that I couldn't grant him absolution if that was what he was looking for, and that if he felt he needed forgiveness from God, then that was between him and his maker. He said in response, 'It's not finding absolution for my many sins I need from you.' He said that he hoped his autobiography *The Moon's a Balloon* would be the official record of his life but he had seen what they did to Errol Flynn with a biography that claimed he was a Nazi and a homosexual. He said, 'I don't want the same thing happening to me after I'm gone. I'm not a Nazi, I'm not a homosexual, I don't take drugs, but I'm sure they'll make something up about me. "Niven was born a woman. He took part in devil worship. David Niven killed JFK." I need to set the record straight, and I feel that if *you* know, then you'll be able to do two things for me.'

I asked him what those two things were.

He said, 'If anyone is going to write about me after I'm gone, I want it to be you. The other thing I'm going to need are your prayers.'

My immediate thoughts were that I felt hugely inadequate to meet the task of writing his biography, and I felt very humbled and privileged that he would ask me to pray for him. It was, in essence, his last confession.

I'd first set eyes upon David Niven, in the flesh, in 1970. And I mean, literally *in the flesh*. He'd opened the door to his suite at the Connaught Hotel in London wearing just a small towel around his waist, revealing surprisingly muscular legs and arms. I had somehow always thought of him as skinny. But he was, even at the age of 60, very well built.

'Do excuse me, gentlemen, I had to have a quick shower or I'd give off an awful pong. Been exercising, you see.' And with that he did a little weight lifting movement, too delicate and comical to be convincing. 'Pumping, you know,' he said with a grin.

The 'gentlemen' were me, just turned 18 years, and my boss, Ron Lee, managing director of Cinerama International Releasing Organisation which was distributing Niven's latest film, *The Statue*. Although it wasn't due for release until early 1971, Ron Lee thought that since Niven was in town for a few days, I should sit with him with my trusty reel to reel tape recorder and get a potted biography of him for publicity purposes. I was little more than a messenger boy and trainee junior publicist but Ron Lee was adamant that I should interview David Niven to produce a biography which, I realised long after, was never intended to be used but was one of Ron's numerous ploys to get me introduced to film stars and directors to satisfy my movie mania. David was in on the ploy too, agreeing to be interviewed by me but knowing it was never going to be used.

I became aware of movement within the suite and saw a half naked young lady tiptoeing around as she collected her clothing.

'She's the cleaner,' said Niven, deadpan. 'Only she makes more mess than she clears. Anyway, do come in, gentlemen.'

We stepped inside the suite and David disappeared into another room to get dressed. The girl was hurriedly getting into her clothes, completely unconcerned by our presence, and by the time David reappeared, buttoning his shirt, she was dressed and fully made-up and ready to go.

'I do hope you won't be late, darling,' he said to her.

'No, my audition won't be for another hour,' she said, and left. I have no idea if she passed her audition, but a few years later she became quite a well known actress. No, I won't name her.

I knew that Niven was married but having been in the film business for a year I was well aware that normal morals didn't apply.

Ron Lee presented Niven with a little present we had prepared. It was a framed sketch of him that I'd done in my spare time at my desk. I could draw, and did a number of sketches which Ron Lee used for publicity purposes, and when possible, he presented the originals to the subjects concerned. Niven appraised the sketch as though it were the best present he'd had in years. 'That's splendid. Really wonderful,' he said, his teeth flashing from his broad smile. 'It's a fine work. You know, I like to draw a bit. Yes, this is really very good.' It *was* good, actually.

'Coffee, I think,' he said, and he picked up the phone and ordered room service.

Ron Lee said he couldn't stay but assured David he was leaving him in my capable hands. My capable hands were shaking with nerves. I was anxious *and* I'd just seen a scantily dressed girl.

After Ron Lee left, and while we were waiting for coffee to arrive, David said, 'Well, young man, tell me about yourself.' I was supposed to be interviewing *him*, but for a few minutes at least, he wanted to know about me. I gave him an extremely brief biography of myself and what my job was at Cinerama, and what my hopes and dreams were. He told me, 'Never let anybody tell you that your dreams can't be realised. If I'd listened to people, I would never have become an actor.'

Back then, as now, my pleasure in meeting actors was because of my great admiration for their body of work or simply because of one or two of their films I particularly liked. I wasn't actually what you would call a fan of Niven's, and I found it difficult to name more than a handful of his films off the cuff, although, of course, I was very aware that he was a famous star. At the time I could only recall seeing him in *The Guns of Navarone* and *55 Days at Peking*. I had seen *The Charge of the Light Brigade* on television but couldn't remember him in it. But I had done my research and knew enough about him to be able to ask at least several reasonably intelligent questions.

I was to discover that I didn't need to ask too many questions. David loved to talk. And talk.

Within a matter of minutes I had formed my first impressions of David Niven. He was a randy fellow and didn't hide the fact. He had tremendous charm and a sense of humour. I hadn't realised he would be so funny. I knew I liked him, and he seemed to like me – perhaps because I had sketched a decent portrait of him. I was also about to discover what a first-rate story-teller he was. My first impressions never changed.

Between 1970 and 1982 I interviewed Niven seven times, and with each interview I learned more about him and, by pressing him further and harder, discovered the man behind his own myth. I also met with him often when he came to London on a social basis. Sometimes we had lunch, always on him, and I will always remember two memorable evenings out to dine with him and Ava Gardner. You learn a lot about people over dinner and lunch.

I also watched him at work just for the pleasure of it, seeing him filming in London and on studio sound stages. I love seeing actors at work. He made it look very easy.

I had learned from Ron Lee almost from my first day at Cinerama – my first day in the film business – to write down everything anyone said to me that I thought was of interest. I had remarkable recall when young and wrote down, at the earliest opportunity, just about everything any film star, director or writer ever said to me. For formal interviews I always used a tape recorder.

Those interviews and conversations make up the main body of this book. The interviews are of specific importance. The first, in 1970, was almost an abridged 'spoken word' recording of *The Moon's a Balloon*. When I met him in 1970 and got his life story over what turned out to be a period of three days, I didn't know that he was in the final stages of writing his famous autobiography, and the many funny stories he had told in that book were ones he repeated for my benefit as easily as if he were reciting the lyrics of a well known song, sung so many times that the words flowed without even the hint of a stumble.

The second interview in September 1975, when I had just started my journalistic career, was about his second book of memories and anecdotes, *Bring on the Empty Horses*. In 1976 I interviewed him on the set of *Candleshoe* at Pinewood Studios. The next year I interviewed him at the time of the paperback publication of *Bring on the Empty Horses*.

Interviews with Niven were always wonderful, hilarious experiences. He related his many funny anecdotes which seemed to change from one interview to the next, but he just wouldn't talk about films. He usually said, 'I never talk about my films. That's so boring,' and then he'd always launch into one of his funny and probably not altogether truthful stories.

But in 1978 I took him completely by surprise by telling him I didn't want to interview him ever again. It happened on the set of the World War II drama *A Man Called Intrepid* when he found me with his co-star Barbara Hershey engaged in conversation in a sound stage complete with sets but bereft of cast and crew as it was lunch time. He seemed his old perky self at first and said, 'Hello, old man, what brings you here?'

'I'm interviewing Barbara.'

'Not going to do one with me?' he asked jovially. Obviously he expected me to say I would.

'No,' I said, and his face changed. He actually looked shocked.

'Why ever not?' he asked.

'Because you won't tell me the things I really want to know.'

My response seemed to sink his spirits like a stone. I hadn't realised it but he was in something of a depression and I wasn't helping through what he perceived to be my lack of interest in him. But as a result of my frankness, he took me aside and after discussing the matter, he said that he would answer all of my questions if I interviewed him. So I agreed, and did two interviews with him, the first back at the Connaught Hotel that evening where he invited me for dinner, the second the next day back at the studio where I asked him if he would talk frankly about the war, something he had never done. But he did for me, partly, I think, because of the subject of the film he was making and also because I related some of the war stories director John Huston had told me.

I think he had always thought of me, like he did a lot of journalists, to be a private audience for him to entertain with his many hilarious and often outrageous anecdotes. One of his favourite journalists was Roddy Mann who also happened to be his good friend. Comparisons of the stories told to different journalists often revealed different versions. His intention was simply to improve on any one story to get the biggest laugh. 'I simply love making people laugh,' he said to me once. 'A day without laughing is a day wasted.'

Even when cornered and forced to tell a more honest version of humorous events, he still made me laugh. But, although he didn't seem to know it, Niven's real world was every bit as entertaining and rich and fascinating as the one he'd invented.

In 1979 I interviewed him when he was making *A Nightingale Sang in Berkeley Square*. Because he was always so bright and cheerful, I challenged him to talk about the things that really made him angry – I called it *Niv's Most Angry Interview Ever*, and intended to publish it in *Photoplay*. It resulted in the darkest interview I ever did with him. I decided to shelve it as I felt it wasn't the right time to reveal some of his darker moments in a fan magazine.

In 1982 came the last interview, done at his request, which proved to be the most revealing, shocking and emotional of all the interviews. It was a dying man's confession.

My first interview with him, in 1970, was by far the longest – it was spread over three days during which he told me the story of his life. On the first day, when I was alone with him in his suite, coffee arrived, I turned on my tape recorder, and we began.

CHAPTER 2

—

A Father and a Farce

According to my research material he was born in Scotland, so I began my interview with, 'You were born in Scotland,' which was hardly the most probing way to begin an interview, but it at least started at the beginning.

'Yes, old boy,' he said. 'At Kirriemuir. We moved to London after my father died in the Great War in 1915.'

In one sentence he had moved swiftly from mentioning his place of birth to talking about his father's death. I now realise he didn't want to dwell on his place of birth. And with good reason. He wasn't born in Scotland but in London and it was a source of embarrassment to him that he had been saying for years that he had been misleading everyone about his place of birth. In fact, he made no mention of his birthplace at all in *The Moon's a Balloon*, published a year after I first met him.

However, it was Niven himself who, in 1978, told me he was born in London. It slipped out over dinner at the Connaught Hotel, in a moment of reflection. He said, 'I do *love* London. I suppose one never stops loving one's first home.'

I said, 'I thought you were born in Scotland.'

Without missing a beat he replied, 'Oh, you don't want to believe all that old tosh. That's old, *old* studio publicity. They lied through their teeth. Thought it would make my life sound more interesting. Maybe it does. I don't know.'

I decided not to remind him that it was he who had told me that old tosh eight years earlier. It is true, however, that his early studio publicity played fast and loose with the facts of his life. They did with a good many film stars back in the 1930s.

'Sometimes even *I* can't tell which is real and which is studio tosh,' he said.

I think there was actually some truth in what he said about him not always knowing what was completely true, but he certainly benefited from playing fast and loose with the facts, making a fortune from writing the most entertaining autobiography ever penned by a Hollywood film star. David's greatest talent was telling a good story and not letting facts get in the way, so he had often talked happily of his Scottish ancestry. The truth was, his father was born in London, and his mother, who was half-French, in Wales.

He was born 1 March 1910 in Belgrave Mansions, in Grosvenor Gardens just around the corner from Victoria station. It's an area of London where many film and TV stars have lived, and over the years I've often been in the neighbourhood to visit actors either socially or to conduct interviews or discuss some other business.

For many years his place of birth had been given as Kirriemuir in Scotland. When he died, some obituaries named Scotland as his homeland. Even *The Macmillan International Film Encyclopaedia* still puts Kirriemuir as his birthplace.

I think it was Sheridan Morley who first revealed publicly that David was born in London when he wrote his excellent biography of Niven, *The Other Side of the Moon*, in 1985, but by then I already knew that. Sheridan told me once, 'I think David came to believe many of the fictions that either he or the studio came up with. He acted as though he wasn't sure where he was born, but I think he chose to gloss over that subject.'

When I asked David how his father died, he said, 'There was a battle with the Turks. My father was a second lieutenant in the Berkshire Yeomanry which went ashore at Sulva Bay in Turkey. The Turks had laid barbed wire in the sea, and there was machine gun fire as they tried to get ashore. Most of them were killed. My father's body was never found.'

He said that he heard the news of his father's death when his family was living at his father's house, Carswell Manor, in Berkshire. 'He was a landowner, you see,' David said. 'Before that we lived in Scotland – after I was born.' They did actually live in Scotland. 'We had all the trimmings; a butler, footmen, gamekeepers, maids. My father was rich when I was born, but he lost a good deal of his money backing the wrong horses. He had his own bookmaker too. So some of the land had to go. But he kept Carswell Manor. That's where I was, with my sister Grizel, when we heard the news our father had been killed.'

David's account can't be true because William Niven sold Carswell Manor in 1910 to help pay off debts he had run up. The family moved to a farm in Cirencester and then to Fairford Park in Gloucestershire by the time war broke out in 1914, and it was most likely there that David lived when the news came.

It doesn't really matter where David was when he heard of his father's death, and I don't think Niven was purposely lying. He was, after all, only five when the news came, and the family moved about a lot.

When I asked him if he could remember how he felt upon hearing of his father's death, he said, 'I don't think it made too much of an impression on me. I hadn't seen that much of him. Children were seen but not heard in those days. So I was little seen or heard by my father.'

In 1982, he told me, 'My father was not my father.'

That didn't so much as take me by surprise as shock me into silence for what was probably only several seconds but seemed like minutes. I said, 'What do you mean?'

'My father – my *real* father – was Thomas Platt. He'd long been in love with my mother.' Thomas Walter Comyn Platt was a Conservative politician.

David's mother was Henriette Degacher. She came from a long line of British military officers on her mother's side. Her grandfather had been a general, so had her great uncle. Her father had been a captain who fought in the Zulu wars.

She had given birth to three children before David was born; Joyce who was 10 years old when David was born, Henry [nicknamed Max], who was seven, and Grizel who was three. 'I don't know if they really were my father's children,' David said. 'I mean by that, if they were Thomas Comyn Platt's. I think Joyce and Max were William's. But they didn't look like Grizel and I. I always thought she and I looked like Thomas.' David had always referred to Thomas Platt as 'Uncle Tommy'.

'My mother wasn't completely unhappy when my father died,' David said. His feelings about his mother were often mixed. When he was a child he was convinced that she didn't care for him, and there were times in his life when he maintained that she didn't love him.

He said, 'She was very beautiful and quite unconcerned with me. I never saw a lot of her. Grizel and I were looked after by our governess. We had a wonderful lady called Whitty who loved us and brought us up. My mother was too busy, but what with I couldn't say. She didn't seem to do *anything*.

'If she was busy it was probably with lovers. She flirted outrageously and showed more attention to other men than she ever did to me.' David would often claim that he was brought up in near poverty. 'After my father was killed, he left everything, including his debts, to my mother. She was just able to afford a house in South Kensington [in London]. She had rather a merry crowd of young men about her, and Uncle Tommy was foremost among them. He got knighted [in 1922] and he hyphenated his last two names, so he became Sir Thomas Comyn-Platt. But we called him Uncle Tommy. He'd been around mother for many years and they got married.'

The wedding was in May 1917 at the House of Commons' own parish church St Margaret's, in the grounds of Westminster Abbey.

David remarked, 'Sir Thomas Comyn-Platt was not a stranger to my mother even when she was with my father.'

I asked him just how long Platt had been around Henrietta and he said, 'Since 1904, at least. He wrote love letters to her.'

'What makes you think he was your real father?' I asked.

'For a start, I look more like him than I ever did my father.'

'But have you proof?'

'My God, yes. He didn't like having me around, that's for certain. Grizel and I were a nuisance. She and I have always been close. Right from our childhood. Max was a fine chap, lots of fun, but he was off to join the Navy when Platt married my mother.

'I'm afraid I didn't care for Joyce. She was always telling Grizel and I what to do. She was the oldest and very bossy. I used to think my mother didn't like me because she once told me, "I wish you'd never been born."'

'She actually said that to you?' I asked.

'Just the once. I had got in her way and she said, "You are the only mistake Tommy and I ever made." I was eight and didn't understand what she meant at the time. It's as clear as crystal to me now.'

I asked him if he was sure that's what his mother had said, and he answered, 'I never forgot it. I didn't understand it when she said it, but I never forgot it. Grizel also believes he was our real father.

'He once said to me, the last time I spoke to him during the war, "I'm as proud of you as any father could be." I saw a look in his eye. It was the look of a proud father. Officially he was my stepfather. But a *real* father looks at you with a very different eye. And then he said, "You know our secret, don't you?" and I said, "That you're my father? Yes, I do." And he said, "I hope you understand why we could never tell anyone, what with my position as a Member of Parliament." I said I understood perfectly, and we parted on good terms.'

That was in contradiction to what he had written in *The Moon's a Balloon* when he maintained that he last saw Sir Thomas before he went off to

Hollywood and that there had been some unkind words from Comyn-Platt and they never saw each other again. All his life, David had kept up the pretence about the true nature of his relationship with Sir Thomas Comyn-Platt, but as he edged towards the final months of his life, David Niven was revealing the truth.

I asked him, at that time, if he thought William Niven had known. 'I have no idea,' he answered. 'I've often wondered that and I've talk to my sister about it. We just don't know. And it's something we agreed to keep to ourselves.'

'Then why are you telling me?' I asked.

'Because when I'm dead, and God knows how long Grizel will live for, no one will know, and somebody should. *You* should.'

'Why me?'

'Because, as I said, you're a friend, an author and a priest.' And then he added, 'But not necessarily in that order.'

He had been convinced as a child that his mother and Tommy had done their best to get him out from under their feet. 'I think I was rather badly behaved as a child,' he said. 'I wasn't into anything criminal. But I did run riot, which is why Tommy and my mother sent me to boarding school. They thought it would instil some discipline in me. It didn't, you know.'

He told me that his time at a private prep school in Worthing was 'one of the worst experiences of my life. The older boys and the masters there bullied the younger boys.' He talked of being whipped with wet towels by the older boys and being hung out of a window by a school master.

'I was terrible in most subjects,' he said. 'I was terribly bad at mathematics, and I was rebelling even though I was really scared.'

In 1979, during the 'angry interview', David told me, 'I had things done to me that were simply horrifying. Younger boys were often abused by boys who would do the most disgusting things. I mean, sexual things. I call them sadistic, not sexual. Sex is a pleasure. This wasn't pleasure. I felt that I would never forgive my mother and stepfather for sending me there.'

He got a terrible boil from bad food which became infected when the school matron cut it off with a pair of scissors and he ended up in hospital. His mother removed him from that school and placed him, in 1919, at Heatherdown, an expensive private school at Ascot, where, he said 'all the snobs went. But it was a good school with kindly masters and good food. I was happy there. My mother must have been up to her ears in debt but I suspect Uncle Tommy handed over some money for not just my schooling but for all of us. Max was at Dartmouth, and Grizel and I were both at boarding schools.'

David revealed that his mother wasn't so poor after all when I had lunch with him and actress Lynne Frederick in London in 1980. During a rather morbid conversation about inheritance – Lynne had just become a millionairess following the death of her husband Peter Sellers – David rather carelessly said, 'We were lucky because my mother had inherited quite a bit from my father and could afford to take care of us very well indeed.'

I told him, 'But you always said your mother was poor and you were always going without.'

He looked sheepish and said, 'Yes, I did say that. It's Flynn's fault.'

'Errol Flynn?' I asked.

'Yes! Him! One of the first things he said to me was, "Tell them a good sob story, sport. They'll love you the more for it." So my sob story was that my mother struggled with money. But she had done really well from the inheritance my father left her.' I reminded him that William Niven had lost a lot of money through bad debts, to which he replied, 'Oh, not all that much. There was plenty left for my mother, and there was also money from Uncle Tommy as well.'

In 1982 I remarked that it would have been natural for his real father, Sir Thomas Comyn-Platt, to have paid for his schooling.

'Yes, that's true,' was his response. 'But I never wanted to acknowledge that. It was very hard to accept that the man I always called Uncle Tommy was my father and was the one who forked out for my education.'

His mother was able to afford to buy a house at Bembridge on the Isle of Wight where the family spent summer holidays and where David discovered a love of sailing. Sir Thomas rarely joined them, preferring to stay in London where he owned a large house in Chelsea.

As a child, David was an attention seeker – something I think never changed. 'I was a clown at school,' David said. 'I was addicted to playing pranks, and it got me into a lot of trouble.'

There was the time when he stole a huge marrow from the nearby girls' school in an attempt to win a prize in the annual Flower Show for the best kept garden which each boy had. He told me, 'I didn't win but I did get the cane for stealing.'

'How did you get found out?' I asked.

'Probably because some snitch couldn't keep his mouth shut. You see, I didn't keep my pranks a secret. I did them to entertain the other boys. By then I'd discovered that by making the other boys laugh, I became popular, and I admit that I wanted to be liked. Well, don't we all? I was liked because I made them laugh. I think they laughed more when I got caught and caned. The pain seemed worth the admiration I received. I think, to be truthful, that it was like an addiction. I still have it. I *must* be the centre of attention. I love making people laugh.

'When I arrived [at Heatherdown], I thought all the other boys were frightful because they were such snobs. I think they all went on to Eton. I felt out of place but had this strange overwhelming need to please them, and the only way I could do that was to play pranks and make them laugh. I still want to please everyone.'

In 1982, in a brief moment of re-evaluation, he asked me, 'Wouldn't you like to be best remembered as someone who made people laugh? Made them happy? Or for just doing your job reasonably competently?'

I answered, 'There can't be anything more important than making people happy.'

'Then it's all been worthwhile. If people laughed then, yes, it's been worthwhile.'

During one interview, he recalled one of his finer pranks.

When I turned 10 my voice broke. I was the envy of many boys who still had their soprano voices. Our headmaster was a wonderful man called Sammy Day. There was a group of boys I liked a lot, and they were being given a hard time by some other boys. So I told my friends to follow me to the nearest public phone box where I made a call to Sammy Day.

In my deepest voice I said that I was a local shopkeeper in a popular sweet shop and that some of the boys from his school had been pilfering. I was able to give a good description of each of the boys. My friends were listening and giggling.

I got carried away and started to give too much information. 'I think I heard one of the boys call another Wainwright. And another went by the nickname of Monkey...yes, a boy with large ears...no, I didn't catch his real name but there was also a boy called Ginger...yes, he had ginger hair.'

I thought I'd done a wonderful job, and my friends all congratulated me on my fine impression of the sweetshop keeper. The next day I was summoned before Sammy Day who had five boys in his office – the five I had turned in. Sammy Day said to me, 'Would these be the five boys you were telling me about?'

'Five boys? Told you? Me, sir?'

'Yes, *you*, sir.'

I knew immediately I'd not fooled him for a minute. He presented them with the sight of me being caned. Six thwacks but it turned out it was worth every thwack because these boys were so impressed by my prank that they not only stopped giving my friends a hard time but they also bought me lots of chocolate and sweets.

Then came the fall from grace with some of the boys, Sammy Day and other masters. I had become quite a nuisance with my pranks, but the more I sensed irritation, the harder I tried.

His last and most audacious prank was to send a large chocolate box to a friend of his at a nearby school. Inside was a smaller box, and then an even smaller box until finally there was a matchbox with some dog's mess inside. His friend was ill with pneumonia so the school Matron opened the box, and David was promptly expelled. 'I was only ten and a half and already an outcast.'

His mother and Sir Thomas were beside themselves with angst and worry over their wayward boy. Because of his interest in sailing, they thought they might have better luck with his discipline if he was in the Navy so they planned to get him into Dartmouth Naval College for which he would need to pass a number of exams. But first they sent him to a school in Southsea which dealt with difficult boys, run by an ex-Royal Naval officer who, David claimed, punished boys by locking them in a dark cellar full of rats, and whose wife was an alcoholic who never fed the boys enough. In a rebellious and neglected state of mind, David joined a local gang of boys who stole from shops.

After a month in Southsea, David was enrolled in an expensive private school run by a vicar in Buckinghamshire where David was much happier, but after two years of schooling, he failed his maths exam which was essential for entry into Dartmouth.

That year, 1923, Stowe School opened at Stowe House near Buckingham. The headmaster, John Fergusson Roxburgh, was to become the father figure David had long needed. He never considered Thomas Comyn-Platt to be a suitable father figure, and for many years he complained that 'Uncle Tommy' didn't care for or about him, but it was Comyn-Platt who was able to get him enrolled, in September, at Stowe School which was a much sought after house of education.

It was only in 1982 that David was able to say to me, 'I never knew it at the time but Thomas took great care of me, in his own way. I suppose a man who had a son who wasn't legally his would try and do something for that boy. I could never call him father – he was always my stepfather – and I always called him Uncle Tommy. It was a farce. When it sunk in that he was actually my father, I think I came to resent and dislike him even more because I felt lost and confused, and I dearly needed someone to be a real father to me. My "real" father had been taken from me in the war, and now I had a stepfather who couldn't even admit that I was his. But I suppose he loved my mother very much and he tried to do what was best for her and for me, and for Grizel. For all of us, really.'

He said, 'I was lucky because I found someone who was the next best thing to a father. He was John Fergusson Roxburgh, the headmaster at Stowe School. He set me such a fine example that I tried hard to emulate throughout my life. He changed me for the better. Well, I couldn't have got much worse. I had been turning into an evil little bastard, but going to Stowe School turned my life around.'

He was also influenced by Major Richard Haworth, the recipient of a Distinguished Service Order, who was master of the 'house' in which David was placed – Chandos House. Major Haworth had been a senior instructor at Sandhurst military college and was, said David, 'a gentleman who received respect through understanding and kindness, but was never less that firm.' He was David's second role model figure at Stowe.

In the five years that David spent at Stowe School, he turned from an 'evil little bastard' into the young charming gentleman that became the hallmark of his screen persona. I asked him how this amazing feat was accomplished. He said,

John Roxburgh was a young man, only 35. He wasn't like the old masters who believed that discipline could only be administered by use of the cane. He was incredibly tolerant and understanding, and he would actually listen to any boy who had a problem or a grievance.

I went to him soon after I started there because I'd decided that I was going to begin as I meant to go on, causing problems and trying to make myself stand out from the crowd and be liked. So I went to him and said, 'Now see hear, Mr Roxburgh. The food here is disgusting. Not fit for animals. Who's doing the cooking? Chimpanzees? Just look at this boil I've got?' And I showed him what looked like a boil on my neck, modelled rather well, I thought, on the one I had at Worthing, only this one was made out of a red chewy sweet I'd sucked on for a while, moulded into shape and then stuck on my neck.

He looked at it very gravely, went 'Tut! Tut!' and said, 'This won't do at all.'

I said, 'I know how to get rid of it. Give me a pair of scissors, please.'

He said, 'But surely you're not going to cut it off. That could give you a terrible infection and you'd become gravely ill.'

I said, 'It's no problem. I have a special antibody in my blood which fights infections.' I was going to snip it off and then baffle him over the next week as I remained perfectly healthy.

He said, 'I have a better idea,' and he reached slowly and carefully out towards my fake boil, and as though he were suddenly grabbing a poisonous spider he whipped the boil off my neck and said, 'Look at that. Not a mark has been left.' And then he ran the boil under his nose, sniffed a bit and said, 'Strawberry. Nice try, Niven. Goodbye.'

I was more annoyed that he'd bested me than anything, and I went out and slammed the door and stood there a moment or two, and then I heard him laughing like a drain. And I knew that he was a good sort after all, and best of all, I'd made him laugh. He was an actual human being, and I made up my mind to be like him and not cause him any more trouble. And that's how I stopped being such a poisonous little bastard!

Because of his love of chocolates, David put on a lot of weight and became quite fat, earning him the nickname Podger. His weight problem subsided as he went through puberty, and by the time he was 14, he was fit and strong and playing rugby. He was also drinking, but not heavily. He told me, 'I only got drunk once as a young man. I'd just turned 14 and polished off half a bottle of brandy. I don't know how I got there but I was found face down under a rhododendron bush. I was so ill that I quickly learned to hold my drink like a gentleman.'

For the rest of his life, like many actors, David drank but, unlike many drinking actors, never got drunk – well, hardly ever.

—

CHAPTER 3

Lovely Delicious Tarts

During the school holidays, David, then 14, returned to his family who had moved to a large house at 110 Sloane Street in Chelsea, London. Joyce, who was then 24, was living at home, and Max had returned from a stint in the Navy and then the Army before resigning his commission. Sixteen-year-old Grizel also returned for the school holidays. 'It was a packed house,' David told me. 'There were a couple of maids, and my whole family, and there was no room for me. So Uncle Tommy sent me away every night to sleep in a boarding house in St James's Place. It was a dreadful hole with an iron bed and a floor with no carpet.

'I made my own way there by bus, and I actually found I enjoyed this new sense of freedom and got more adventurous and went exploring Piccadilly Circus where there were lots of lovely young prostitutes.'

David began *The Moon's a Balloon* by writing about Nessie, a 17-year-old blonde prostitute with 'a pair of legs that went on for ever', who he met during his Easter holiday. He followed her for three nights until she noticed him, took him to her flat and, upon discovering he didn't have the three pounds required for her services, took pity on him and gave him his first taste of sex without charge.

His description of that first night as written in his book, and in the abbreviated version he gave to me in 1970, was hilarious, and he entertained many people with it, especially TV audiences, when *The Moon's a Balloon* was published in 1971.

He met her often to go to music halls and theatres, and then returned to her flat for more sexual antics. He said to me, 'She was my sex education. But she meant a whole lot more than that to me. She was my first love. I know it sounds unlikely, but I was 14 years old and I had the most enormous crush on this slightly older girl who taught me how to fuck. I lost a lot of my fat through plenty of wonderful fucking. I can recommend it as a way to lose weight. Much better than dieting.

'She came to Stowe to watch a cricket match. She wanted to meet Mr Roxburgh. I was mortified what he might think of her, but she didn't look like a tart at all, and he was quite taken with her. She talked with such a strong Cockney accent that she sounded like Eliza Doolittle in *Pygmalion*, but she charmed Roxburgh and everyone who met her.'

David did an impression of her for me, and it sounded like the worst kind of Hollywood version of a Cockney accent, but it was hilarious. David and I often did impressions, possibly giving the best worst impressions ever, and we always got into hysterics when we did them, such as when we compared Cary Grant impressions. Those are the kinds of moments I shared with David that I treasure. I did, however, do a much better Cockney than he since that was the accent I had as a kid.

Over the years since *The Moon's a Balloon* which introduced Nessie to the world, there has been much speculation over whether she was an invention, or maybe a composite of several different prostitutes. He certainly took advantage of prostitutes now and then. 'Sometimes I just want the pleasure without the pain of emotion,' he once told me.

I discovered more about the authenticity of Nessie when, in 1985, I interviewed actress Ann Todd – she was making a film called *The McGuffin* – and she told me that she had actually met Nessie. 'He brought her to see a play I was in,' she said. 'He'd never mentioned her before and he just turned up at the theatre with this girl and said, "Ann, this is my dear friend Nessie," and I wondered how dear she was to him. When I read *The Moon's a Balloon*, I found out.'

When he talked enthusiastically about Nessie to me in 1970, he said, 'Can you imagine what it was like for a 14-year-old boy with testosterone surging to find himself the benefactor of a generous and very pretty little whore?'

He obviously expected me to say no, but I took him by surprise by saying, 'Yes.' Then I added, 'Well, not at 14. I was 17.'

That intrigued and fascinated him and he demanded that I elucidate, and I only do so here, briefly, because it led to something that happened. I had been making my way through St Anne's Court, an alley leading off Wardour Steet which was jammed with strip clubs, porn shops and doorways that had cards reading 'French Model first floor', when I was hailed by a young woman leaning out of a first floor window. I thought she needed my help so up I went, and met Annie, a prostitute who discovered that not only did I not have a clue why she had invited me up to her room but also that I couldn't afford to pay her for what she was offering on my £5 a week salary. So she gave me a freebie, followed by tea and biscuits. From then on I popped in at least one morning every week – just for tea and biscuits and a chat. There were no more freebies, and I never paid. But I did enjoy her company and she seemed to like mine.

David was delighted by my story and, seemingly desperate to meet her, positively insisted I introduced him. I resisted his request, but he was adamant, so I arranged for an introduction. She was extremely excited at the prospect of meeting David Niven, and so on what was my last day with him I took him to meet her. Not surprisingly, she was immediately won over by his charm, and he was equally won over by her Cockney wit and fine legs. Annie wasn't what you would call beautiful but she was appealing and voluptuous.

David insisted that he take Annie and I for lunch, and so off we went to an Italian restaurant nearby called Quo Vadis where he entertained us with stories of Nessie and many of his other exploits that may or may not have ever really happened.

After that, David often met Annie on his visits to London when she provided him with the kind of 'pleasure without the pain of emotion' he often sought. I think she reminded him of Nessie. She was a common girl, very much a tart, but literally the tart with a heart of gold. She was also very fussy about her clients and always insisted they used condoms. David always carried a supply, just in case.

He once told me, 'I do love tarts. Always have.'

He called her Saint Annie of St Anne's Court.

He didn't just use Annie for sex. He really liked her company and often took her for lunch. Sometimes I'd go along too.

David told me that if I wanted to take advantage of Saint Annie's services he would gladly pay because he knew I couldn't afford to. I asked him why he would do such a thing and he replied, 'Because I can.'

I thanked him and said that I had a girlfriend who I wouldn't be unfaithful to.

'It's not cheating,' he said. 'Not when you pay. Besides, you're not married, are you?'

I liked David a great deal, but I never understood his moral values. And I never took him up on his generous offer. That always baffled him.

One day in 1972 Annie simply disappeared, moving away without telling me, and I never saw her again. When David was in London to promote the paperback edition of *The Moon's a Balloon* in 1973, he said to me, 'Where on earth is Saint Annie?' I told him I had no idea.

'What a pity,' he said. 'I did love seeing her. She reminded me so much of my Nessie. Both of them were tarts. Lovely delicious tarts.'

In 1982 he recalled Annie and asked me what I thought had happened to her. I said that I hoped she had simply given up her profession and perhaps married someone who could take care of her.

He said, 'That's what happened to Nessie.'

'Did you ever see her again?' I asked.

'I did, as a matter of fact. In 1973. I was in the States doing a tour, and she got in touch with me and asked if we could meet. I hadn't seen her for many years. I waited in a coffee shop on the highway, and in walked a rather matronly, stout, middle-aged lady with a tight grey perm who sat down and said, "I married an American who's done rather well for himself, and we live in Seattle and I'm head of the Women's Institute." She was a grandmother, and sad to say there was nothing between us. No spark of friendship at all. People change and move on.'

He looked genuinely sad.

'So Nessie was really real,' I said, having been dying to ask him outright for so many years.

'Oh my God, yes. So long ago.'

I asked him how he had been able to cope with having a girlfriend who was a prostitute. He said, 'I was totally obsessed by her. She could have been a mass murderer and I would have still loved her. I was young and infatuated, and I had wonderful sex with her. I've been addicted to sex ever since.'

And so at the age of 14 David was having what he said was 'very good sex' and was a lot happier for it. He was also happy at Stowe School, and had begun to entertain friends and teachers by creating characters, such as a man who had eaten mothballs, having mistaken them for peppermints, or an elegant, gracious lady trying to be polite about a Christmas present she detested. He turned these impressions into short sketches to perform on stage in shows that he helped to put on at the end of each term.

'My first taste of being on stage,' he told me, 'was being in the Chandos House end of term concerts which I did because I simply wanted to be liked. I had no thought at all of being an actor. It never occurred to me.'

When Major Richard Haworth founded an Officer Training Corps, David joined and spent 10 days during the summer of 1925 at an Officer Training Camp in Salisbury Plain where he performed in the camp concert, held in a huge tent, before hundreds of his peers. He portrayed a dull-witted officer, Major General Sir Useless Eunuch, complete with a wispy grey moustache and a monocle. Despite suffering terrible stage fright, he received a standing ovation. His impressions turned into an annual event at the camp.

His mother, pleased with the way he had settled down, bought a 14ft (4.5m) sailing dinghy, *Merlin*, at the Isle of White for him and Grizel. 'It took me a long time to realise that my mother really loved me,' he said to me in 1982. 'I was actually getting to know her, and like her. My life felt very secure, very happy.'

He discovered a love for skiing when he went on a two-week break on the slopes of Savognin in Switzerland with the school. Skiing, sailing and sex were to be his three favourite pastimes throughout his life.

During his second term at Stowe, David helped to start a Chandos House magazine, *The Chandosian*. He also played drums and trombone in the school jazz band, and joined a drama group for which he wrote one-act plays.

He was persuaded by Major Haworth to join the Army and try for Sandhurst, which meant he needed to pass several specific exams in 1926. He was given special coaching in his weakest subject, maths, while he excelled at English. He also began writing published articles.

'We had a school magazine called *The Stoic*,' he told me in 1975 when I interviewed him about the publication of *Bring on the Empty Horses*. 'I was 15 when I wrote an article for it, called *A Tailing Party at the Swiss Camp*, which told, very wittily I thought, of a school expedition in Switzerland. My English teacher, Mr Arnold, said he thought it indicated a real flair and talent and he said he thought my future as a writer was secure. Which was very nice. But I felt quite ashamed really, because I'd stolen it, you see, from A.A Milne, who wrote a story called *The Tailing Party* in *Punch* a few years earlier. I changed the names and made a few necessary alterations. But I think *that* demonstrates a creative flair, all the same.'

By 1926 David had progressed and matured so well that he was made a prefect in a new house, Grafton. He had to prepare to re-sit his exams at the end of the next year, putting him a year behind almost everyone else.

At the end of 1926 he spent another two weeks skiing in Switzerland, then began 1927 by joining the Debating Society. In February he played his first rugby match for Grafton House against Cobham House, and he learned to play tennis and squash. He also swam for Grafton, winning a 100-yard race and being awarded a medal in life saving. His fitness continued to improve and he grew into a very solid, strong young man who would remain physically active throughout his life.

He was promoted to lance-corporal in the Officer Training Corps in May, and began to play in the school cricket team in which he excelled as a fast bowler. But at the end of July, before the summer holiday, he again failed the School Certificate exams. He was promoted to corporal in the Officer Training Corps but the next year he failed his exams a third time.

He worked solidly through the next term, was promoted to sergeant, played cricket regularly, and won the senior backstroke in the school's swimming sports. In June 1928 he passed the entrance exam for Sandhurst, but he still needed to pass his School Certificate exams, which he took for the fourth time in July – and passed.

David was now on his way to becoming a professional soldier, a career that he said 'wasn't a passion for me but it was a job I could get immediately and be well paid for it'. It was also a profession he never really shook off even as an actor because, as an actor, he often had his greatest success as a gentleman and an officer. In fact he said, 'The Army was the only formal training I had as an actor.'

Laurence Olivier had RADA. David Niven had Sandhurst.

CHAPTER 4

—

Sandhurst

On 31 August 1928 David Niven joined the Royal Military College at Sandhurst to begin 15 months of training as an officer in the British Army. 'I was used to parading at the Officer Training Corps,' he told me, 'but the real thing came as a tremendous culture shock. The first 10 weeks were spent being drilled and paraded, shouted at, sworn at and being made to drill in full battle gear if you hadn't polished your boots beyond perfection. It was absolute hell, I swear. But at the end of it I was as fit as I would ever be. It got better after that as I studied tactics, admin and management and even military law.

'We even had leisure time at last. We would go to the pub which was at Frimley Green, and to the cinema at Aldershot and to a lovely pair of prostitutes at Camberley.' He still loved those tarts.

At the end of his first 10 weeks at boot camp he was promoted to lance-corporal and was chosen to be one of the commandment's two orderlies. One of his perks was to be excused from Saturday morning drill parades, allowing him to go to London for the day.

He performed in the college theatre, sharing a duologue, *Searching for the Supernatural*, with a fellow recruit, and that sketch earned him his first rave review; 'A valuable recruit, who deservedly made the hit of the evening, was David Niven,' wrote the college's *R.M.C. Magazine and Record*. 'He is a great find, with the most exquisite meandering manner.'

He also performed in his first full length play at Sandhurst, *The Creaking Chair*, playing a crime reporter which the college magazine described as 'an irresistible hero'.

Early in 1929 he appeared in the Sandhurst variety show in a sketch he wrote himself, *Why Every Married G. C. Should Have a Wife*, and a few weeks later he did another play, *It Pays to Advertise*, playing a charming layabout. He was developing a good light comedic touch.

'I was fortunate to get the chance to do a few plays at Sandhurst while I was struggling to make a soldier of myself,' he told me, 'and, I suppose, my screen persona sprung from all that. I didn't invent myself for the screen. What you got was what you saw, a man with a military background speaking ever so nicely and trying not to stretch himself beyond his abilities as an actor. If the audience laughed, I felt I'd done well.'

But behind the wit and the charm, the twinkle in the eye and mischievous manner, and the often impeccable manners was a very different man – someone even his closest friends rarely got to see.

He told me in 1982,

I was often petrified that I would disappoint everyone. I don't think there was a great deal of substance to me. I was far more insecure than anyone would have realised. That's why I worked so hard to be liked. If I hadn't done that I think I would have been a basket case. There were times in my life when terrible depression overcame me, and when it did I had to give in to it. But most of the time I fought off depressing thoughts.

There were two versions of the younger me. There was the poisonous little me who got into trouble and even crime – I could have easily gone on to become a criminal and would no doubt have been a dismal failure and ended up in prison – and there was the 'life can't get me down' young me charming everyone he could with banter and wit, which is the preferable me. I think because that was the more successful me, it was the one that took over, and thank God for that. Thank God for the people in my life who had the tolerance and patience to put up with me and also to inspire me to want to better myself. Perhaps coming from my background, I could only go in two directions; either become an officer and a gentleman, or become a crook. Maybe even a gentleman crook.

I told him that was an interesting analogy because James Cagney had told me something similar; he came from a deprived background from which you became a gangster, a priest or an actor. That almost made David laugh but because of the Motor Neurone Disease he stifled it and said, 'Thank God I didn't have to decide between those three options. I would never have cut the mustard as a priest. I mean, how do they get by without *girls*?'

By his own admission, in 1970, he was, as a young man, before, during and after Sandhurst, 'a randy fellow with an unfortunate tendency to get an erection on all forms of transportation, and the best way to work it off was with the local prostitutes. There was little time to find girlfriends, although Nessie came down to Sandhurst for the Ball we had that summer of 1929. She made it very clear to me. "David, we're only together for the larfs and the fuckin', so don't go gettin' all serious on me." I think by then I knew the score, and my crush on her had waned.'

By then he was seeing Ann Todd regularly. He had first seen her in a play in London and was so taken with her that he went to see her perform whenever he could.

She told me,

He would hang around the stage doors. He wanted to meet all the actors, or mostly the actresses. He seemed to have a liking for me especially. I was always bothered by what we called stage-door Johnnies.

I went on tour in a play by Ian Hay, and David started turning up to see this play in Portsmouth – every night – and he drew love hearts against my name in the programme and sent them to my dressing room. That got very irritating because it was so childish and I didn't believe he was really in love with me. We hadn't even met. I was desperate that he shouldn't come near me and on the last night I was waiting for Ian Hay to come and see me and I was going to tell him to make sure that a chap called David Niven didn't come to my dressing room, and as soon as Ian walked in he said, 'I'd like you to meet David Niven. I knew his father.' And there he was, right behind Ian Hay, smiling and full of charm and very handsome. But I was still annoyed. I got to realise that David directly or indirectly knew *everybody*.

He was so charming and funny that it was impossible not to accept his invitation to dinner one night. So when the tour was over, I met him for dinner. He wasn't earning much but he insisted that he pay for everything. He was very old fashioned about that sort of thing. He must have borrowed the money to pay for the meal. He was always very keen to impress me, probably because I was an actress and he was very keen on the theatre. I don't think he was thinking too much about becoming an actor at first.

I went to see some of the Army concerts he was in, and he was very funny. David was funny all the time. If he wasn't on stage being funny he was telling stories that were funny.

One evening when we were out to dinner, I said, 'David, don't you take anything seriously?'

He said, 'I take *you* very seriously.'

I thought, *Uh-oh, here it comes, the declaration of love.* And then he said, 'Have you got a shilling? I don't think I have enough to leave a tip.'

I was relieved and annoyed. I had feelings for him but I didn't want to be tied down to a soldier who could end up anywhere in the world. So I wanted to hear him say something sweet but also I didn't want to hear it.

One day I couldn't bear it any longer and I said, very earnestly, 'David, where are we going?'

He said, 'To a party, darling.' He *knew* what I meant but he dodged the question.

He continued to spend his summer holidays at Bembridge with his mother who was suffering considerable pain from a mysterious illness. David spent his hours sailing and working off his frustrations on the local girls. He would later regret not spending more time with his mother.

He returned to Sandhurst in September 1929 for his final term and was promoted to junior under-officer. In October he performed in another variety show and later played the juvenile lead in *The Speckled Band*, a Sherlock Holmes mystery. He continued to excel in rugby, but he did poorly in his final exams.

He had long wanted to get into the Argyll and Sutherland Highlanders and had even learned to play the bagpipes in readiness. He got his chance formally to request his admission into the regiment of his choice when he filled in a War Office form. He had to list three regiments in order of preference. His first was the Argyll and Sutherland Highlanders. His second choice was the Black Watch. For his third choice he wrote, 'Anything but the Highland Light Infantry.' He thought that a funny joke. Somebody didn't laugh at his joke and that's possibly why he was sent to the Highland Light Infantry.

He left Sandhurst a few days before Christmas, 1929, depressed about his fortunes, and at the end of February joined the Highland Light Infantry. He spent nine months learning how to command a platoon and, at the beginning of October 1930, was posted to Malta where he was put in charge of No. 3 platoon which was made up of around 30 tough Glaswegians.

Ann Todd was the girl he left behind. She told me, 'I knew the Army would send him away. I didn't want to fall madly in love with him because it would hurt. But it hurt all the same when he went to Malta.' She recalled,

We had a quiet dinner on our last night together. He said, 'Darling, will you wait for me?' I would have laughed if I hadn't felt like crying.

I said, 'And while I'm waiting for you, will you be confining yourself to barracks?'

'What do you mean?'

I said, 'I'm sure there are plenty of pretty girls on Malta.'

He said, 'I'll be far too busy for that sort of thing. I doubt I'll have a minute to myself.' He looked sincere but it was almost melodramatic. Over the top. Like in a silent movie.

When we were saying goodbye, he kissed me and said 'You do know that I love you,' and he said it very lightly but that meant he really meant it.

Leaving Ann and just about everything else he loved in life behind, he was shipped off to Malta.

CHAPTER 5

—

Malta

'I hated Malta from the moment I arrived,' David told me in 1970.

I was still a young man, only 21, but my fellow officers were almost all middle aged and they didn't want anything to do with me. Even my commanding officer wouldn't talk to me. The first thing he ever said to me, at a regimental dinner, was, 'I have fucked women of every nationality and most animals, but the one thing I cannot abide is a girl with a Glaswegian accent. Pass the port.' He never spoke to me again.

I had hoped to join the 2nd Battalion in India which would have been far more exciting than policing a huge rock in the Mediterranean. The only excitement we had was when stones were thrown at a Customs shed in the harbour one night during an anti-demonstration. It was terribly depressing.

The only good thing was that I met a big fellow, standing six feet and six inches [1.98m] with a bushy handlebar moustache and the most wonderful and often bizarre taste in humour, and that was Michael Trubshawe.

I interviewed Michael Trubshawe in 1984 and he was more than happy to talk about his friendship with David as long as I also asked him plenty of questions about his career because he became an actor and appeared in small roles in many films, mainly World War II pictures.

Trubshawe, a big bear of a man with a bushy moustache he'd sported since his Army days, told me, 'We were almost made for each other on Malta. He was a second lieutenant and I was another second lieutenant, and we both loved sex and alcohol, and a combination of those two things meant trouble. We loved trouble too.

'The men I commanded in B Company seemed to like my peculiar ways but my fellow officers thought I was pretty disgraceful. Nivvy wasn't much liked by his fellow officers either, but he and I took to each other straight away. We met at a cricket match. Our battalion versus the Royal Artillery.'

Trubshawe had strode over to David, shook him by the hand and offered him a generous helping of whiskey and soda. Said Trubshawe,

Niv was an immediately likeable person. He was very outgoing with his friends but could be quite anxious when surrounded by people he didn't like or with whom he had nothing in common.

I saw him one night at a regimental dinner stuck between two officers, one of whom was his commanding officer. Niv had put back several glasses of wine and from the look on his face I figured that his bladder was close to bursting. But he couldn't leave his seat because no one was allowed to leave the table until a toast to the king had been made at the end of the meal. So he put away his soup and three courses, and I thought that I could help the poor chap out. So I got our mess steward to push an empty magnum under the table where he sat and let Niv know that it was with my compliments. So Niv relieved himself into the magnum, and the look on his face as he emptied his bladder over the next several minutes was priceless.

He helped me out one time the way only a good friend like that can. We were at an Army function and one of my superior officers asked me to dance with his wife. That wouldn't normally be a problem but this woman always stank of something I can only describe as lavatory cleaner which is why none of the other men would dance with her. I think her husband must have suffered – or been blessed – with absolutely no sense of smell. Suddenly the fire alarm was sounded and the whole place was quickly evacuated. But no one could find a fire. I said to David, 'Damn funny that fire alarm and no fire,' and he said, 'That was me, old boy. I saw you dancing with that dreadful woman and could see you were holding your breath and thought if I didn't do something soon you would probably pass out or die, so the only thing I could think of was to sound the alarm.'

Trubshawe said that David would have been a 'really good soldier because he took the whole thing very seriously. I didn't.' He continued,

The Army wrecked any chance of him becoming a good soldier by sending him to Malta where we were just a Home Service station on domestic duties. That depressed him.

He knew how to be a good soldier, and he knew how to gain the respect of the men. He *commanded* their respect. He was just like a regular soldier when he was on parade or in the mess. But something was *missing*. He didn't have the fire for it. By day he was a soldier, but late at night if you went into his room you'd find him leafing through theatre programmes or reading the society pages of the *Tatler*.

I said to him, 'What are you reading those things for?' and he said, 'Because right now I'd rather be an actor than a soldier, and I'd rather be at a dinner party among high society than stuck here on this bloody rock.' He was so bored and frustrated that he started getting into trouble.

David always tried to fit in, wherever he was. But when he found himself a square peg trying to fit into a round hole, he rebelled. When he met me he was delighted because I rebelled too. I'd been thrown out of Cambridge because I spent all my time on the hunting field instead of at lectures. So we were like two peas in a pod.

At first we were unable to get out of the barracks often because the second-in-command, who had no friends and hated seeing all the young officers going off to cocktail parties, decided we all had to do fencing every evening at six o'clock. The young men, who hadn't learned to fence, were being cut to ribbons. So finally, after a week of this, David said to me, 'I think something needs to be done about this waste of good drinking time,' and without giving me a clue what he was up to, he started fencing with the fencing tutor. My God, he looked as good as Douglas Fairbanks in one of his swashbuckling pictures. He made the fencing tutor look like a beginner.

Afterwards David said, 'No, I'm not really that good, but I was taught by a staff sergeant at Sandhurst how to fence dirty.' He'd used all the dirty tricks he knew with a sword, and after that demonstration of his skills fencing was no longer compulsory and we used our drinking time wisely.

I was two years older than David and I had a private income whereas he was struggling to manage on the nine shillings a day the Army paid him. So I took care of all bills – drink, food and girls, that sort of thing.

I knew the best whores on the island. David was bursting for some hanky panky and said he hadn't had any since he left England. So I took him to a very good brothel called Auntie's.

I also knew a very nice Maltese girl who was not a regular prostitute but would often give me a good time for payment. I asked her if she had a friend for David, and she did, but the friend wanted paying also. So I arranged for us to meet them in a little hotel, and he took a liking to my usual girl, and I said, 'Sorry, old boy, but *that* one's for me.'

He said, 'That's utter rubbish and you know it. No one has exclusive rights when you pay for it.'

I said, 'Well *I* do when *I'm* paying,' and he said, 'Oh, right, yes, of course. Yes, the other girl is most pretty.'

So the next time I said to him, 'Right old man, you can have my girl,' and he said, 'Thanks all the same but I like the one I've got.'

So I said, 'But you said you fancied mine,' and he said, 'I know, but my girl knows some really good tricks.'

I said, 'Are *you* paying for her?'

He said, 'Ah…no!'

'Very well,' I said, 'then yours is mine and mine is yours, and I don't think you'll be disappointed.'

Afterwards, I said to him, 'How was it?'

He said, 'Oh marvellous. Your girl was very good. Funny thing, though. She said it made a nice change not to have a rash all over her face and tits.'

I said, 'What is she talking about?'

'That moustache of yours, old boy,' he said. 'Gives her a terrible rash.'

'Why didn't she mention it before?' I said, and Niv replied, 'Because *you're* the one who pays.'

After that I thought we should try the non-professional girls of which there were many on the island. They were daughters of officers, even wives of officers, and the lonely wives of sailors who were always off to sea, leaving their poor wives behind with no one to take care of their needs. So David and I volunteered. Often.

There was never any shortage of women. I said to him that we should try the older women – the officers' wives. He said, 'I'm not into old ladies.' But then he realised that a lot of the wives were only in their early 30s and still very nice looking, so he said, 'I always fancied trying an older woman,' and he got very involved with a captain's wife.

The captain found out and called Niv into his office and said, 'Look here, Niven, are you very much in love with my wife?'

Niv said, 'No, sir. Not at all, sir.'

So the captain said, 'Then will you *please* stop telling her you are. It upsets her.'

So Niv found he had the captain's blessing. That put him off. 'What's the fun in poking a man's wife if he knows it and doesn't care?' he asked. So he moved on to somebody else's wife.

Apart from keeping other men's wives happy, David's other great talent was telling anecdotes that captured the interest of everyone around him. Trubshawe said, 'He told the best stories, or rather he was the best at telling stories. I remember him at a dinner party given by the Commander-in-Chief on board ship where there were two dozen guests, and Niv was able to manipulate the conversation until he was the centre of attention, telling stories that had them all in hysterics. He had a single pip on his shoulder yet even the most senior officers were his captive audience. It was just astonishing the way he could tell an anecdote. He was a raconteur even at that young age.'

In the summer of 1931 David returned to England for two months' leave and was shocked by two discoveries. The first was that Nessie had gone. The second was that his mother, holidaying at Bembridge on the Isle of Wight, had cancer of the colon. But she didn't complain. She was just happy to be surrounded by her family because Max was briefly home from the South Pacific where he managed a banana plantation, and Grizel was home too, having just given up on an acting career. She had studied at RADA but decided she would do better to study sculpting at the Chelsea Polytechnic. She had also discovered that she was a lesbian, and David lovingly referred to her as 'my sister the dyke'.

Max needed money so Henrietta loaned him £3,000, a huge amount in 1931, and told him he needn't repay the loan until after her death. The seriousness of her illness still didn't dawn on David, and he concentrated his energies that summer on his favourite subjects – boats, booze and girls.

When he returned to Malta, he and Trubshawe continued their antics 'because it was so bloody boring there,' said Trubshawe.

> We got drunk quite a lot, and when we did, we got up to all sorts of things that seemed like a good idea at the time. One night we decided it would be a bit of a wheeze to dress as women, and the Madame at Auntie's allowed us to mingle with her girls who all helped to dress us and put make-up on us. Of course, I had this moustache! When I asked Niv how I looked, he said, 'Nobody will want to poke you. You've got a hairy face.'
>
> I said, 'I don't want anyone to poke me.'
>
> He said, 'But you want them to *think* they are going to poke you. That moustache will have to go.'
>
> I said, 'Come one step nearer and I'll drop you where you stand.' Then David had an idea. He got a veil and put it over my face but the moustache is so big that the veil had to be huge and it covered almost all my face. He said, 'We'll say you're an exotic Turkish whore.'

I said, 'Nobody will believe that,' but Niv said, 'Want to bet?'

So we joined the girls and waited for some customers. Niv looked like Clara Bow with little cupid lips. We were the ugliest whores in the brothel. But a couple of Naval officers took a shine to us. 'Here we go,' he said when he spotted these two officers giving us the eye. I thought they would spot us as fakes in a minute and give us hell. But they were really interested. They knew we were men – that was obvious. We didn't fool them for a minute, which was what the joke was supposed to be. They were willing to pay top price for us. The Madame was haggling. David whispered to me, 'Get rid of the veil. That'll make them change their minds.'

So I whipped off the veil and one of the officers said, 'Christ, even *better!*'

Then Niv said, 'Discretion, old man – better part of valour and all that,' and we shot out of there, still in our frocks, and arrived back at barracks like that. We just marched past the guard and saluted, and he stood there with his mouth gaping open as we strode by in our frocks.

Despite these escapades, David was restless in Malta and asked to be transferred to the West Africa Frontier Force, but his request was denied.

'If it wasn't for Trubshawe,' David said, 'I would have gone insane. We started running out of ideas how to keep ourselves entertained. We tried joining the Malta Amateur Drama Society but were rejected, so we decided to put on our own show in a canteen at the docks. Not the most glamorous of venues, but we ran for three nights. Our show consisted of funny sketches and highland dancing. We were surprisingly successful and it reminded me how much I enjoyed performing.'

Niven and Trubshawe were relieved to be returned to England in December 1931 and stationed at the Citadel barracks above the town of Dover overlooking the English Channel. Trubshawe bought a car so they could occasionally race off to London, more than 70 miles (112 km) away, to meet girls.

David finally bought his own car, purchased with a small inheritance of £200 left to him by his grandmother who died that spring. In his Morris Cowley he was able to run around, finding girls here and there, while Trubshawe made plans to settle down, having got engaged to a girl, Margie Macdougall, he had met in Malta.

That pretty much brought an end to the Niven–Trubshawe era of schoolboy escapades, and their friendship would never be the same again.

CHAPTER 6

America

Now that Trubshawe was no longer single and fancy free, David went to parties on his own, and at several very fashionable social events in London that summer he kept meeting Barbara Hutton, the beautiful 19-year-old American Woolworths heiress. She was engaged to a Georgian prince, Alex Mdivani, but she liked David so much that they became firm friends and when the time came for her to return to the United States she invited him to join her for Christmas in New York.

Around that time he was seeing a beautiful hostess at the Café de Paris called Merle Oberon who was trying to become an actress and had appeared fleetingly and uncredited in a number of British movies. She was half-Indian, half-British – her ethnicity was kept a secret for many years – and possessed stunning exotic looks which captivated David.

That November, in 1932, David received word from Sir Thomas Comyn-Platt that Henrietta was dying in a nursing home in South Kensington in London. He rushed from Aldershot, where he was on a training course, to be with her. She had undergone an operation but peritonitis had set in and she was unconscious.

In 1982 David said to me, 'I was too selfish at such a young age when we holidayed at Bembridge to realise I should have spent more time with my mother. It was only in those last years that I really came to understand that she had loved me very much. I had grown up thinking I was unwanted and unloved. I suppose that was my naturally selfish attitude. But by the time she died it was too late.

'I saw her before she passed away but she couldn't recognise me. I felt crushed and ashamed, and I didn't want to lose my mother now that I had realised what a wonderful mother she was. I took her for granted and didn't make the effort to make her more happy. I didn't spend enough time with her.'

David had also been seeing Ann Todd regularly; she had become a rising star having made five films in two years. She told me, 'His mother hoped that I'd marry him. She told me that if I ever had children I should not feel hurt if they spent their school holidays off with friends or going to parties instead of staying home. She never resented David enjoying his life while she was ill. I went with him to see her in hospital when she was dying. He suddenly seemed quite lost.'

It was a time when David was trying to come to terms with issues he had. He had neglected to realise how much his mother loved him, and he was also dealing with the truth about Sir Thomas Comyn-Platt being his father. 'It took me a long time to realise that the man who was my real father had made her happy,' he said in 1982. 'I think I always resented that he seemed to have her more than I did, and I never wanted to acknowledge that he was my father, and it rankled that he never publicly acknowledged that I was his son.

'One day when we were on holiday at Bembridge, she said to me, "David, please try and understand the position he is in. He's an important public figure and it would cause a scandal if it were known that he had illegitimate children." I took that to mean that neither of them cared for me enough. I understand perfectly now.

'I think I understood it when my mother was dying and I wanted her to know how happy I was to be her son. But it was too late. She never regained consciousness.'

Henrietta died at the age of 52 on 12 November with Sir Thomas Comyn-Platt at her side. She left an estate worth more than £14,000 which was a lot more than she had inherited from William Niven. It turned out she had left most of her money untouched all those years so it grew with interest while Sir Thomas Comyn-Platt paid for David's and Grizel's educations and all their living expenses.

Most of Henrietta's estate was left in the care of trustees for use by Sir Thomas who would receive the entire income from the estate until he died, after which it would pass to her four children. David received half the family silver with the Niven crest and a grand butterfly brooch. Max received the other half of the silver along with some jewellery, and to Grizel and Joyce went diamonds, sapphires, brooches, earrings and pearl and platinum rings.

As well as intense grief, David also suffered from confusion and uncertainty. He knew he had made a grave error in choosing the Army over the Navy, and he began to wonder what he would do with the rest of his life. He certainly didn't foresee a future as a solider. One day, Ann Todd introduced him to Laurence Olivier, another rising star of the theatre, and David thinks that was the moment he began to wonder if he could make a career for himself as an actor.

Olivier told me that initially he saw no potential in David as an actor. 'I thought he was really rather silly when I first saw him. He obviously loved mixing with actors and seemed to want to impress them all, so he would put on very silly voices and make funny faces, and Merle clearly thought a lot of him and she was very sweet to him. He was seeing both Merle and Ann, you know, and hoped they could help him. I think he was trying hard to be an actor, but he really was just someone who created funny characters.'

Ann Todd wasn't convinced that David could ever be an actor. She said, 'Around the time his mother died he told me he was thinking of becoming an actor. He wanted to know what I thought about him leaving the Army and going into the Theatre. He always enjoyed seeing plays and I knew he enjoyed performing. I'd seen some of his sketches he did at Army concerts and he was very funny, but it was always him impersonating somebody or pretending to skate without any ice; that kind of thing. It wasn't acting. So I said to him, "David, you are *not* an actor. If you said '*I love you*,' nobody would believe you." I'm afraid that rather crushed him.'

The death of Henrietta was a crossroads in David's life. He felt extreme guilt and grief, and now he was uncertain about his future. What he was sure about was that the Army wasn't a part of it.

David's commanding officer at Aldershot gave him a month's leave, so David cabled Barbara Hutton in New York to ask if he could visit. She cabled him to come immediately, so he sold his car, borrowed money from the bank and from Grizel, and bought the cheapest ticket to sail to New York, arriving on Christmas Eve.

'I'd not experienced American hospitality before,' David said, 'but I stepped ashore and was immediately met by Barbara and some of her friends and was made to feel unbelievably welcome. I was whisked off to the Pierre Hotel, a very elegant and exclusive place where Barbara's family lived in several swish suites. I wasn't allowed to pay for a single thing and I lived like a millionaire for a week. I was really overwhelmed by their warmth and generosity. I simply wasn't allowed to pay for anything – not that I could have afforded to.'

He was treated to a night at the Central Park Casino where bootleg liquor was flowing despite Prohibition, and he spent Christmas Day with Barbara's family and was showered with presents. He was introduced to

American football and an assortment of nightclubs. He also had a girlfriend which I only heard about in 1980 when I had lunch with him and Lynne Frederick. He said, 'I met a very nice girl in New York on my first trip there, called Maureen Brennan, a fitness therapist with a very nice line in acrobatic sex. I was fit but not that fit, and I hurt my back rather badly. From time to time my bad back has returned but I've always told people I damaged it during the war. I was too embarrassed to say I hurt it having intercourse. Not that I was embarrassed to have intercourse. Everybody does. I was embarrassed to say I got *damaged* having intercourse.'

He had, of course, experienced high society life, something reserved for the lucky few. It was only a fantasy that many European immigrants to America dreamed about, thinking the streets were paved with gold. David would become one of the lucky ones because most immigrants wound up living in poverty. David wound up living in Hollywood. But Hollywood was still a long way from Aldershot.

'I'd realised that there was a way of life in America that was like a dream,' he told me. 'I couldn't wait to go back and I knew that when I did it would be for good – or at least, for a very long time. Even on the voyage home I benefited from the generosity of an American who was a passenger and who shared with me his daily sweepstake ticket, and I won £160.'

In late February 1933 he sailed back to England, vowing to return to America at the earliest opportunity. Trubshawe had left the regiment to marry Margie Macdougall, and Army life became ever more dull.

Niven was promoted to full lieutenant and bought a sports Bentley with his sweepstake winnings and drove to London whenever he could to be with Ann Todd and Merle Oberon. Ann seemed not to know about Merle, and told me, 'David was getting very serious about me and I think we might have got married, perhaps. But we were just never alone. He liked to be in a crowd, always wanting to be at the centre of it all. I didn't like crowds. We just weren't suited.'

David didn't let the grass grow under his feet. He had yet another girlfriend, Priscilla Weigall, voted Deb of the Year. She had friends in high society, among them Douglas Fairbanks, the swashbuckling actor from the days of silent movies who was now living in Hertfordshire. Knowing that David wanted to be an actor, Priscilla introduced him to Fairbanks and the two hit it off immediately, but David couldn't find the nerve to ask Fairbanks outright for help in becoming an actor.

Priscilla then introduced him to film producer Bunty Watts who gave him a job as an extra in a film she was making, *All the Winners*. David appeared briefly as one of a crowd at the races, but it wasn't enough to get him noticed so he went back to soldiering.

Things suddenly improved for him when a new commanding officer was appointed in the spring, Colonel Alec Telfer-Smollett. The regiment was revitalised under his command and David found him very approachable. Before long the colonel was inviting him to dine and play golf.

'He was someone who believed in the ancient concept of a regiment. That it should be a family,' he told me in 1970.

I said to him, 'You seem to have taken to men in authority who treated the people around them almost like family.'

'Yes, I suppose I have. I suppose I never really felt I had enjoyed a family life so I took what substitutes came along.'

'Were these men father figures to you?' I asked.

'Yes, they were, because I lost my father when I was five.' This, of course, was what David said in 1970 when he was still referring to Sir Thomas Comyn-Platt as 'Uncle Tommy'. He said that in the spring of 1933, he was invited to lunch by Uncle Tommy at the Carlton Club. 'Apart from seeing him at my mother's funeral, I hadn't seen him for many years. As I approached him at his table, he rose from his chair and I extended my hand to him, and he said, "The solicitors tell me that you've paid nothing towards the grave." I felt that was unkind and I realised that I never wanted to see "dear old Uncle Tommy" ever again.'

That didn't turn out to be the case. They would meet again, cordially, within weeks.

David's spirits sunk when half his platoon went to India but he was among those sent to Salisbury Plain to learn all about machine-gunnery. He decided he'd finally had enough and resigned his commission so he could head for Canada to stay with an old friend and former soldier Victor Gordon-Lennox who had married a Canadian girl. Her family was in oil, but David's intention was to head for Hollywood.

He said, 'Sir Thomas was really rather kind to me after my mother died. He *was* upset that I'd neglected to contribute to the grave, that's true. But he was not unkind, and when he heard I was intending to become an actor in Hollywood he was very worried that I might starve in the process of trying. So I told him I was going to work in the oil business, which I think impressed him. He understood I no longer wanted to remain in the Army and he gave me his blessing.

'I only wish I had appreciated him more at the time. I think, you know, that it must have hurt him not to be able to acknowledge me or Grizel.'

Of his proposed trip, David said, 'I really believed I could make it in America. When I said goodbye to the Army I wasn't at all afraid. I suddenly felt like the world was finally my oyster. That's the audacity of youth, and you have to take advantage of it before you grow out of it. The trouble was,

I didn't have enough money to get to Canada so I sold my body to science.' It sounds like an extraordinary claim, which he made to me in 1970 and also in *The Moon's a Balloon*, but he insisted he really had sold his body – or at least, the rights to use it after his death for medical research. 'I got six pounds and ten shillings for it. And I had to sign a pledge that I would never smoke.'

He bought a return fare to Canada just in case things didn't go well and sailed on 6 September 1933. He was 23 and had no real idea how he was going to achieve his dream of becoming a film star. 'That's the only way to do what you really want to do. You take a chance. The biggest chances can reap the biggest rewards. They can also bury you. I got lucky.'

He stayed with his former Army friend Victor Gordon-Lennox and his wife Diana whose parents were Admiral Charles and Lady Kingsmill. David stayed for a few weeks, fishing and exploring the countryside, and then headed for New York. He paid for his fair by cashing in his return ticket. He claimed that in Ottawa he came down with severe tonsillitis and had to have his tonsils removed. A few days later his throat bled so profusely that he had to be hospitalised again and given blood transfusions to save his life.

It was around the middle of October when he finally arrived by train in New York, virtually broke and barely able to afford to rent a small room in a cheap hotel. This was the era of the Great Depression and millions of Americans were unemployed but David landed a $40 a week job selling liquor for 21 Brands, a wholesale company that was part of the 21 Club where he had once been a regular guest with Barbara Hutton. It's probable that she helped to land him the job, and his first sale was made to Barbara's rich cousin, Woolworth Donahue.

'I wasn't a very good salesman,' he said, 'because I was always hanging around the 21 Club with Barbara and her many rich friends, and I just couldn't bring myself to sell liquor to people who were buying me drinks and meals.'

He didn't want his rich friends to know that he was staying in a cheap hotel so he told them he was staying at the Waldorf-Astoria. Every morning he entered the hotel through the back door and left through the front, and each evening before returning to his cheap lodgings, he walked through the front doors of the Waldorf and left by the back. In the Waldorf lobby he bumped into Tommy Phipps, an old friend from England and the brother of actress Joyce Grenfell. Phipps introduced David to his father-in-law 'Lefty' Flynn who had once been an actor in Hollywood. Flynn in turn introduced David to Elsa Maxwell, a New York social fixer. She immediately took a liking to David and decided that he would do well in Hollywood because he spoke like Ronald Colman.

David had made no mention to any of his new friends that he wanted to be a Hollywood actor. 'I thought that if I failed, I'd simply make a bloody fool of myself and look bloody ridiculous,' he told me. 'But I did get excited when Elsa invited me to a party that was in honour of Ernst Lubitsch [the film director]. Unfortunately, he ignored me.'

David lost his job selling liquor because of his poor sales figures, and he had to move out of his cheap hotel and into even cheaper lodgings, a basement room on Second Avenue. He wasn't prepared to admit defeat just yet, and in March 1934, in a bar on 58th Street, he met a cowboy, Doug Hertz, who persuaded him to join him in an indoor novelty horse race venture. Lefty Flynn and Elsa Maxwell helped out, getting friends to invest in ponies and hiring cowboys to ride them. Writer Damon Runyon also got in on the act, buying $1,000 worth of shares in what became the American Pony Express Racing Association.

The grand opening was in May at the municipal auditorium of Atlantic City where 15,000 people came to bet on the ponies. Its success quickly came to the attention of the local Mafia who demanded a large share of the profits. Doug Hertz refused to pay up, and the mobsters closed the business down within days.

Broke again, David was saved by Sir Thomas Comyn-Platt who sent him a cheque for what might have been as much as $3,000. It was enough to send a happy David off on a holiday with Lefty and his wife Norah to Bermuda where David had a fling with an 18-year-old girl from Virginia.

In Bermuda, David listened in fascination as Lefty Flynn reminisced about his days in Hollywood. David's dreams of movie stardom were further fuelled when he got a letter from an English friend, Dennis Smith-Bingham, who was now living in Los Angeles and urging David to join him out there. At the end of July, David set sail for Cuba and waited in Havana for a ship to take him through the Panama Canal and on to Los Angeles.

He claimed that while in Havana he met an Irishman in Sloppy Joe's Bar who tried to persuade him to join a troop of mercenaries who planned to overthrow the Cuban government. In 1970 he said, 'I became a Cuban rebel and because of my Army training I was able to train the rebels in the use of machine guns.'

Just five years later, unable to recall which version of events he had given me, he told a different story. 'I used to drink every night in a bar called Sloppy Joe's where I met a mad Irishman who was looking for mercenaries. I told him I wasn't interested in getting myself killed. It turned out he was being watched, and then I discovered I was being watched also. I was warned by the British Embassy in Havana that the local police were watching me and it would be best if I got out of town. I couldn't go anywhere because I had passage booked on a liner called the *President Piece* and there were still two days to go. So I steered clear of Sloppy Joe's and was very relieved to get on board and sail on through the Panama Canal and on to Los Angeles.'

He told me that the story of him becoming a Cuban mercenary was made up by a publicist at the Samuel Goldwyn Studios and he liked the story so much he occasionally related it among his many other highly exaggerated tales. But I doubt either version was true. He just couldn't resist adding colour to an already colourful life.

—

CHAPTER 7

Hollywood

U pon his arrival in Los Angeles he was met by Dennis Smith-Bingham and a 24-year-old actress, Sally Blane, whose mother allowed David to stay in her guest house on Sunset Boulevard for a while. He was immediately struck by the sights of Los Angeles and the film star mansions of Beverly Hills, and he knew this was where he wanted to live and work.

Sally, whose real name was Elizabeth Young, had three sisters – 10-year-old Georgina, 21-year-old Gretchen, and 25-year-old Polly Ann Young who under her own name was a successful actress and had appeared in a number of films. The middle sister, Gretchen, was also a successful actress with the screen name of Loretta Young.

I became acquainted with Loretta through a series of transatlantic telephone conversations which began in 1974 (thanks to John Wayne who gave me her number when I worked on the film *Brannigan* – Loretta was Michael Wayne's godmother). We hit it off and became friends – over the years, I took an interest in her many charities – which made it easy for me to talk to David about his relationship with her. On the set of *Candleshoe* at Pinewood Studios in England in 1976, he said,

> I fell instantly in love with her. By the time she was 18, she'd already been married and divorced. There was a lot of competition for her and I didn't stand a chance. She was seeing Spencer Tracy. Now Spence was a man of charm and wit and a good friend if he liked you, but when he was drunk he could be a dangerous enemy.

Unfortunately he didn't like me, not at first, so we weren't going to be good friends in a hurry. One evening he became quite drunk and was convinced I was flirting with Loretta – which I probably was. I'm a terrible flirt. I see a pretty girl and away I go, even if I don't intend to actually follow it up.

He'd come over to collect her from her house, and she was with me in the house by the pool where I lived with all my worldly belongings which I carted from England to Canada to New York and finally to Hollywood. And they had grown on the way because you pick so much up, like presents from friends and odd souvenirs you simply can't resist. Among these souvenirs was a war lance I'd been given in New York by an Indian who was one of the jockeys in our indoor horse racing business.

Spence didn't like the way we were talking and laughing, or how she would hold my hand or pat it. I think I was in love with her, and when her eyes locked onto mine it was impossible for me to look away. Well, Spence had put away a few and although not blindly drunk, he was past the point of being polite. He picked up the lance and came at me with it. I ran outside with him in hot pursuit, and Loretta was yelling at him to stop being so damn silly. I tried to stand my ground for only a second, and as he came charging at me with the lance aimed right at me, I side stepped and he ran straight into the pool.

He disappeared under the surface. Loretta and I got on our hands and knees and peered into the water where we could see him but he didn't seem to be in a hurry to come up for air. 'Maybe he's drowned,' I said.

Loretta said, 'Do something.'

I said, 'Like what?'

She said, 'Jump in and save him.'

I said, 'It might have slipped your mind but he was trying to kill me.'

She said, 'You can't just let him drown.'

I said, 'Oh, very well,' and I took off my shoes and was about to take off my trousers when he gently bobbed to the surface like a buoy, blinked several times and then blew out a spout of water from his mouth and began laughing.

Of course, Loretta was very relieved, and I was delighted I didn't have to dive in after him as I was convinced he would just try and pull me under with him and we'd both drown. He climbed out of the pool and also managed to retrieve the lance, and when he stood up, he held it out to me and said, 'This is yours, I believe. You really must be more careful with that, it could hurt someone.'

After that I avoided being alone with Loretta for a long time in case he came back. But I needn't have worried. Their affair didn't last long, and the next year she was involved with Clark Gable.

Now Gable was the most handsome man in Hollywood, and so I knew I had no chance against him, and so I gave up on Loretta. Fortunately there were hundreds of young starlets and would be starlets around and I was never at a loss for female company.

In 1979 I told David I was going to be speaking to Loretta, primarily for a tribute I was writing about John Wayne who had just died, and he said, 'Give her all my love,' so I did, to which she replied, 'David's one of my oldest and dearest friends. I knew him when he first came out to Hollywood. He came to stay with me and my family. I think he was rather overwhelmed by it all. He was like a little boy with eyes like saucers.'

'Because of the girls?' I asked.

'Oh yes, them too, but I mean the sights and sounds of Hollywood. It was a wonderful place back then, like a small community. Not sprawling and overgrown and overcrowded like it is today. The air was clean, the sun was warm and shone virtually all day, every day, and he thought it was like a playground.'

When I spoke to Loretta after David died in 1983, she said,

> He was very serious about becoming an actor. None of us knew if he could act or not, but he was very handsome, very well built and he had that wonderful Niven charm. But you never know if all that is enough until you get before a camera. He told me he was desperate to try acting and wanted to get into a studio, so I took him with me to Twentieth Century-Fox where I was filming [*The White Parade*]. He had to get down on the floor of my car and I covered him with a blanket so I could get him through the gate. He came to my dressing room and watched me being made-up. He kept saying to me, 'You don't need make-up. You're perfectly beautiful as you are.' I told him everyone needed make-up for the camera. He didn't understand that and said, 'The camera obviously doesn't recognise perfection when it sees it.' It was that Niven charm. But he was sincere, it wasn't just flattery.

I told her, 'He said he was quite in love with you.'

'Oh yes. Well, we did enjoy some time together. He was very attractive and very funny which girls can't resist. He had a lot of girlfriends, and he was so charming that people just took to him. We had a lot of movie actors come to our house and they were intrigued by this young Englishman, and before they knew it he was telling them funny stories and making friends. That's a special gift.'

I told her that David had said that he often went with her and her sister Sally to various nightspots such as the Coconut Grove, the King's Club and the Clover Club. Loretta recalled, 'He'd go with us but usually ended up with some beautiful girl he'd spotted, and so we'd go home without him.'

I told her that in the years I'd known David I had discovered that sometimes his cheerful demeanour disguised a certain amount of insecurity and even depression.

'I think you're right,' she said, and added,

He was very anxious when I first knew him. He was quite nervous and twitchy, especially when he met people for the first time, and he overcame that by being so funny. He was very affected by not having his father in his life. He always wanted to have a father. When he was a child he thought his mother didn't love him. He had a sister he adored, Grizel, and another sister and a brother, but he hardly saw them, hardly knew them. He said he never had a family life and was very insecure. But he became very independent quite young.

Coming out to Hollywood all by himself was a remarkable demonstration of his strong sense of independence. He was quite anxious, quite nervous, but he *made* himself do all those things like coming to a foreign country and trying to get into pictures which thousands of people tried to do every day. I think he didn't really have a clue how difficult it could be to get into pictures, so he had the benefit of ignorance and youthful ambition on his side.

I never tried to dissuade him from becoming an actor but I told him to be prepared for a difficult time. I knew that if the camera liked him then he had a good chance. He just needed the opportunity.

I wondered if he'd ever asked her directly for help in becoming an actor, to which she replied, 'No, he never asked. I think he might have felt that living with us he might get to meet the right people. We must have been a useful family for him to settle in with,' she laughed.

I asked her if she felt that he adopted himself into her family.

'Oh yes. He did. I could tell he wanted to be a part of our family. My mother began to wonder when he was going to go because she said he could only stay a week or two until he found somewhere to live, but he arrived with tons of baggage and he settled very quickly and was in no hurry to leave. My sisters and I liked having him there.'

After living rent-free with Loretta's family for six weeks, he realised he was outwearing his welcome, so he looked for somewhere else to live. He told me, 'I thought I'd try my luck at the Roosevelt Hotel on Hollywood Boulevard. It turned out to be half empty, so I thought I'd see if I could persuade the manager, a nice chap called Alvin C. Weingand who later became a Congressman, if he would let me have a room for $65 a month and defer all my rent until I got a job. Of course, I told him I was expecting to get work any day, and he agreed.'

David often played cards with Alvin Weingand who knew just about everybody who was anybody in Hollywood, and so through him and Loretta as well as Sally Blane, he soon got to know a number of important actors in Hollywood. He also became reacquainted with Douglas Fairbanks and often played tennis and golf with him.

David admitted to me, 'I thought these people, when they became my friends, would easily get me into the movies. There was Charlie Chaplin and Ronnie Colman, all eager to give me advice, but none of them offered me any help, and I can see why. I had no background in the theatre which they all had. They had worked hard to get where they were and I was trying to just jump in and hope to land on my feet.'

Laurence Olivier, another British actor arriving in Hollywood at that time to make his first Shakespeare film, *As You Like It*, saw through Niven straight away. 'He was always trying to be *liked*. Well, I understand that. So did I. So does every actor. But he was an *expert* at it because he entertained people with silly stories that had people in stitches. But that was going to wear thin eventually.'

Deciding he might find his way into movies by becoming an extra, David tried to sign on at the Central Casting Office but was turned away because he didn't have a work permit.

He had once met the sister of Fred Astaire, Adèle, in London, so he took a chance and called at Astaire's home after playing tennis nearby.

'Fred and [his wife] Phyllis were probably my dearest friends when I first got to Hollywood,' David said. 'But I failed to make a good first impression when I turned up at their house without my shirt on and all hot and sweaty from a game of tennis. Phyllis answered the door and I started to explain that I knew Fred's sister, and she just shut the door and I heard her cry, "Fred, there's a dreadful man at the door with no shirt on who says he knows your sister."

'Fred came to the door, invited me in, we had a few drinks and chatted, Phyllis changed her mind about me and I stayed all day. We always remained especially close.'

David admitted to me, 'I made as many contacts as I could because I'd learned years before that it's not what you know but who you know, and I needed to know as many people as possible in Hollywood. So I ingratiated myself. I played cricket every Sunday with the British contingent and that way I got to know some marvellous character actors like Cedric Hardwicke and C. Aubrey Smith, and they had as many good stories to tell as I did, but because I was young they indulged me. I was just a kid to them, and they took a liking to me.'

He also made sure he got to know, and be liked by, stars like Cary Grant and Henry Fonda. He also played golf with Jean Harlow and her fiancé William Powell. 'It was important to let them win,' he told me.

Despite all these Hollywood stars who liked him, few of them were actively helping him break into movies. His break came through a series of events started, not by anyone in Hollywood, but an old Naval friend of David's.

It began on a weekend he spent in Montecito, near Santa Barbara, with a girl he had met in New York, Lydia Macy. From the window of the cheap room in the hotel where they were staying, David saw a sight that took his breath away. He recalled,

In the bay was HMS *Norfolk*, a battleship which had been in Malta, and I wanted to pay her a visit. By a happy coincidence the ship's officers were throwing a party and all of Montecito was invited, so that night in a rather frayed dinner jacket – the only one I owned – I escorted Lydia on board *Norfolk*. By good fortune, among the officers was a friend of mine, Anthony Pleydell-Bouverie who was flag lieutenant to Admiral Sir Ernle Erle Drax who also on board. Then I saw other officers I knew, and poor Lydia ended up leaving the ship at the end of the party on her own while I stayed the night.

The next day I was invited to have lunch with the Admiral, and just as we were finishing a message was brought to the Admiral that HMS *Bounty* was off the starboard bow. And sure enough, when I looked out of the port-hole, there was a beautiful re-creation of the *Bounty*, the ship on which Fletcher Christian had led the famous mutiny against Captain Bligh.

Anthony told me that the ship was there as a publicity stunt for *Mutiny on the Bounty* which was going to be filmed. This beautiful ship had been built at great cost to Metro-Goldwyn-Mayer and they were looking to get as much advance publicity as possible, so there were scores of Hollywood reporters and photographers on a tender alongside of the *Bounty*. Anthony knew that I wanted to be an actor, so he and the Admiral had decided that I should gatecrash the *Bounty*.

I was still in my frayed dinner jacket and rather shabby trousers because I had no other clothing to change into, and I climbed down a rope ladder over the side and onto the tender with all the press watching and wondering who this gatecrasher from a battleship was.

I was welcomed onto the tender by the film's director, Frank Lloyd, and the stars Clark Gable and Charles Laughton. Robert Montgomery, who was a bigger star than Gable at that time, was along for the ride. Bob Montgomery and I got along like a house on fire, and Frank Lloyd was very hospitable indeed. I must have made an impression upon him because he suggested he meet me later back at the studios of Metro-Goldwyn-Mayer.

We arrived at San Pedro where Bob had his car waiting, and we arrived at MGM in the early evening just as filming was winding down for the day. I went to Frank Lloyd's office and there met another great director, Edmund Goulding, who was very amused by the story Frank told of my arrival on the *Bounty*.

He said, 'Ever done any acting?'

I said, 'None to speak of,' and he said, 'Good. I'm looking for a new face to play the drunken, dissolute, younger brother of Ruth Chatterton in my next film. Come and make a test for me tomorrow.' I told him that I didn't have a work permit, and he said, 'You don't need a permit to make a test, and if it works out, the studio will arrange everything.'

I asked what he expected me to do for the test, and he said, 'Just be yourself.' Then he invited me to have dinner at his house with him and his wife, Marjorie Moss, who was a famous dancer, and then he insisted I stay the night. I wanted to go home and change my clothes, but he said, 'I want you to make the test in that dinner jacket.' I obviously looked suitably drunken and dissolute in it.

In the morning I presented myself at stage 29 as ordered where the director making the test was Harry Bouquet who was in a great hurry. I'd been made up by Bill Tuttle and was painted a peculiar yellow ochre, and my eyes and lips were painted so I thought I looked like a tart. I knew nothing about film make-up, and felt ridiculous.

The director told me to stand on the set which was a New York apartment. I was blinded by the lights and couldn't see anyone. Bouquet was very impatient and said, 'Start by facing the camera, then turn slowly and hold it for a beat. Then face the camera again. You got it?' 'Yes, sir.' 'Okay, turn 'em over.' I had no idea what that meant, but the camera started running and Bouquet said, 'Okay, now turn slowly, hold the profile....I said *hold it*, goddammit...okay, now hold the full face...Jesus, try to come alive for Chrissake...tell a funny story, do *something*.'

I still couldn't see because of the lights, and I was getting in a panic, and I suddenly remembered a limerick, and said

> There once was an old man of Leeds
> Who swallowed a packet of seeds,
> Great tufts of grass
> Shot out of his arse
> And his cock was covered in weeds.

'Cut! Jesus, what are you trying to do? Get me fired? Louis Mayer's gonna see this. So's Eddie Mannix. Okay, now just relax kid and think of some little story. But keep it *clean.*'

So I told them a story about Tommy Phipps's first trip to an automat. He didn't know how it worked, and put five cents into the slot for a cup of coffee but didn't get his cup in place and hot coffee squirted him in the groin. He finally managed to get a cup of coffee but meanwhile someone had eaten his sandwich, and then someone dunked their doughnut in his coffee. Well, it seemed to go down well.

The next day I went to see Goulding who said the test was bad except for the limerick. He said I wasn't being given the part but he would help me anyway.

Edmund Goulding was actually one of the very first British film directors to become a success in Hollywood, having scored a huge hit with *Grand Hotel* in 1932, and this perhaps explains why he was so determined to help the young Englishman with aspirations of being an actor. It's also likely that Goulding was quickly won over by Niven's charm and wit. David told me once, 'I knew I could get people to like me if I told a good story, and that was my talent. I couldn't act when I first got to Hollywood but I told funny tales, and some of them were even true.'

The actor who did get the role Niven had tested for was Louis Hayward, a South African who had been raised in London where he became an actor in plays and then films. As far as Hollywood was concerned that made Hayward a British actor, complete with authentic English accent who arrived in America around the same time Niven did but with the advantage of theatrical training. Niven had no acting training at all but fortunately for him, Goulding saw something in him that made him believe the young Niven could become an actor.

Goulding and Frank Lloyd made sure that David got introduced to Irving Thalberg, the boy wonder producer at Metro-Goldwyn-Mayer who took an immediate liking to David and they became firm friends. David said,

Irving Thalberg was the most important producer at Metro. Every film he produced was gold. He had the magic touch. He had the most wonderful wife, Norma Shearer, who was a great actress and very beautiful. That Christmas [1934] they bought me the most marvellous Christmas present – a Studebaker car – brand new. I gave them a set of handkerchiefs with the letters I and N embroidered on. I felt very embarrassed that my gift to them was so meagre, but Norma said, 'We can afford to buy a dozen cars, and most of our friends can buy us a car each, but none of our friends would think of getting us something as wonderfully personal as handkerchiefs with our letters embroidered on.' Irving said it was the best present he'd ever had, and they made me feel on top of the world. Unfortunately, I was so broke that I couldn't afford to buy petrol for the car, so I sold it to eat and pay for rent.

Edmund Goulding was so convinced that David had potential that he recommended him to director Al Hall who was about to make a film with Mae West, *Goin' to Town*. David met both star and director for an unusual audition – they wanted to see David without his shirt on. Mae West was impressed by his muscular build; he was no Tarzan but sports and Army life had given his lean frame impressive strong muscles.

They said they would want to see him again, but before that could happen he was caught up by an immigration official who told him that his 10-day visitor's visa was long expired and he was now an illegal immigrant with 24 hours to leave the country or be arrested.

David Niven was on the verge of becoming a criminal.

CHAPTER 8

—

An Anglo Saxon Extra

To avoid deportation, David went to Mexico by train and arrived in a small border town called Mexicali where he applied to the local American consul for a resident alien visa so he could work in Hollywood. A police report from England was requested by the consul but it took a few weeks for his visa to come through, during which time he earned money by working in a bar, washing up in a restaurant and cleaning the guns of visiting American tourists who were on a shooting holiday.

In January 1935 he returned to Los Angeles to discover that the part in the Mae West film had been taken by Paul Cavanagh, an English actor with stage experience. There was quite an influx of British stage talent arriving in Hollywood around that time, and Niven was in competition with them all.

He reported back to Central Casting and was signed on as 'Anglo-Saxon Type No. 2008'. He said that his first job was in a Western playing a Mexican. I doubt that is true as there were plenty of Mexican extras in Los Angeles. He also claimed he was a half naked slave in Cecil B. DeMille's *Cleopatra*, but that film was made and released in 1934 before he had his work permit.

The life of an extra was very mundane, turning up for work early, being sent to a sound stage or to the backlot and trying not to get lost, getting into an ill-fitting costume, being part of a crowd, maybe just walking a street as a 'passer by', or sitting in a restaurant, often not knowing what the film was or even seeing any of the major stars. (I speak from personal experience.) I said to David, 'I bet you can't remember half the films you were an extra in,' and he replied, 'My dear chap, I can't remember *any* of them.'

I don't think he worked that often as an extra and had to supplement his income by working as a deckhand on a 45-foot (13.5m) charter fishing boat, the *König*, out of Balboa.

'I did love that life,' he told me. 'It was hard work, very dangerous but I was young and strong, and I got $6 a day plus tips. One day Clark Gable came on board with a pretty blonde. When he heard me speak, he said, "You're English." I said, "Yes, I am." "You sound like Ronald Colman." I said, "Yes, so I'm told." He said, "What the devil are you doing out here?" So I told him I was hoping to be an actor, and then I told him our paths had crossed, so to speak, when I transferred from *Norfolk* to the *Bounty*. "That's right, I remember," he said. "Say, aren't you the guy who was living at Loretta Young's home?" I said, "Yes, I am actually." He raised his famous eyebrow and said, "That Loretta, huh?" Of course, he'd had a fling with her when they made *Call of the Wild*.'

That 'fling' resulted in a daughter, Judy, who had to be kept secret. Loretta claimed that Judy was an orphan and she had adopted her. I found out about that in 1975 when it was still a secret, and I asked David if he had known.

'Who the devil told you about that?' he asked.

I told him it was Ava Gardner. Ava was a friend of mine for many years, and also a long time friend of David's.

'Hollywood is full of secrets that everyone knows,' he said. 'What I loved about the "old Hollywood" was the true camaraderie they had there. If you got yourself into trouble, there was always someone to get you out of it and even if everybody knew, nobody talked of it openly. When Loretta had her little girl, Gable had to pretend for years he wasn't her father. That was a terrible thing for him and for Judy.' I can see that Niven identified with Judy in that respect.

I consider myself lucky to have been in the company of both David and Ava Gardner a number of times. One night in 1975 David treated us to dinner at a small intimate and very exclusive Italian restaurant in West London. Something happened there that was a personal revelation to me of his generosity. He was dressed casually but still very smartly in what must have been a crisp new shirt and a casual jacket that also looked brand spanking new. He wore no tie and his shirt collar was open, yet he still looked immaculate. Ava had dressed what I would call comfortably. I was in my best and only rather shabby three-piece suit, looking over-dressed but hardly dazzling.

David said, 'You look dressed for a wedding or a funeral.'

I said, 'This is the suit I got married in.' (That was two years earlier.)

'Oh my God,' laughed Ava, 'you really *are* dressed for a wedding.'

David suddenly announced, 'Tomorrow I will buy you a new suit. What would you like. I mean, *really* like?'

I admitted that I really rather admired the way Tony Curtis dressed in the 1971 TV series he did with Roger Moore called *The Persuaders* and was particularly fond of a dark suit he wore in the pilot episode. David said, 'I haven't a clue what that looks like but tomorrow we'll go to King's Road and you can look for that suit and I'll buy it for you.'

He did, too, complete with shirt, shoes and a chunky tie. When David saw me with it all on, he said, 'Yes, well, you do look a lot like Tony Curtis now.' I think I did; I styled my hair on the way he wore his in *The Persuaders*. (Yes, sad, I know, but I was a young fan, you see.)

Then David asked if I could do an impression of Curtis. I could but it wasn't very good but I could do a good impression of Curtis doing an impression of Cary Grant, and David responded as though I had given an award-winning performance, laughing and applauding in the shop. He said, 'I'll tell Roger that if he ever decides to do another *Persuaders* but doesn't want Tony Curtis, I have the perfect substitute for him.'

I don't think he ever did tell Roger Moore that, but his purchase of a suit that I really loved and his kind words have always been one of my most abiding memories of him.

Over dinner that night in 1975 Ava talked about having moved from Spain to London in 1969 and of the horror of finding that the IRA was bombing the city. She also talked about some frightening encounters with the Mafia during her marriage to Frank Sinatra which, in turn, led David to relate the following experience he had during the time when he was working as an extra.

He said there was an extra called Eddie Hunnicut who told him, 'How about I fix you up with a great little prostitute. You'll love her and what she does.'

David told him that he was very tired and didn't think he could 'even raise a smile'! Eddie told him, 'You won't be too tired for this. She gives the best blow job in Los Angeles.'

As David told it, 'Well, that got my interest. I mean, it wasn't like I had to *do* anything. So I said, "Okay, let me know where and when."'

Eddie told David to be at a certain place at a certain time. 'I was really looking forward to it after a long day's work. The trouble was, he had neglected to tell me how much it was going to cost me, and I hadn't even thought about that. So after what was really only a regular blow job – I mean, I've certainly had a lot better – in the front seat of her car, she asked for $50. Well, that was a *fortune*.' David told her that he couldn't pay that much and the next thing he knew a couple of hoods were getting in the car and pointing guns at him and saying they were going to lend him the money and he was going to repay them with a hundred per cent interest.

David had no option but to agree to their extortionate terms, and then he got out of the car and walked back to his room at the Roosevelt Hotel, wondering how he was going to pay a hundred dollars when he only got paid $2.50 a day as an extra. The three days' work he had on the picture barely paid for his meals for the week.

In desperation he decided to see if he could borrow the money, and that night called a number of the rich people he knew. He told the ones he could reach that he was in debt for his rent and needed $25. 'I figured it was a downright cheek asking for a hundred in one go,' he told us. 'So I thought that I needed just twenty-five dollars from four people. I didn't think it would be so hard.' He didn't say which ones he couldn't reach or which ones refused to loan him any money, but the one guy who did lend him $25 was Clark Gable. 'I told Clark I'd pay him back as soon as I could, and he said, "Oh, forget it, I don't want it back. You helped me catch a blue marlin the other day and I didn't tip you enough." Well, that wasn't quite true. I did help him catch a marlin but he tipped me very nicely.'

Twenty-five dollars was all he had been able to get together so far and he hoped that would be enough to keep the hoods happy. The next day at the studio, he was approached by an extra he knew quite well, an Irish American called Gerry O'Hara who said to him, 'I hear Eddie fixed you up and you got rolled over.'

'How did you know about that?' David asked.

'He was bragging about it last night in a bar. He figured that because you're a limey nobody's gonna give a fuck what happens to you. To tell you the truth, as an Irishman I couldn't give a fuck about an Englishman, but you're okay and I hate to see you end up in the morgue which is what's gonna happen when you don't pay. So we're gonna fix things.'

David asked him what he had in mind, and all O'Hara would say was, 'Just try not to worry.'

David recalled, 'That was easier said than done. I'm due to be bumped off the next day, and I'm not to *worry?*'

He described the next day as 'one of the worst days of my life because I thought it might be the last'.

He finished the day's work on the studio backlot and after the extras were dismissed, he was on his way to return his costume and collect his $2.50 when the two hoods caught up with him and, taking him by the arms, forced him to a quiet corner and said, 'Now pay up.'

David recalled, 'I was shaking, really ready to pee in my pants, and I told them I only had twenty-five dollars and it would take more time to get the rest.' They took his $25 and David hoped he had a reprieve, but then they grabbed him and dragged him off to somewhere even quieter. He told us, 'I thought, *This is it. I'm a dead man. But I'm taking at least one of them with me.* I knew unarmed combat and I was going to put it to the test.'

Suddenly O'Hara and half a dozen other guys, all extras and all Irish Americans, appeared; they'd been keeping an eye on David. They told him to clear off, which he did, he said, 'without any further persuasion'.

He didn't see Gerry for a week or so, but when he did, he asked what had happened to the two hoods. O'Hara told him, 'You don't want to know.' David recalled, 'And he said it like I really *didn't* want to know.'

Then O'Hara told David that he and his friends were leaving Hollywood to go to Ireland. 'Ah, going back to the old country, eh?' asked David.

O'Hara laughed and said, 'Aye, that's right, to drive the bloody English out. We're going back with a few things we need,' and then he imitated firing a rifle. David suddenly realised they were with the IRA.

He said that he became desperately worried and went to the British consul and told him what had happened. The consul said they could handle this in two ways. One way was to bring in the police and the FBI because the chances were that the two gangsters were dead and that would put Niven in a difficult situation and he could say goodbye to his Hollywood career.

David said, 'What's the other option?'

'You can walk out and go home and not say another word and stay away from whores in future.'

'But what will *you* do?'

The consul said, 'I'm going to have lunch with some VIPs.'

'But those men are heading back to Ireland with weapons that will be used on our soldiers.'

The consul said, 'Calm yourself. Our men in Ireland will be patrolling the coasts, watching roads, as they always do. There'll be nothing we can do to find these friends of yours so let our boys do their job. You were in the Army, weren't you?'

'Yes!'

'Then have a little faith in our soldiers. And keep your mouth shut. You've done all you can do. Thank you, Mr Niven, and goodbye!'

David said he despised the IRA and felt guilty that he couldn't do anything to stop those men, but he said he also had a sneaking admiration for them because they probably saved his life.

He wondered what happened to Eddie who he never saw again. Ava told him, 'That guy must have been a soldier in the Mob and running a scam, and once his cover was blown, he just got out of there.'

David said that he later told Clark Gable the whole sorry episode, and Gable said to him, 'Why the hell didn't you say, for crissakes? I would have given you the full amount.'

David said, 'I'm sorry, Clark, but I really only wanted what I thought was going to be the best blow job in town.'

Gable said, 'Jesus, David, if that's all you want, I can *tell* you where you can get that, and it won't cost you a dime.'

David told us, 'Dear old Gable, he understood.'

Ava said, 'Yes, and knowing Clark, he *did* know the girl in Hollywood who gave the best blow job.'

David continued to sign on each day as an extra, hoping for more work and maybe a break that would turn him into an actor. But he knew the chances of that were next to nothing because every extra in Hollywood, hundreds of them, all wanted to be movie stars. But Niven had the advantage of friends like Edmund Goulding who found him an agent, Bill Hawks who in turn got David a screen test with Claudette Colbert for her next movie, *The Gilded Lily*.

There were two other actors also being tested, Ray Milland and Fred MacMurray. Milland was another British actor in Hollywood, having made steady progress since arriving there in 1930.

I interviewed Milland in 1980 in London. He remembered David Niven's early days in Hollywood. 'He was without any acting ability and I think he knew it. He was always ready with a funny anecdote but in front of a camera he dried. I don't think it had dawned on him at first that there would be other actors from Britain; maybe he thought he would be the next Ronald Colman. In fact he became very friendly with Colman, but he was nervous and I think jealous with other British actors in Hollywood and with a background in stage and British films. I wasn't around him very much, but when I was I felt that he was giving me the cold shoulder. If you weren't a big star, he didn't want to know you.'

It didn't help Niven's confidence when both Milland and MacMurray got the parts they tested for *and* a contract at Paramount while David was shown the door. Shortly after that, he was signed to a contract by Samuel Goldwyn, one of the most powerful independent producers in Hollywood.

The story of how David came to be signed by Goldwyn is almost apocryphal. David always said that Thalberg decided to give him a tiny part in *Mutiny on the Bounty*, playing one of the mutineers, but there is no evidence he appeared in the film. A rumour spread that Thalberg was about to put David Niven under contract to MGM, which created sudden interest from other studios. If there was a rumour, I suspect that David started it. The rumour got Samuel Goldwyn's interest and he signed David before anyone else could. That was Niven's version of events.

Another account that I read said Goulding persuaded Goldwyn to take a look at David's one and only screen test and Goldwyn decided that was enough to sign him up. But the screen test, by David's own admission, was pretty awful.

I asked Loretta Young if she knew what happened, and she said she did. She told me that her mother advised David to play tennis regularly with Frances Goldwyn, Sam Goldwyn's wife. Loretta's mother knew that Frances would immediately like David, and she persuaded her husband to give David a break.

David once said to me, 'I suppose I got signed because Frances Goldwyn liked me.' He had got his start in movies because Sam Goldwyn was just pleasing his wife.

David might well have been considered by Thalberg. Niven told me, 'I was good friends with Irving Thalberg. He said to me once, "I could have done better things for you than Goldwyn." I had to tell him, "Then why didn't you say something before I signed with Goldwyn?" He said, "I would have but you rushed into that contract while I was producing *Mutiny on the Bounty*, but I would have got around to it. Tell you what, when your seven years with Sam is up, *I'll* sign you." By the time my seven years were up, Irving had died.'

It was late February 1935 when Goldwyn signed David to a seven-year contract, starting at $125 a week, a fortune to David back then. His salary would increase to $150, then to $200 in the third year, and then by a hundred each year until he was earning $600 in the seventh year.

For the rest of his life, David had very mixed feelings about Goldwyn. He told me, 'Without Goldwyn, I might never have made it. Or that's what he wanted me to believe. I think it's possible that I could have done better at Metro-Goldwyn-Mayer. But I did have a career, and I suppose I should be thankful to Goldwyn for that. He could be very kind, and sometimes he was very generous, but then he made a lot of money by loaning me out to other studios. I remember when I told Ronnie Colman I was going to work for Goldwyn. Ronnie was just leaving Goldwyn, and he was horrified. He told me that Goldwyn was by far the best producer in Hollywood, but he could be a real bastard. Well, he *was* a bastard at times. But maybe you have to be a bastard to be a successful producer in Hollywood.'

Whatever kind of man Goldwyn was, he got David started in movies. That's a lot more than most other extras in movies ever got.

—

CHAPTER 9

A Great Big Star

David was able to afford to pay Al Weingand his bill and then move into a small house on North Vista. He told me that he was so overjoyed at his new-found wealth that he rushed out and bought a car for $500, only then to discover that his contract allowed Goldwyn to lay him off unpaid for 12 weeks every year, and that his annual 12 weeks unpaid layoff had started with immediate effect. So he had to return his car.

I wasn't totally convinced about this so I mentioned this tale of David's misfortune to Joseph Cotten when I interviewed him in London in 1980; Cotten had been under exclusive contract to David Selznick, another of Hollywood's powerful independent producers, and he said, 'I think Niven has spent his life thinking up things he can say about Sam Goldwyn. It's all garbage! An unpaid layoff was never a part of any contract from a major independent or studio. Men like Goldwyn and Selznick survived by loaning out their stars for considerable amounts of money and they couldn't afford for a studio to ask for a contract player only to be told, "I'm sorry but he's on a 10 or 12 week layoff and can't work."

'You were *employed* by the studio, and you negotiated when you could have time off, all paid for at your usual weekly rate. No, I'm sorry, David Niven was never put on an immediate layoff. I knew Sam Goldwyn. He was a very good, very shrewd producer. He would have been wanting to loan Niven out and make some money from him from the moment he signed him.'

David often made out that Goldwyn was a cruel tyrant, telling me in 1970, 'Goldwyn told me he wouldn't be looking for work for me and I had to find it myself. So I put the word about that I was under contract to Goldwyn and waited for the offers to trickle in.'

But Goldwyn *was* finding David work, at Paramount, in *Without Regret*. Elissa Landi was the star, playing a woman who escapes from bandits in China and unwittingly becomes a bigamist. Goldwyn secured David sixth place in the billing, despite the fact that he delivered only one line, 'Goodbye, my dear.'

It was about this time Merle Oberon arrived in Hollywood. She had become the biggest female movie star in Britain and was under contract to Alexander Korda, the Hungarian born British based film producer who was very powerful in the British film industry. In 1935 Goldwyn bought a share of her contract from Korda to star her in American films, and so Merle arrived in Hollywood to star in *The Dark Angel*.

David's affair with Oberon continued in the US but Niven never spoke publicly of this throughout his life. When he wrote about it in *The Moon's a Balloon* he tried to disguise her identity by referring to her as a 'Great Big Star'. But it was an open secret in Hollywood. Laurence Olivier had seen the romance kindle just a few years before in London. 'By the time I arrived in Hollywood,' he told me, 'Merle and David were very much in love. He'd changed a great deal since I first saw them together. She was obviously a big help to him professionally, teaching him how to behave with more confidence for the camera, and she was able to get him to deliver his natural charm for the camera. He was likeable and natural on screen, which is as much as any successful screen actor needed to be.'

David and Merle spent weekends up at San Ysidro, a ranch owned by Ronald Colman and Al Weingand near Santa Barbara, where many friends of Colman and Weingand carried out their secret rendezvous. There Merle coached David for the camera and then persuaded Goldwyn to use him in *Barbary Coast*. He didn't get billing at all, but as a Cockney sailor thrown out of a San Francisco brothel during the gold rush of 1850, he delivered one line as he was being pushed out of a window. Nobody heard what he said as his line was lost amid the general noise of the scene but David said that his line was, 'Orl rite – I'll go.'

Merle's private coaching paid off when he was tested for a small speaking role in *A Feather in Her Hat* and got the part. Goldwyn would have collected a good fee from Columbia for the loan of Niven for this film, and David would have received his usual hundred dollars a week salary. At this stage of his career David didn't care too much, or even think a great deal, about how Goldwyn made money from loaning him out. All he cared about was actually getting a part where he had a scene in which he was the centre of attention as a witty poet enlivening a literary party.

The film featured a British actress, Wendy Barrie, who would later become one of gangster Benny 'Bugsy' Siegel's girlfriends. David took her dancing a number of times; she was just one of numerous actresses and starlets he went dancing with. In 1975, when he was in London promoting *Bring on the Empty Horses*, he said to me, 'I used to go dancing a lot with the girls I met in Hollywood. Of course, the word "dancing" is just a synonym for something a little more intimate, you understand.'

The fact that he was seeing Merle didn't prevent him from 'dancing' with many other women.

David landed a decent supporting role in Goldwyn's *Splendour*, a romantic drama in which he played a failed crook who attempts to marry a rich girl because his family has fallen on hard times. Joel McCrea, who was the film's leading man, and Merle Oberon persuaded Elliot Nugent, the director of the film, to give David the role.

David liked Joel McCrea but was also a little jealous of him. 'We both started at Goldwyn the same time,' he said, 'and I was a little put out that Goldwyn was giving him starring roles while I was billed about sixth and seventh most of the time. Goldwyn was very busy building McCrea's career with the right kind of parts. I began wondering why Goldwyn even took me on when he didn't know what the bloody hell to do with me. But it was good of McCrea to lobby the director and Goldwyn to give me a decent part.'

David recalled the horrors that awaited him on that film.

I was trying to marry a rich girl and had a line which I'll never forget. 'I'd marry her millions if she had two heads and a club foot.' I said it over and over before we filmed it so it would be stuck in my head. But when we came to shoot it, I was so nervous, I said, 'I'd marry her club foot and two heads for her millions.'

'Cut!' The director, Elliot Nugent, was patient at first, and he just said, 'Take two!'

'I'd marry her twenty heads and club foot for…!'

'Cut!'

'I'm sorry, Elliot, I *do* know it.'

'Then say the goddam line. Take three!'

'I'd marry her millions if she had two feet and a club head.'

'Cut!' It took me nine or ten takes to finally get the line right. Now I can't ever forget that line!

The film earned David his first professional review when the *New York Times* noted, 'The unpleasant Lorrimores are acted with poisonous effectiveness by Helen Westley…Katherine Alexander…and David Niven as the useless son.'

David made a fourth film before the year was out, *Rose Marie*, a Jeanette MacDonald/Nelson Eddy musical for Metro-Goldwyn-Mayer. David had little chance to shine in this because, as the *New York Times* noted, 'Since this is Miss MacDonald's and Mr Eddy's picture there can be no important place for other members of the cast.' Another newcomer, James Stewart, also had trouble getting noticed.

David said in 1978, 'I had thought that acting in a film would be easy, but I found that when it came down to it I had very little confidence and was extremely nervous. I had trouble saying the few lines I had in each picture.'

Merle suggested to Goldwyn that it might help David if he was to do a stage play. Without mentioning Merle's part in the plan, David told me,

> Goldwyn really hadn't a clue what kind of parts to put me in. He'd taken me on as a sort of successor to Ronald Colman but he didn't have the scripts that called for that kind of part. So he thought I needed to learn more about acting and the best way to do that was to put me in a play, *Wedding*, which played at the Pasadena Playhouse. I only had three scenes and didn't speak until the third scene when I had just two lines.
>
> I couldn't resist putting it about that I had the starring role but that backfired because on the opening night I was horrified when I made my first entrance to tremendous applause. All my Hollywood friends, the Colmans, the Fairbankses, the Goldwyns, had decided to surprise me by turning up to see my starring role on the stage. I was terrified, and after my first scene I got back to my dressing room and drank three great slugs of whiskey, staggered back on for the second scene, just about made it back on for the third and made a total mess of my only two lines of the play. So to cover, I told a dirty story and then as I made my exit I walked into the scenery. I didn't do a second night – I was fired.
>
> Goldwyn was furious with me and my punishment was to be laid off for six weeks – unpaid.

It's difficult to know if Goldwyn really did lay him off as punishment. David was hardly in demand by other studios, and Goldwyn didn't produce enough pictures to feature all of his contract players, so it may be that David was simply out of work for a while, and probably not unpaid.

Merle had to return to England to make two films for Alexander Korda. When she returned to America in October, David met with her in New York and they decided to drive the 3,000 miles (4,800 km) back to Los Angeles. David recalled some of this adventure to me without ever mentioning that he was travelling with Merle but did refer to the 'Great Big Star'.

They stopped at a hotel, possibly in Chicago, where they booked in under a false name. 'I was absolutely broke so she was paying the bill. I didn't mind being a kept man at all for the trip.' Actually, Merle was paying for most things; they were living together and she was paying the rent on their house. He really was a kept man.

On route from New York to Los Angeles, Merle had to let Goldwyn know where she was at all times and telephoned him at every stop. 'The upshot of this,' said David, 'was that Goldwyn got wind of where I was and started sending me telegrams telling me to get back to Los Angeles immediately, but I figured that since I was on suspension I would just ignore them. Telegrams followed us right across America, each one angrier than the last. When we finally got back to Los Angeles Goldwyn fired me.'

Laurence Olivier later heard about this episode but had a lot more insight into what really happened. He told me in an interview I did with him in at Shepperton Studios when he was making *Dracula* in 1979,

Goldwyn was furious with David for risking the career of Merle because she was under contract to him and he was trying to present her as a sweet, virginal heroine – well, Merle was sweet, but *virginal?* That didn't matter; there were precious few virgins in Hollywood, male or female. As far as Goldwyn was concerned David had risked everything he'd invested in Merle, and worse still, he had broken the strange law they have in America which forbids a man to take a woman across state lines for what they call 'immoral purposes'. Hollywood stars were doing that all the time, and the women all went very willingly. But it would have caused a terrible scandal if he had been arrested or if someone had leaked the story to the press. The scandal would have been enormous. David just didn't understand all that. He said to me, 'A little car ride, that's all it was.' I said, 'Yes, from East to West Coast. That's a very long little car ride.'

When Goldwyn fired him, Merle fixed it. She went to Goldwyn and she was so sweet and charming that he couldn't resist her when she urged him to keep David on.

I really think that without Merle, David would never have had a film career. He was very nearly a disaster from the start, but she kept coaching him, encouraging him, and she kept him working for Goldwyn who would have fired him and that would have been that.

As much as David loved Merle and she loved him, he was unable to stay faithful to her. He had an insatiable sex drive. He admitted to me, 'I just couldn't get enough when I was a young man.'

When I asked him if he was faithful to the Great Big Star, he said, 'Oh, how I wanted to be, old man. But I just couldn't. If a pretty girl came on to me, I couldn't resist. Now, who could?'

On Christmas Day 1935 Merle and David were among the guests at Clifton Webb's house. Sam Goldwyn may have disapproved of David's affair with Merle but the couple were the Goldwyns' guests on New Year's Eve.

Before January was out, David was relieved to be back at work. He told me, 'I was always sure that each film I made would be my last. I had no track record and I was sure somebody was going to tap me on the shoulder and say, "Sorry, old man, but you really don't cut it so off you go and don't come back." I was always surprised and delighted when I found myself with another job.'

His first film of 1936 was at Paramount, *Palm Springs Affair*, a musical comedy that cast him as a debonair character that finally suited his own personality which may have encouraged Twentieth Century-Fox then to give him his biggest role so far, as Bertie Wooster in *Thank You, Jeeves* from the writings of P.G. Wodehouse. Arthur Treacher starred as Jeeves.

Although it was a B-picture, it gave David his first leading role, and with his incurable charm, he was able to make the upper-class nitwit Wooster into a character of elegance and wit. Both Niven and Treacher were perfectly cast as Wooster and Jeeves, as the *New York Times* noted: 'Mr Wodehouse must have been one of the fates in attendance at their births, marking them to play the characters he has been writing about these many years.'

Although the film gave David a taste of being a leading man, few people got to see it. It ran barely an hour and was played only as a second feature in major cities in America. It didn't play at all in the UK because at that time the British government imposed a very strict quota on how many films could be imported. Only A-list films from America were shown in Britain, and *Thank You, Jeeves* was undeniably a B-movie.

His next film put him back into the league of a supporting actor again, but it was worth it because the picture was a Warner Brothers epic, *The Charge of the Light Brigade*, staring Errol Flynn and Olivia de Havilland, and directed by Michael Curtiz who had turned Flynn into a star the previous year in *Captain Blood*. Curtiz and Flynn would repeat their success with a number of other swashbuckling epics, notably *The Adventures of Robin Hood* and *The Sea Hawk*.

Famously, the title of Niven's second book of Hollywood memoirs were inspired by Curtiz's bad English: 'Curtiz had a rather bad command of the English language,' David told me in 1975, 'which was fair enough as he was, after all, a Hungarian. He wanted to film a stampede of horses, and the order he barked was, "Bring on the empty horses!"'

Niven had a major supporting role, that of an English cavalry captain whose main function in the film was to be charming and dashing and die a decent death halfway through the film. During the filming, he and Flynn became good friends.

'Flynn was an Australian,' David said, 'but he spoke with a clear English accent and so he was perfect casting as Captain Blood and Robin Hood. He called everyone "Sport", and he was a sex maniac! So he reminded me a lot of me and we got on famously.

'I had met him a couple of times before we worked together, and at first I found him to be very arrogant and didn't like him at all. But when we worked together I suppose something clicked between us and since we both had a fondness for women and booze and getting into trouble we realised we actually had enough in common to be friends.'

Much of the filming took place near the town of Bishop, some 200 miles (320 km) from Los Angeles. 'The town had only one hotel,' David recalled, 'but it burned down a week after we started filming and we had to freeze our arses off, sleeping in tents. Flynn and I tried to keep ourselves warm by drinking alcohol and sleeping with as many girls as we could find. It is quite surprising how many willing young ladies there were in the small town of Bishop who wanted to sleep with movie stars in tents on cold desert nights.'

Although the film featured the famous charge which occurred during the Crimean War, most of the film was set on the North Western Frontier. In 1978 Niven gave me what he thought was the reason for this meddling with history. 'Hollywood simply didn't feel that the Crimean War, in which the British aided the French against the Russians, was glamorous enough. The North West Frontier had elements of the Bengal Lancers and *Gunga Din* which was popular with Hollywood studios, so the film became an Indian epic.

'All my scenes were set in India. Flynn and I found ourselves sitting in a basket on top of an elephant for a scene in which we were hunting tigers, and the damn thing suddenly went berserk and began running about and turning round and round and crashing into things in an effort to get us and the basket off its back.'

Interior scenes were shot back at the Warner Brothers studio and allowed Flynn and Niven to drink and carouse in the evenings and often well into the night despite having to rise early each morning to begin filming. 'Flynn had a greater capacity for booze than I did,' David said. 'Most men as drunk as him wouldn't be able to *get it up*, but Flynn had no problem. One morning he appeared bright and breezy and I asked him how he had fared the night before after I'd left him with two girls – *he* had the two girls, not me! He said, "I needed a few more drinks, old sport." I said, "You needed *more*?" He said, "Hadn't had enough to get the old cock hard enough for two girls." I said to him, "But surely more alcohol would have made it harder – that is, *difficult* to keep it up." He said, "Not with my metabolism, sport." He pointed at his crotch and said, "He needs plenty of alcohol coursing through his veins."'

The Charge of the Light Brigade was a tremendous success and, despite being killed off midway through the story, Niven acquitted himself admirably.

At this time, he proved to be a valuable and faithful friend to Douglas Fairbanks who had been through a tough time when he and his wife Mary Pickford divorced. Fairbanks was in love with Lady Sylvia Ashley but she was unpopular with many of Doug's Hollywood friends.

'Sylvia was a lovely lady and so good for Doug at the time,' David said. 'She was kind to me and so hospitable when I first got to Hollywood. But a lot of Doug's older friends who were also friends of Mary Pickford didn't like the fact that Sylvia and Doug were getting married. I heard people call her a gold digger. That was nonsense. She made Doug very happy.'

Fairbanks and Lady Ashley married on 7 March 1936 in Paris. Niven was unable to attend, but to show his friendship and gratitude to the couple that much of Hollywood looked down on, he and Merle threw a party for them when they got back to Los Angeles.

'Hollywood could be a cruel place,' Niven told me in 1979. 'If you stepped out of line, you paid the penalty. Doug's career never recovered after he married Sylvia. That was a salutary lesson I learned quickly. You can be forgiven for many things in Hollywood, but marrying the wrong person – never. I think that destroyed Doug and he died just a few years later [on 12 December 1939].'

In May, David was given a decent part in a good movie, *Dodsworth*. Based on a best selling novel, it starred Walter Huston as American busi-nessman Samuel Dodsworth who takes his wife, played by Ruth Chatterton, on a trip to Europe where their lives change dramatically. Niven's role was brief but effective as a suave Englishman who has a flirtation with Dodworth's wife. He had little to do but be charming, and that he did very well.

He might have thanked the film's director, William Wyler, for casting him in such a huge success, but he didn't. 'Willie Wyler was a Jekyll and Hyde,' he said. 'He was absolutely charming and friendly, but as soon as he placed his arse on his director's chair he became a monster. His technique was to reduce actors to shambling wrecks by making them do take after take without ever giving any direction whatsoever. He even reduced Ruth Chatterton to tears.'

I was puzzled by Niven's hatred of Wyler who had the reputation of getting Oscar-winning performances from actors. What I came to know about him, talking to many actors who worked with him, such as Charlton Heston, Stephen Boyd (both in *Ben-Hur*) and Audrey Hepburn (*The Children's Hour*) was that he did put actors through take after take, but he always told them to try different things in each take, often changing his mind, even contradicting himself, getting every possible version of a scene before deciding he had the best he could get. What he didn't do, as Stephen Boyd noted when I interviewed him in 1977, was to tell actors how to act. 'I learned that his gift isn't in *directing* actors, because he can't direct actors to act – his gift is in casting the *right* actors and letting them work through the role and the scenes to discover for themselves what they can do with it.'

Wyler agreed that he was a tough director when I talked to him by telephone in 1976. 'I can't tell an actor how to act, any more than they can tell me where to put the camera. I choose the best actors and the best technicians, and then it's hard work for everyone. I'm not a terrible person. I get on with people, but I can't make good films being nice.'

Wyler did admit that he was 'a lot harder on actors in the early days. I was still learning.' He spoke well of Niven, saying, 'David Niven was still new to films, but he was *exactly* what I wanted to play that character. He was still unsure of himself as an actor, and the more takes he did, the better he got. He was *good* in the part, and that was because I didn't stifle him with too many instructions. I think, perhaps, he wanted to be told how to do it because he was still a new boy in Hollywood and quite unsure of himself.'

Niven didn't remember it being quite that way. He said, 'It seems to me that Wyler's method was to actually destroy an actor's self-confidence – and God knows I had little to start with – and go from there. I gave so many takes that in the end I didn't know what the hell I was supposed to do. Wyler would shout at me, *"Do it again! Be better!"*'

Dodsworth was a critical and box office hit. *Variety* was spot on when it noted that the three men who played the lovers of Ruth Chatterton's character, including the 'suave Englishman played by David Niven' was 'a case of slick casting'. Wyler's great talent was casting the right actors.

David, forever refusing to credit Wyler for his success in the film, said that it was Walter Huston who was responsible for what he was able to deliver in his part. He said, 'What saved me was Walter Huston and [his son] John who was working on the film. Walter Huston was a big star. A major actor. He had played in the stage version of *Dodsworth*. He knew what to do with the role, and he didn't take any nonsense from Wyler, and Wyler knew that, so he hammered everybody else *but* Huston.

'John Huston was a scriptwriter. He worked on the film but didn't get any credit. He became a fine director, a very different director to Wyler. I think he must have learned how *not* to be a director like Wyler by watching him.'

I knew John Huston – I did some work for him in 1972 and 1974 as well interviewing him in 1981 – and he said that his father never helped David at all. He recalled that it was Merle who gave him additional help when he was making *Dodsworth*. Of course, in 1970, nobody was supposed to know about Niven's romance with Merle.

Merle continued to promote David's career and persuaded Goldwyn to cast him in her next film, *Beloved Enemy*, made in September 1937. Merle was to play the daughter of a top British civil servant serving in Dublin in 1921 who falls for an Irishman, played by Brian Aherne, but discovers that he is an IRA leader and betrays him. David had a supporting role, as her father's secretary.

There was some tension on the set because Brian Aherne was rather enamoured of Miss Oberon, and Niven was jealous of their love scenes. Merle knew that Niven was unfaithful and it seems that she took the opportunity to get even by sleeping with Aherne. David very nearly caught them, turning up at Aherne's house one afternoon while Merle was there. Niven and Aherne went for a long walk while Merle hid inside the house. Aherne told Sheridan Morley that he was sure David knew Merle was there but never mentioned her, and Sheridan told me, 'I think Merle was thoroughly fed up with Niven's rakish behaviour and she was beginning to feel humiliated. So she taught him a lesson, and it hurt him. It didn't make for a very happy experience on the set [of *Beloved Enemy*].'

Like almost everyone else in Hollywood, John Huston was aware of the 'secret' romance between David and Merle, and he told me about it in 1974. 'I thought they made a wonderful couple. David was kind of an outdoors man. He liked playing tennis and fishing, and once or twice he and I sailed out and caught some marlin. Merle wasn't too keen on that, but she liked to play tennis and golf. And she went to watch him play cricket.

'I wasn't a part of mainstream Hollywood, so I wasn't at all the big society events that Niven and Oberon attended, but he would tell me how he and Merle had dinner with the Colmans. They'd go up to a ranch Colman owned where a good many couples who were either cohabitating or just having an extramarital fling would spend time. I myself enjoyed a few weekends there and met them there one time. I was with a rather nice young actress I was quite infatuated with, and David and Merle wanted us to join them on a picnic.'

Huston's enduring memory of Niven was that he was 'a wonderful storyteller – I can tell a few tales myself – and he and I swapped stories'.

There was a particular story Huston told which David especially liked. When Huston was a young man he went to Mexico City by mule train from Acapulco and got fleas. After the first few days of travelling three Mexicans with guns came into camp and asked for tobacco and food and which they were given. Then they asked for ammunition. Huston and his companions gave them some but they wanted more. The bandits left but began shooting into the camp. There was a brief gunfight and then another the next night. The captain of the mule train left four men to set an ambush for the bandits. One bandit was wounded and got away, one escaped unharmed and the third they captured, turned him over to the *rurales* at the next town, and he was duly executed. It was a story Huston wrote into *The Treasure of the Sierra Madre*.

Niven loved Huston's story and told him about his own time in Mexico when his visa had run out. He added some spice to his story, saying that while he was there he taught the local rebels how to use various firearms. Huston told me, 'I knew this wasn't true because I knew a little about the Mexicans, but I let him tell his tale because he told it so well.'

David said that while he was instructing these rebels a notorious Mexican bandit rode in and asked him to join his band of outlaws and he politely refused. He told the outlaw leader, 'Sorry, old bean, but I'm rather tied up with the local peons and their cause for liberty,' to which the bandit responded by opening fire on him. There was a gun battle, and Niven said he thought he had got shot in the arse but it turned out to be just a splinter from a nearby tree which was shattered when gunfire hit it.

Huston told me, 'He had Merle and the young lady I was with enthralled by this escapade which I knew was a complete fantasy, but he made it sound so funny. He painted this picture of how they had to take down his pants and remove this splinter from his ass which he claimed he kept as a souvenir of the time he nearly died in a shootout in Mexico. I asked him where he kept it. He said, "I'll show it to you when we get back to Los Angeles."

'Some days later he turned up with a six-inch [15cm] wooden splinter attached to a piece of string which, he said, he hung on his bed post at night. That's when Merle realised he wasn't being entirely truthful and playfully slapped him on the ass.'

Huston said that about a year later he was having dinner with a couple of Hollywood writers, and one said, 'Did you hear about David Niven's adventure in a Mexican mule train. He got covered in fleas, and then the outfit was attacked by Mexican bandits.'

As Huston said, 'That was Niven; he loved to tell a good story, and if he heard one that might be better, he'd end up telling that as well. But he told that story of mine to the wrong person though, one time. He told [Humphrey] Bogart who listened very politely, laughing in all the right spots, and when David had finished telling it, Bogie said, "You know, David, I was *in* that movie. You should have seen it. It was pretty good. It was called *The Treasure of the Sierra Madre*. John Huston wrote and directed it." And David, without batting an eye, replied, "That's the trouble with John Huston. You tell him a marvellous story and the next thing you know he's turned it into a movie."'

Huston had originally let me in on the Niven/Oberon secret in early 1974. When I saw David next, which was in October 1974, I told him that I knew who the Great Big Star was and that it was John Huston who gave the game away. He said, 'Keep that to yourself, *please*. Merle wouldn't be happy at all if it got out. I *knew* I shouldn't have trusted that big Irishman. He told me stories of gunfights with Mexican bandits. Of course, I didn't believe a word of it.'

David shared the shock felt by the whole of Hollywood at the sudden death of Irving Thalberg on 14 September 1936. He was just 37. His widow, Norma Shearer, asked David to be an usher at the funeral. She thereafter became a recluse but was visited often by David who was one of the very few friends she would agree to see.

In October, to David's horror – and also Goldwyn's – Merle announced to a news agency that she and David were going to get married. It seems he had finally decided he would marry her after all. She had told him she was prepared to forgive his sins if he settled down with her permanently and stopped his philandering. 'He must have agreed in a moment of passion,' John Huston said. 'I can imagine him saying, "Yes, darling, anything you say," as she brought him to the brink of ecstasy. I dare say he regretted it the moment it was all over.'

I think Huston could be right. Whether it actually happened that way or not, David wouldn't have agreed to marry Merle for any rational reason, and certainly not just so he could win her forgiveness for all past deeds. As

Michael Trubshawe told me, 'Nivvy couldn't be faithful to any of his wives. If he'd married Merle, he would never have been faithful to her, no matter how much he loved her.'

I suspect that David intended to renege on his marriage acceptance and was mortified to find that before he had found a way to do so, Merle was making public announcements of a forthcoming wedding. He must have made a conscious decision not to bring it all to a sudden end because she was still helping with his career.

Laurence Olivier wasn't convinced that Niven wanted to get married. He told me, 'There's no doubt in my mind that Merle wanted to marry Niven, but he wasn't keen to settle down. I don't think they would have been happily married. David didn't want a wife who was a film star. He wanted a wife who would stay at home. Merle pined for him for many years and she believed she and Niv would have been very happy.'

John Huston said that a marriage between David and Merle would 'probably have ended in disaster. That's the way it is in Hollywood. But for a while they would have been deliriously happy. Merle was good for him. He never would have been an actor if it wasn't for her. I think she made him as good as he was in *Dodsworth*.'

Following newspaper reports of their impending wedding, Goldwyn made them both write denials of any engagement.

David rarely spoke to me about Merle Oberon, but in 1982 he had two things to say about her. The first was, 'She made me into an actor. I couldn't do the bloody thing. But she taught me. She helped me when I made *Dodsworth* while Wyler just sat reading a copy of a Hollywood trade newspaper without even watching me and just kept repeating, "Do it again!" If it wasn't for Merle, I would never have made it as an actor.'

The second thing he said was, 'You know, I have just a few regrets. One of the biggest is not marrying Merle when I had the chance.'

There's no doubt in my mind that David carried a torch for Merle to the day he died.

CHAPTER 10

The Best of Times, The Worst of Times With Flynn

Befor the year was out, Niven managed to fit in one more film, *We Have Our Moments*. He was on loan to Universal, not at that time one of the biggest of studios. The film was very much a B-picture, made only as a supporting feature running just over an hour. He played one of a trio of crooks who frame a school teacher on a European cruise. It was a frothy little comedy, and David earned some fair reviews for his efforts. *Kine Weekly* called it a 'preposterous but entertaining story', in which 'Thurston Hall, David Niven and Warren Hymer mix effectively as the crooks'.

By the end of 1936, Goldwyn had become so pleased with David's progress – which meant that other studios were prepared to pay increasingly larger amounts to use Niven in their pictures – that Goldwyn raised David's weekly salary from $150 to $250 and gave him a new contract so that he would go on to earn $1,000 a week by his seventh year with Goldwyn and not the $600 as originally agreed.

He desperately wanted to have a part in the upcoming David Selznick production of *The Prisoner of Zenda* which was to star Ronald Colman in the dual role of the Ruritanian king and his look-alike cousin Rassendyll. The British contingent of Hollywood often gathered on Sundays at Colman's house and there Colman and Merle decided Niven would be well cast as the king's aide, Fritz von Tarlenheim, a very decent role in what was expected to be a prestigious movie. Douglas Fairbanks Jnr, who was already cast in the film, was enlisted to join Merle and Colman in trying to persuade Selznick to cast David.

Niven was invited to play some tennis and lunch with Selznick and they were joined by Selznick's wife Irene and his brother, Myron, a respected agent. The socialising went on late into the evening by which time David Selznick had made up his mind that Niven would be ideal for the part of the king's aide.

Niven received an unusual present from his brother Max for Christmas 1936. He bought back David's body from the hospital he had sold it to and now David owned his body once more.

In January 1937 Merle was due to fly to England to spend six months making *I, Claudius*, but before she left America, David joined her for a week in Philadelphia, and then another week in Boston where Merle introduced him to her good friend Noël Coward. Then she flew to England and Niven moved in with Errol Flynn. It was not a move to inspire David with thoughts of fidelity.

Flynn had just split from his wife Lili Damita and, in need of a bachelor pad, he and Niven decided to rent Rosalind Russell's house at 601 Linden Drive. As Trubshawe noted, 'David wasn't just finding a place to live while Merle was away for half a year. He was putting himself into a situation where Merle wouldn't *want* to marry him.'

In 1970, and again in 1971 when *The Moon's a Balloon* was published, David spoke of his time with Errol Flynn as if it had been the greatest of friendships. But in 1979 he told me, 'It's true that Flynn and I had a great time. But he wasn't a real friend. He was just a great pal, someone to have fun with. You couldn't rely on Flynn at all.'

In *Bring on the Empty Horses*, David famously wrote of Flynn, 'You always knew precisely where you stood with him because he would always let you down.' Behind the humour of that line was the truth of their friendship. As far as Flynn was concerned David was someone to share in his love of booze and women. For David it was an opportunity to sow enough wild oats that Merle would never want to marry him. It's true that he enjoyed Flynn's company, and they certainly shared a common bond in seeking out the pleasures of bachelorhood. David, at the age of 26, was reliving his youth. As Sheridan Morley noted, he was able to find with Flynn the kind of schoolboy life he had enjoyed with Michael Trubshawe on Malta.

Part of Flynn's appeal as far as Niven was concerned was a 65ft (20m) ketch called the *Sirocco* which Flynn owned. They went sailing every weekend with plenty of booze and girls on board. I don't think David ever drank as much as Flynn did, but their boozy antics at 610 Linden Drive inspired Rosalind Russell to call the house 'Cirrhosis-by-the-Sea'.

Flynn and Niven were not the only occupants there. Robert Coote, another British actor trying to find success in Hollywood, also moved in, and Niven and Coote became great friends. 'Robert Coote was a greater friend to David than Flynn ever was,' said Michael Trubshawe. 'I've no doubt that for a brief period of time Niv thought Flynn to be the best thing since sliced bread. But Flynn had a nasty side to him, and he could be cruel to even those he thought of as his best friends.'

In 1979, during his 'angry interview', I heard David talk about Flynn in a whole new light.

> There was a time when Flynn made me angrier than I can ever remember being. I was out of the house and he took a call from George Stevens who was one of the best directors in Hollywood. He wanted to know if I would be interested in a part in *Gunga Din*. Of course, he should have gone through Goldwyn, but he wanted to talk to me initially. Fred Astaire had worked with him and recommended me. Flynn never passed on the message.
>
> Not long after, Fred said to me, 'Did you accept George's offer?'
> I said, 'What offer?'
> He said, 'I think you better call George Stevens.'
> So I did, and he said, 'I'm sorry you chose to ignore my offer.' I said I didn't know what offer he was talking about. So he told me about his conversation with Flynn on the telephone. He wanted me to play one of the key characters in *Gunga Din* but because I hadn't had the decency to call him back, he gave the part to Doug Fairbanks [Junior]. He had also told Flynn to let me know that if I wanted, he was prepared to get RKO Studios to buy my contract from Goldwyn and they'd do more for me than Goldwyn ever did.
>
> I said, 'I swear, George, Flynn never said a word to me or I would have been on the phone to you the moment I'd heard.'
>
> Stevens said, 'If you want to get on in Hollywood, don't hang around with sons of bitches like Flynn who doesn't give a damn for anyone but himself. He'll ruin you.' And he was right. Flynn almost wrecked my career because he thought it was funny not to tell me about the most important phone call I ever had at that stage of my career. I never forgave him for that.

In *The Moon's a Balloon* David wrote affectionately about Flynn, and he told me, 'He was a shit, of course, but once you knew that it didn't matter because we all have our faults, and we should love our friends complete with their faults.'

But in the 1979 'angry interview' he said to me, 'There never was a bigger shit than Flynn. For a short time it was a lot of fun, but I knew I could never trust him. If I told him a secret, he would tell someone else –

always. I told him something very important once, and I told him not to tell a certain person, and he told, and I found myself in hot water. I could have done without Flynn in my life.'

Flynn may have let David down badly, but David was responsible for his own actions which landed him in the veritable hot water. No sooner had Merle left America to head for England than David began a fling with actress Virginia Bruce. 'I swear, that fucking Flynn blabbed to someone knowing it would get into the newspapers,' David told me. Sure enough, the newspapers in January 1937 were reporting on the romance between Niven and Virginia Bruce. 'I really didn't know what to tell reporters.'

Merle, of course, got to hear about it and was extremely distressed as she began work on *I, Claudius*. Goldwyn wasn't pleased either and told Niven, according to Ray Milland, 'Keep your dick in your pants and out of the newspapers.' David Selznick, who David was about to go to work for on *The Prisoner of Zenda*, also berated him. Studios and independent producers were very wary about the public perception of their stars.

Filming began on *The Prisoner of Zenda* in early 1937 and Niven began it with trepidation. He told me,

I really wasn't sure how best to play the part. It was such a dull character. Out of sheer desperation I started playing it for laughs, thinking this would brighten the role and the scenes I was in. But the director wasn't impressed when he saw what I was doing and he threatened to fire me from the film. I was so depressed I got home and Flynn and I drank our way into near oblivion. I said to him, 'This is it. The end has come for me.'

He said, 'Cheer up, sport, there'll be plenty more offers of work.' That was easy for him to say. He had a watertight contract with Warner Brothers. And he'd already lost me an important role in an important film and maybe a better contract.

I was convinced my Hollywood career was over. Myron Selznick actually told me that my carousing with Flynn wasn't helping my career at all. He said that studios were becoming reluctant to use me because of my reputation as a hellraising chum of Flynn's rather than a serious and hard working actor. I began to realise I really needed to distance myself from Flynn.

I returned to the *Zenda* set the next morning, expecting to be fired, only to discover that director John Cromwell and David Selznick had viewed the rushes from the day before and discovered to their surprise that they really liked what I was doing in the part, and I was told to carry on. I've rarely been so relieved in my life.

It was a difficult film to make and, typical of Selznick, he brought in other directors to shoot retakes, including W.S. 'Woody' Van Dyke and George Cukor. It was a formula that worked for Selznick who was to hire several directors to get *Gone With the Wind* onto film a couple of years later; it certainly worked on *The Prisoner of Zenda* which was a popular success.

In England, shooting on *I, Claudius* had come to a stop in March when a car crash left Merle with concussion and a cut over her left eye and ear. She needed four weeks convalescence but Charles Laughton, who was playing Claudius, was not going to be available due to other obligations so the film was abandoned.

The time that Niven and Flynn shared at 'Cirrhosis-by-the-Sea' was not as long as one might assume by the amount of space David gave to it in *The Moon's a Balloon*. In fact, when Flynn's wife Lili returned to him, David moved out and rented a bungalow at 8425 De Longpre Avenue.

Still depressed over losing the chance George Stevens had offered him, David cheered a little when he was given top billing with French actress Annabella in *Dinner at the Ritz*, a romantic murder story set in London, Paris and the French Riviera. Despite the seemingly glamorous backdrop to the film, it was filmed over six weeks at Denham Studios in England and was produced by New World which Twentieth Century-Fox had set up primarily as a vehicle for Fox's new discovery, Annabella, whose career had gone well in France. But *Dinner at the Ritz* was typical of the poor films Fox was finding for her and her career diminished and she became better known, in 1939, as the wife of Tyrone Power. The film was another low point in Niven's career.

Making the film did, at least, allow him his first return to England, in July 1937. He looked up old friends, particularly Michael Trubshawe who lived in Norfolk, and he was reunited with Merle Oberon.

'I think by then Merle had realised that she couldn't have Niv exclusively,' Trubshawe told me. 'She was really charming to him, and when he was with her one could see he was certainly in love with her. I think she gave him a certain sophistication that he certainly didn't have in the Army. He still told stories and did his impressions of peculiar people, but there was a polish to him, and a new confidence. He was also enjoying his fame a great deal, but he wasn't big headed about it.'

Curiously, Niven *did* think he was big headed at the time. He told me in 1978, 'With *The Prisoner of Zenda* I thought I was a better actor than I was and a bigger star than I was. I got a little cocky, you see. And I didn't feel that Goldwyn was doing his best for me. He put me into some stinkers.'

Trubshawe didn't notice the cockiness. 'I asked him to come and open a village fete and to play for our village cricket team. In many ways he hadn't changed at all. He was happy to do all those things and we had a fine time. He said to me, "I'm sure all this success I'm having isn't going to last." I told him he'd be a star for the rest of his life. He said, "You are a good chum, Trubshawe." We talked about the old days, and it was a lot like old times. I had no idea that things would change so much for him and between us.'

David also took the opportunity to spend time with his sisters Grizel and Joyce – and also with Sir Thomas Comyn-Platt. In 1982 David said, 'I had begun to have success in Hollywood, and he said, "Well, done, my boy. At least you didn't end up in prison."'

I don't think Trubshawe ever knew that Sir Thomas Comyn-Platt was Niven's real father, but he knew that David and 'Uncle Tommy' had had a difficult relationship.

'I think that summer was the last time they ever met,' said Trubshawe. 'I don't think there was any hostility between them any more. David told me he wanted to see if the old man was proud of his achievements. Apparently, he was. He told Niv he and David's mother never really expected David to ever achieve much in life. They even thought he might end up a criminal and behind bars, which Niv found very amusing.'

Niven confided to Trubshawe that he felt it was time to end his womanising. 'He told me he felt he needed to settle down, if only he could find the right woman,' said Trubshawe. 'I told him he had Merle. He had already blown it with Ann Todd. He had glamorous actresses falling over themselves to sleep with him. So I asked him, "Which one of them do you want to marry? Is it Merle?" He said, "Good God, old bean, I don't want to marry an *actress*." He wanted a wife who wasn't in the business, who wouldn't be doing love scenes with Tyrone Power or Clark Gable. He said, "I couldn't bear to see a wife of mine making love on the screen to another man."

'He just didn't think a typical Hollywood marriage could work. He saw what happened to those big star marriages and the high divorce rate in Hollywood. He said, "When I get married, there'll be no divorce." And he was true to his word, despite some terrible times ahead.'

Niven returned to America without Merle who was still working in England. He recalled, 'I went to stay with Edmund Goulding for the weekend at his home in the desert of Palm Springs and was delighted and surprised to find Greta Garbo standing naked in his swimming pool. She would later come to my house, when I was first married, and my two sons had to get used to seeing Greta Garbo naked in their swimming pool.'

Niven spent time at San Ysidro ranch with Virginia Bruce, whom he was still seeing, and they also enjoyed the hospitality of William Randolph Hearst and his mistress Marion Davies at their grand and legendary San Simeon castle.

He had also begun an affair with Norma Shearer. For him, she would emerge from her reclusive shadows, and they often dined and danced. Dancing, as Niven had told me, often involved a lot more than moving around a ball room.

Goldwyn next loaned David out to Paramount to co-star with Gary Cooper and Claudette Colbert in *Bluebeard's Eighth Wife*. Niven's role was brief, as a charming and elegant foil to Cooper who played a much married millionaire. The film didn't do well, being made at a time when America had little sympathy for millionaires. 'In these days it's bad enough to have to admire millionaires in any circumstance,' wrote the film critic of the *New York Times*, 'but a millionaire with a harem complex simply can't help starting the bristles on the back of a sensitive neck.' That critic did, however, feel that the film was 'enlivened by the supporting presence of Edward Everett Horton, Herman Bing, David Niven and Warren Hymer'.

Although David was still with Merle Oberon, now back in the US, as well as seeing Virginia Bruce and Norma Shearer, he saw the New Year in with Loretta Young, along with Ronald Colman and some other Hollywood luminaries at a mountain resort at Lake Arrowhead.

Niven enjoyed the Hollywood life to the hilt: 'There was nothing like it, old bean, if I wasn't filming, I was at Ronnie Colman's or at San Simeon, or skiing.'

He discovered a great love for skiing at the new ski resort at Sun Valley in Idaho. He recalled, 'My instructor was a nice young fellow called Marti Arrougé. I called Norma Shearer from there and she was so desperately lonely that I said, "Come and join me," and when she met Marti, who was 12 years younger than she, they fell in love and got married.'

Niven moved out of his bungalow and, with Robert Coote and an Australian fortune hunter called Walter Kerry Davis, rented one of Marion Davies's guest cottages on Ocean Front at Santa Monica. Flynn, still one of Niven's closest friends, occasionally stayed with them whenever his marriage was going through yet another sticky patch. Douglas Fairbanks Jnr also moved in for a while, and in March 1938 Noël Coward came to stay, and although they'd met before, this visit established a friendship with Niven that lasted until Coward died. The house on Ocean Front was a place of fun, laughter, booze and girls.

Merle Oberon had not completely given up on David, and she was able to get him a part in a film she made with Gary Cooper, *The Cowboy and the Lady*, but every one of his scenes was cut from the film for reasons not at all clear. David thought it was because he was 'so bloody awful in it'. That was bad news because other producers suddenly lost interest in him.

Loretta Young came to his aid, persuading director John Ford to cast him in *Four Men and a Prayer* in which Loretta starred as an American girl in love with one of four brothers whose father, a British colonel, played by C. Aubrey Smith, is court-martialled. David played one of the colonel's four sons.

Loretta's love interest in the picture was played by British actor Richard Greene, a new arrival in Hollywood and one which David eyed with some envy. I interviewed Greene in Norfolk in 1981, and found him to be frank about his uneasy working relationship with Niven. He told me,

> *Four Men and a Prayer* was not only my first film in Hollywood but my first film, *period*. Niven was rather put out that I was coming in with what was the lead male role – that is, I was the one who got Loretta Young – while he had been working for four years or so in Hollywood and still wasn't getting top billing. I quickly noticed that he would look at me – *glance* at me – rather enviously and suspiciously.
>
> He wasn't unpleasant to me when we spoke, although he didn't speak to me much at all when we weren't in front of the camera. I thought he seemed rather nervous, as if I was the opposition and he was afraid I would be better than him. I suppose that was his own lack of confidence as an actor. He made up for it by being the life and soul of the party, telling endless anecdotes in a state of never ending good cheer and bonhomie. But I could never figure out what was really going on behind that grin of his. I felt that he'd smile at me and be thinking, 'Who do you think you are, you bastard, coming onto my territory and thinking you can be better than me?' Well, I never did think I was better than he, and I can admit that he was the one who went on to greater stardom than I ever did.
>
> I would like to have liked him more but I could tell that he didn't like me, and we never got together much after that. We saw each other at social events, but we were never great pals.
>
> It was apparent that he didn't much care for me being overfriendly with Loretta Young even though it was only for the film we were making. I think he must have been in love with her – he certainly seemed jealous, or maybe it was just that he was jealous that I was her love interest and he wasn't.
>
> But despite all that, at the wrap party he shook my hand and said, 'I think you have a wonderful career ahead of you and I wish you the best of luck.' All the same, I couldn't be sure if he was sincere or not. I'd like

to think he was, but I think he could be very shallow. I heard and saw him talk to some people like he was their best friend, but when he walked away from them his smile disappeared and he'd say something terrible about them under his breath.

During that interview, I told Greene that David had been diagnosed with a terminal illness, although I didn't say what it was as it hadn't been publicly announced that he had Motor Neurone Disease. Shocked by this news, Richard Greene said, 'I really should write to him.' I don't know if he ever did. Not long after I interviewed him, he had a fall and suffered head injuries that resulted in a brain tumour that killed him in 1985.

Niven admitted to me once, 'I wasn't the nicest of people in Hollywood to start with.' In 1980, when he was in London for Peter Sellers' memorial service, he talked about how actors – Sellers in particular – were so insecure that they could be 'real bitches'. He said, 'Before the war, just as I was getting some success in films in Hollywood, I was so insecure that I saw every new English actor who came along as a threat to me. I felt that some of them just turned up and had instant success while I was jumping through Goldwyn's hoops.'

He also admitted that he made an effort to get on with the established stars 'because they were the ones it was important to get on with', rather than the newcomers. He said, 'I suppose it was shallow of me, but that's what show business can be like. I'm lucky that I do have some truly wonderful friends, and have had many, but there were and always are plenty just waiting for you to fall.'

Four Men and a Prayer was not destined to be a classic John Ford film.

Loretta Young did her best for David, landing him a major supporting role in her next picture, *Three Blind Mice*. This time he got the girl – but not for long, as the leading man Joel McCrea won her in the end. Loretta played one of three sisters who all inherit $5,000 and decide to invest it in finding them all rich husbands. Niven, as a playboy, and McCrea, as a man of high society, vie for the affections of Miss Young and Niven wins until she discovers he is just a pauper and she ultimately winds up with the wealthy one. I suppose there is a moral in there somewhere, but for now it eludes me.

When I talked to Loretta following Niven's death, she remembered him as 'a great friend and a really ambitious actor, though one who struggled to be good'.

I asked her if she felt she had contributed to his success considering that she did get him work in several of her films. She said, 'I hope I helped him some of the way. Sam Goldwyn wasn't doing much for him at that time.

He was just loaning him out and taking good money that other studios paid for him but Goldwyn still only paid him his weekly salary. It was difficult to cast David because he was a certain type of Englishman, and there weren't that many parts being written like that. He had to just sort of fit in wherever he could, and I convinced my studio [Twentieth Century-Fox] to put him in good supporting roles in my films. At best, that made sure he kept working.'

I told her that David had expressed how a number of people like her had actually helped him in those early days, to which she replied, 'We all loved David. That was the great thing about him – he was very easy to love.'

And that opened the door for me to ask her if she and David ever really were in love. She said, 'Oh yes, we were. We even talked about getting married, but he didn't want a movie star for a wife. I said, "That's good because I don't want an actor for a husband," because I'd already done that.' She had married Grant Withers in 1930 and divorced him the following year.

Although he had Merle Oberon and Loretta Young helping to guide his career, what Niven really needed was an unqualified success – something that turned him into a star. But a star part for an Englishman who had plenty of charm and wit and an authentic British stiff upper lip was rare in Hollywood. And then one came along, thanks to his friend Edmund Goulding who cast him opposite Errol Flynn in *The Dawn Patrol*.

This was a remake of a 1930 World War I drama about the Royal Flying Corps. Rare for an American movie, this had an almost entirely British cast – Flynn was Australian, but his English accent made him a Hollywood Brit. He took top honours as Captain Courtney, a member of a daring squad of British pilots flying in inadequate aeroplanes in an effort to beat off the German aces and their more superior aircraft.

Niven played Lieutenant Scott, a derring-do or die pilot who shares danger in equal measures with Courtney. It was a perfect role for Niven, and he gave the best performance of his career up till then. *Film Weekly* noted David Niven's 'clever changes of mood, from wild gaiety to agonised worry prove him to be a deeply sensitive, natural actor'.

The critic of *Picturegoer* wrote, 'Acting honours are fairly divided, but I would give pride of place to David Niven. It is a finely balanced, sincere performance.'

Variety observed that the film 'sparkles because of vigorous performances of the entire cast', and added, 'David Niven makes the character of Flynn's great friend stand out.'

The Dawn Patrol was filmed in early 1938, and gave the Niven–Flynn friendship a final hurrah. 'It was wonderful to have such a good part in a good film and to work with Flynn on pretty much equal terms,' David told me, 'but I'd learned by then that while it was good to have a good role in a good Flynn film, it wasn't so good to be in Flynn's company after hours. I'd moved on, I suppose, from what we had before.'

Many people, including Merle Oberon and Loretta Young, were urging him to distance himself from Flynn. 'I told David he needed to be seen to be taking his career seriously if he wanted others to take him seriously,' Young told me. 'All that in-like-Flynn stuff wasn't good for David. When I think back now on how I used to sit him down and give him pep talks makes me smile. He was often like a naughty schoolboy and needed to be put right. Flynn was good for his career at that time but not good for him personally, especially considering the trouble Flynn got into later.' Loretta was referring to the case of statutory rape that was brought against Flynn in 1942.

But there was more to the breakdown of Niven's friendship with Flynn than a gradual breaking away from Flynn-induced antics. There was a very sudden and permanent rift between them. As Laurence Olivier put it to me, 'Flynn goosed Niven, and Niven didn't take kindly to that at all.'

Ava Gardner also once referred to an episode Niven had told her about when Flynn 'goosed' him. So I asked David about the 'goosing' incident when I interviewed him in 1979. He said,

> Flynn would get very drunk, and even though I could put away a fair bit, I didn't get smashed the way Flynn did. We had finished making *The Dawn Patrol* and we were celebrating our success with a couple of girls, and after we had sent the girls home, Flynn…well, he grabbed me…where a man doesn't expect another man to be grabbed. That's the sort of thing school boys might do, and I felt that it was time he really grew up, and I told him so, and he said, 'Oh come on, sport, you and I, we're pals, and there's nothing wrong in a couple of pals having a little fun together.' And then he tried to grab me again. I had no idea where this came from. I told him he should grow up and that I was heading home, and he got rather nasty and was almost spitting with rage. He yelled, 'I think you're the one who should grow up, Niven. This is Hollywood. People here are phoneys. They fuck anything that moves. What makes you so fucking different?' And I said, 'Being loyal to my friends. You should try it.' And after that I never wanted to see him again.
>
> He tried calling me, and he even wrote me a letter saying how sorry he was. I came to realise that most of the people who called themselves his friends were hangers on. I felt very sorry for him, and I was sorry our

friendship ended the way it did. I'm still angry about what happened, and I'm sad too. I had the best times with Flynn, and I had the worst. What did Dickens say? It was the best of times, it was the worst of times, and that's what I had with Flynn.

Over the years Niven's path rarely crossed with Flynn's. David did all he could to put distance between them, especially when Flynn became embroiled in a series of public scandals. I asked David in 1975 if he could remember the last time he saw Flynn. He said it was many years later, when Flynn was about 50 and looked more like 70. He said that it was a 'joyful reunion' during which Flynn apologised for not ever contacting him after Niven's first wife, Primmie, died in a tragic accident.

Niven and Flynn had a drink and then Flynn said that he had taken to reading the Bible. That's also the story David told in *Bring on the Empty Horses*. It was a sentimental finale to their one time hellraising friendship. But it wasn't what really happened.

In 1979 David told me that in 1958 he came across Flynn in a London restaurant. 'He looked ghastly. The drugs and the booze had bloated him and he looked like a man who should have died a long time before. I tried to avoid him but he came over and sat down, drunk, of course, and then he said, "You know, sport, when Primmie died I never came to see you, never did a goddamn thing to help. But you know how it is."

'My hackles were up and I said very coldly, "Yes, Errol, I daresay I do. You were too busy what with all the lawsuits," and by that I meant he was probably ravaging some underage girl or getting arrested, and I think he got my meaning. He stood up and yelled, "Well you can go to hell." I said, "I've been there. When my wife died. Funny that I never saw you there."

'And he threw the chair over and staggered out, and I never saw him again. I felt very sorry we couldn't have parted as friends, but he touched a very raw nerve. He was always selfish and I guess he died selfish.'

Dawn Patrol may have signalled the end of Niven's friendship with Flynn but it also signalled the dawn of Niven's film stardom. It wasn't the kind of stardom that Colman or Cary Grant enjoyed – they were able to have films built around them and their names usually guaranteed an audience; that's the true meaning of 'star' – but at last Hollywood began taking Niven more seriously.

'I didn't have to stretch myself too much,' David told me in regards to his performance in *Dawn Patrol*. 'I had the kind of military training that the character might have had, at least as far as the discipline was concerned. And I knew many men who came back from the Great War who had survived. I knew officers who had found themselves with the responsibility of sending men to certain death. And it's true to say that the part had a lot of *me* in it. I'd learned a little about acting by then, but I had my own personal traits to fall back on. It didn't require any great leap for me.'

It was only years later, when I saw the film again on TV after David was dead, that what he had told me about his acting was true; it is all there on the screen – the British stiff upper lip, the jovial personality, the authentic military background, and the understanding of what officers of the Great War had gone through. It was, in fact, a lesson in method acting long before the term 'method acting' had been coined. He had learned one of the most important lessons of acting – that an actor draws on personal experience whenever he can.

What David didn't completely learn was to lean on the smaller experiences of life that many actors draw on. That is why there were so many David Niven performances that lacked depth; he could impersonate a skater without ice to skate on but he couldn't always get under the skater's skin.

That was no great setback for a screen actor; many stars endure with just the basic understanding of acting and a whole lot of charisma. But Niven never really had quite enough charisma to make it as a major star. He was invariably someone the audience could enjoy seeing in a film that was generally crafted around somebody else. That was the rule in Niven's career, and there were very few exceptions to the rule.

The fact that his career lasted as long as it did, when greater stars fell by the wayside much sooner, is a testament to his sheer likeability – the audience has always liked him, but they haven't necessarily wanted to see a film just because he was in it. He was invariably an added bonus, or sometimes he turned out to be the only worthwhile element of a rather bad movie.

Somebody who understood this was William Wyler who wanted to cast Niven as Edgar Linton in his up-coming production for Samuel Goldwyn, *Wuthering Heights*. But David had sworn that he would never work for Wyler again.

—

CHAPTER 11

Wuthering Wyler

W hen I talked to Wyler in 1976, he told me, 'I had two wonderful stars, Merle Oberon and Laurence Olivier, to play Cathy and Heathcliff, but what I needed was someone who could play the hapless Edgar and still make him more than he is in the book or the script. Cathy has to marry Edgar when she could have had Heathcliff, and she and the audience know it is a mistake, but you can't make Edgar into a villain. He is a victim of circumstance. That makes the audience all the more torn, that makes for good drama. Principally I had to choose someone who was under contract to Goldwyn, and of all his contract players, David Niven was the one actor I knew could make Edgar into the kind of character I wanted Edgar to be.'

But Niven was having none of it – to start with. He told me,

I had two objections to that picture. Samuel Goldwyn told me I was going to play Edgar, which was a part I hated and didn't want to do. Who can even *like* that idiot? The second objection I had was working for Wyler again, and I didn't want to work for Wyler again…ever. So Wyler called me and said, 'David, why don't you want to play Edgar?'

I said, 'Because it is such an awful part.'

He said, 'It's not, you know,' and then he hit the ego button with 'and you're one of the few people who can make it better than it is.'

So I said, 'But Willie, I was so bloody miserable working for you on *Dodsworth*, and I just couldn't go through it again. You're a son of a bitch to work with.'

That just made him laugh, and he said, 'I've changed. I'm not a son of a bitch any more.'

Niven was convinced. There were other reasons he did the film. One was that if he didn't, Goldwyn was going to put him on suspension. The other reason was Merle Oberon. She, naively, felt that it would help their relationship if they worked together again, and she was the one who had suggested to Goldwyn that David should play Edgar. That, it turned out, was a mistake because Niven, always happy to be helped along in previous years by his famous friends, now resented being handed a part he simply hated. It was compounded by his dislike of Wyler.

Merle took the same view that Wyler had, which was that Niven was one of the few actors who could make something of the role, and she also pushed David's ego button. In the end, Niven had no good argument to turn the part down, and he went to work on *Wuthering Heights* in December 1938. He recalled,

> The first day of shooting, I had to drive up in a two-horse buggy with Merle at my side. We had a line of dialogue each. She would say, 'Come in, Edgar, and have some tea.' And I would say, 'As soon as I've put the horses away.' Not difficult stuff.
>
> We did the first take and Wyler said, 'Cut! Just play it straight, David, this isn't a comedy.'
>
> I had no idea I'd played it for laughs, so we did the second take, and he said, 'Cut! What's so funny, David? This is not a Marx Brothers picture. Do it again.'
>
> And we did it 40-something times, and finally Wyler said, 'Well, if that's the best you can do, we'd better print the first take I suppose.'
>
> I said, 'Willie, you really are a son of a bitch, aren't you?' and he said, 'Yes, and I'm going to be one for the next 14 weeks.' And he was.

David said that it was an unhappy experience all round, not just because of Wyler but because Olivier and Oberon didn't care too much for each other, probably because Olivier had wanted the love of his own life, Vivien Leigh, to play Cathy. If Merle thought that David would come to her rescue when Olivier called her an 'amateur little bitch', and just 'a little pick-up by Korda', she was wrong. Displaying a less than gallant stance, Niven kept his distance, partly because his ardour for her had considerably cooled, and also because the friendship between him and Olivier was strengthening.

Niven recalled, 'Larry and I had been friends for some time and our friendship was further grounded when we both started *Wuthering Heights* sharing a deep hatred for Willie Wyler.'

Olivier actually came to like and respect Wyler a great deal, even if it was tough going, and he learned from Wyler much about the film medium which stood him in good stead later, not just as an actor but also as a very fine director. But Niven simply hated Wyler even though Wyler proved to be right about casting him – Niven *was* good as Edgar. Olivier thought so too. He told me, 'He carried off the part of Edgar wonderfully. In fact, I'd say he was better than Merle in her role. He had an impossible part and he hated it, but he was perfect in it. I would watch him on set and think, "He isn't even trying to act and here I am working my bloody guts out, and he is going to look bad on screen." But he wasn't bad at all.'

Olivier even admitted that he learned from Niven. 'David and I are very different kinds of actors and I think that is why we got on so well. He was, with all respect and love for the man, a lightweight actor and he couldn't have performed in a stage classic ever in his life, but he could easily breathe into any part his own great charm and humour and also sincerity, which was all very much his own. And also, when it was needed, he had tremendous pathos. I learned a lot about screen acting from him, although I thought when we first started working on the picture that I knew more about acting than he did. And I did, when it comes to acting on stage, but he had a natural gift for screen acting which I had to work at. So when I call him a lightweight, it is not a criticism.'

Although a box office success, the film was not received well critically at the time of its release in 1939, although Niven got good personal notices. The *New York Times* noted that, 'the Lintons, so pallid, so namby-pamby in the novel, have been more charitably reflected in the picture. David Niven's Edgar (and) Geraldine Fitzgerald's Isabella are dignified and poignant characterisations of young people whose tragedy was not in being weak themselves but in being weaker than the abnormal pair whose destinies involved their destruction.'

A casualty of the film was the Niven/Oberon love affair – by the time filming was over, so was their affair. Merle married Alexander Korda and David began seeing actress Evelyn Keyes who moved in with him. He could cope with cohabiting with an actress but not marrying one.

The success of *Wuthering Heights* did a great deal for Niven, but it also inflated his ego further, as he admitted to me later. 'I thought that to be able to play that awful Edgar and still get noticed when playing against two such excellent people as Merle and Larry meant that I was a star of great magnitude, especially coming after *The Dawn Patrol*. I began doing Lux Radio Theatre programmes on the wireless and decided that I wouldn't even get Goldwyn's permission because I was too big a star to have to ask him for his permission. A great mistake! I was under contract to him and *all* freelance work had to be passed by him. He wanted half of everything I earned, so when I was awarded with a glorious food hamper by one of the radio producers, I cut it in half and sent it to him.'

Actually, Goldwyn was contractually owed *everything* David earned freelance and Niven was supposed to settle for his weekly wage of $500 from Goldwyn, so in a sense Goldwyn was being generous by insisting on only half of David's earnings from radio work.

Niven discovered that Warners had paid Goldwyn $175,000 to rent him for *The Dawn Patrol* so he decided to consult a leading agent, Leland Hayward, who took a look at his contract with Goldwyn and told David that Goldwyn had been making a fortune from loaning him to other studios.

When Goldwyn heard that David had been secretly meeting with Leland, he got revenge by planting a story in the *Los Angeles Examiner* that success had gone to Niven's head and he was becoming impossible to work with. Goldwyn banned Hayward from his studio and put Niven on suspension for several weeks.

Goldwyn, however, recognised that Niven was becoming a better actor, and I think he really was fond of David. In February 1939 David's weekly salary had been due to rise to $650 a week but Goldwyn raised it to $750 and amended his contract so that the annual increases would result in $2,250 a week in 1945. He also allowed David the use of a large suite on the studio lot and promised to give him star billing in all Goldwyn productions in which he appeared.

His first film under the new terms was *Bachelor Mother* with Ginger Rogers. For the first time, David's name appeared above the title.

Forty years later Niven was still unimpressed by what Goldwyn intended as a show of generosity. 'It's true that Goldwyn gave me a career in films,' he told me. 'But who's to say I wouldn't have made it without him? He earned a fortune by loaning me to other studios, and by [1939] I felt I was actually worth a lot more than I was getting. I should have been earning $2,000 a week *then*, not having to wait another five or six years for that amount.

'My head grew enormously. My ego was inflated like a giant balloon. I was so full of myself because I was at last a big star and I revelled in it and became very conceited. I even believed all the publicity that was being written about me.'

With *Bachelor Mother* Goldwyn came up with a part that perfectly suited Niven's talents. He played a charming playboy whose father owns a major store where Ginger Rogers, working in the toy department, finds an abandoned baby. She and David are wrongly assumed to be the parents but they nevertheless marry, and it all ends happily.

The film opened on 1 September 1939 just 18 days before the outbreak of World War II, and it delighted critics and audiences alike. The *New York Times* reported, 'The spectacle of Miss Rogers and David Niven struggling forlornly to prove their innocence of parenthood and winning co credence at al is made triply hilarious by the sobriety of their performances. That is the way farce should be handled, with just enough conviction to season its extravagances.'

The *Observer* critic said, 'I must insist that the most timely as well as the most engaging film of the week is a little thing call *Bachelor Mother*,' and added, 'Mr Niven is growing, film by film, into one of the best romantic comedians in the cinema.'

The *Daily Sketch* enthused, 'As good as Miss Rogers is, Mr Niven is better. He races through the film with so much gaiety and sophistication, with so much charm and understanding, I'd advise you to keep your girl friend from going to see this picture.'

His next film was another with Loretta Young, and this time he shared top billing with her, in *Eternally Yours*. It wasn't a Goldwyn picture, but Niven was very happy now that he was getting star billing, and I suspect he was also happy to be working with Loretta again.

Eternally Yours was not in the same league as *Bachelor Mother*, telling the strange tale of the Great Arturo, a hypnotist, illusionist and daring stuntman whose wife and stage partner, played by Loretta, leaves him when he goes on a world tour. I suspect that David and Loretta made more magic off stage than on, and the outcome for audiences was a huge disappointment. The *New York Times* said it was 'an amusing and irresponsible picture, though, on the whole, more irresponsible than amusing'.

Goldwyn had something special in store for Niven – the starring role in a remake of a 1930 film, *Raffles*, about a cricket-playing English gentleman thief. 'I was desperate to have that role,' David said. 'I almost begged Goldwyn to give it to me, but the old bastard just kept saying, "We'll see, we'll see." The next thing I knew was, I was being heroic in the Philippines.' He was referring to *The Real Glory* in which he co-starred with Gary Cooper. It was an action adventure about American officers, led by Cooper, who join local forces against a terrorist uprising in the Philippines. Niven played a lieutenant, something he was perfectly capable of doing, and would do so often, although the military rank would alter from film to film – but he was always an officer and a gentleman. 'All I had to do,' he said, 'was pretend to be Irish among American officers and die bravely at the end while rallying the troops.'

Directed by Henry Hathaway, it was a good, spectacular and noisy action film which the *New Statesman* said was 'recommended to adolescents of all ages,' and pointed out that 'David Niven dies pleasantly and quietly'.

Goldwyn then rewarded David with the role of Raffles. He was over the moon about it, feeling it would be the part that would really shoot him into the top league of movie stars. He had top billing, and his leading lady, Olivia de Havilland, had to settle for second billing. 'It seems awfully trite to worry about billing,' Niven told me once, 'and I'm sure the public couldn't give a flying fart who gets billed first or second or even third, but it matters to *us*. It matters to our vanity and our ego.'

He was alarmed, however, when the film's director, Sam Wood, fell ill and was replaced by William Wyler. 'I thought it was an evil trick being played on me by Goldwyn because I'd become so big headed,' David said. 'But to my great delight and surprise, Willie was incredibly pleasant and very helpful.'

When I spoke to Wyler in 1976, I told him that David had called him 'pleasant and helpful' and he said, 'That job was a piece of cake. I always believe that if the casting is right, the director doesn't have to worry. Niven was so perfect for that part that he didn't even have to try. So I didn't have to be a mean guy!'

I relayed this later to Niven – I often wished I could have got those two together, or any other combination of actors and directors – and he said, 'My confidence was soaring and I felt I could do no wrong, so maybe I was actually really good and Wyler didn't have anything objectionable to say to me. A lot of Hollywood directors can be pussy cats away from the set and ogres on the set. I later learned to deal with directors like that.'

Raffles was popular with the public. The *New York Times* noted, 'Mr Niven makes the game worth playing and the film worth seeing. His Raffles is one of the nicest tributes to burglary we have seen in many a year.'

It would have been the first in a series of films, but halfway through production, England declared war on Germany.

CHAPTER 12

—

Not a Mere Prop

David and Robert Coote were asleep after a night's drinking in a small sloop moored at the Balboa Yacht Club when they were awakened at six in the morning by someone banging on the side of their boat. Niven and Coote looked over the side at a man in a dinghy who said, 'Are you guys English?'

'We are.'

'Then good luck to ya – you just declared war on Germany.'

Niven and Coote were due to join a party on Douglas Fairbanks Jnr's yacht just off Catalina but were late because they had drunk too much at the Balboa Yacht Club. They gave themselves a quick toast with gin and set sail for Catalina where they met up with Fairbanks, his wife Mary Lee, and their guests Laurence Olivier and Vivien Leigh, Nigel Bruce, and Ronald Colman and his wife Benita Hume. As Niven noted upon their arrival, 'Nobody felt like celebrating any more.'

Olivier said he would try to join the RAF. Robert Coote said he would head for Canada to join the RCAF. Niven would try to get back home and try to join whatever military service he could get into.

Fairbanks gathered his guests together and opened champagne. 'Well, here's to whatever it is,' he said.

Olivier said solemnly, 'To victory.'

The British consul in Los Angeles advised the Brits that turned up to ask for help getting home to volunteer that they would be of greater service to their country to remain. The exceptions were those who were in the reserves who had to return to Britain. Niven was no longer in the reserves, having resigned his commission from the Highland Light Infantry, but he was determined he would enlist, possibly in the RAF. But getting out of Hollywood was not an easy task as he was still under contract to Goldwyn. He said,

> I wanted to get home and join up, but Goldwyn refused to release me. I told him that I'd been called up, which was a lie of course, and had to return to England immediately.
>
> He said, 'I'll get back to you,' and half an hour later he called and said, 'David, I just checked with the British Embassy in Washington. They said nobody's been called up yet. They said the best thing for you to do is stay right here and carry on as normal.'
>
> So I cabled my brother Max with instructions to send me a cable, sating 'Report regimental depot immediately Adjutant.' I went to Goldwyn with this cable. He knew very well that I had served with the Highland Light Infantry years before but didn't know that I had resigned my commission. So Goldwyn felt he had no choice but to release me.
>
> The thing was, I didn't quite know what I was going back to. I didn't want to go back into the British Army, so I made enquiries about joining the Canadian Army but was told they didn't need me.

When David abandoned plans to go to Canada, he went to Washington where Lord Lothian, the British Ambassador, encouraged him to remain in Hollywood to represent his country on the screen.

Much of what Niven told me about his war experiences came in an interview I did with him when he was making *A Man Called Intrepid* in England in 1978. That interview included a great deal of detail that David generally never discussed, and it revealed many of his feelings about warfare and his personal experience of it. In it, he also spilled the beans rather carelessly about a secret Laurence Olivier had kept for many years, but once the cat was out of the bag, he told me much more, but only because it indirectly involved him.

In 1979 I learned just a little more from him: 'Before I was able to leave America, I was asked to remain to try and drum up support for the war effort. We were hoping America would join us, you see, but there was a lot of opposition to the very idea among many Americans, and it was to be a very secretive and really very difficult task because to do that very thing could result in one being arrested and charged. The isolationists in America were very strong, even though [President] Roosevelt was prepared to support us. So the British Government required people who could come and go at liberty in America and who could use their influence to increase support for the British.

'I wasn't against doing that, but I wanted to enlist and fight the war where it was happening. So I said, "Why don't you ask Larry Olivier? He's dying to do something for the war effort, and it'll be a while before he gets home."'

I asked Niven, 'And did they ask him?'

'Oh, yes.'

'Did he do it?'

'Larry isn't the kind of man to turn down that kind of request from his country.'

I asked David who it was who had actually asked him to stay. He answered, 'The British Embassy in Washington.'

'And then they asked Olivier?' I asked.

'Oh yes.'

Instead of going straight to England, Niven very curiously decided to head for Italy. Sheridan Morley, in his biography of David Niven, wrote that Niven met up with several Italian skiers that he knew from Sun Valley. In *The Moon's a Balloon* Niven claimed he met up with an Austrian friend, Felix Scaffcotsch – who had designed a skiing resort on Sun Valley and had never made a secret of his admiration for Adolf Hitler – in Naples for a final drink before they became official enemies. Morley wasn't entirely convinced of that account. He told me, 'I can't see David enjoying a farewell drink with a Nazi SS officer. But he did go to Italy and then made his way to Paris from there.'

The next curious event happened when David got to Paris. He told me that there he met with Noël Coward who was working in naval intelligence. 'Noël tried to persuade me to return to America to work for naval intelligence, but I insisted I was returning to Britain, but I once more suggested that Larry Olivier might be willing. I believe it might have been Noël Coward who put Larry's name to Churchill. In fact, Coward told me that he personally asked Larry to assist.'

So Laurence Olivier remained in America and was recruited by SOE, working for Alexander Korda who was an SOE operative. Korda set up offices in New York which were a front for SOE while Olivier's mission was to gain support for the British war effort in a generally isolationist America.

When I talked to Sheridan Morley about this, he said he thought that it was very likely that Coward had tried to enlist Niven and that his whole purpose in going first to Europe rather than straight to England may have been because Coward had summoned him there.

In Paris, Niven presented himself to the air attaché, John Acheson, at the British Embassy in Paris and announced he wanted to join the RAF. He told me,

> He said to me, 'Oh no, you can't do that, not here. You must go back to England,' and he secretly put me on a mail plane that evening. So I flew back to Britain in a plane full of mail bags and a few days later presented myself to the Air Ministry.
>
> I was ushered before a group captain who asked me my name although it was obvious he knew who I was.
>
> 'And what do you want?'
>
> 'I want to join the RAF,' I told him.
>
> He shook his head. 'Ever heard of Wilfred Lawson?'
>
> 'Of course. A wonderful actor,' I said.
>
> 'He's also a heavy drinker. We took him on and we've had trouble with him ever since.'
>
> I was pretty pissed off by now and I said, 'Look, I've just come seven thousand miles [11,250 km] at my own expense and I'd like to join up.'
>
> 'We don't encourage actors to join this service.'
>
> This made me so angry I said, 'Then fuck you!'
>
> He herded me to the door, shouting, 'Get out! Get out of my office *now*.' I was on my way out when I passed an air commodore, and I said, 'And fuck you, too!'
>
> I tried the Scots Guards, but they turned me down. It was very depressing. It just seemed that, after I'd come all the way back from Hollywood, every door was slammed in my face. The problem was, nobody wanted to see a film star in uniform at that time unless he was in a film, being kept safe from the real action.
>
> Goldwyn didn't help because he turned it into a publicity stunt; I had a couple of films opening in London, and he wanted my arrival in London to reap all the publicity he could get. So he got his London office on to it and I found myself giving a press conference explaining that I hoped to get into the RAF.
>
> The next day the papers came out with headlines like, RELAX, THE DAWN PATROL IS HERE and NIVEN SPURNS THE ARMY. There was one London film critic [Caroline Lejune] who wrote an article that said, 'The British film fan does not want to see David Niven in the Army, the Navy or the air force. We want to see him in his proper place, up there on the silver screen helping us to forget this war.'

This critical response depressed and distressed him. By early 1940 he was still a civilian, and little had happened in the war – it was known as 'the phoney war'.

One evening, sitting in the Café de Paris in London, while watching the dancers on the floor and aware that many of the young men around him were in the Rifle Brigade, he heard an announcement by the band leader: 'Ladies and gentlemen, if anyone is interested, the air-raid warning has just sounded.' David recalled for me,

> There were cheers and cat-calls and the music started playing again and people were dancing. Nobody was fooled any longer by the phoney war. Then I was suddenly struck by the sight of a beautiful WAAF but she didn't seem to notice me, so I was about to remedy that and go over to speak to her when someone said to me, 'Excuse me but my name is Jimmy Bosville.' There was this young man in uniform, and he said, 'I recognised you.'
>
> I said, feeling rather depressed, 'Oh, please don't ask for an autograph or expect me to talk about my pictures.'
>
> He said, 'Oh, no, you see, I was with an air commodore this morning who was talking about a visit you paid to his office. I wish I'd been there.' So I told him to sit down, and he said 'Look, old man, why don't you come to the Rifle Brigade?'
>
> I told him, 'You couldn't get me into a ladies' lavatory at Leicester Square.'
>
> It turned out he was in the Rifle Brigade and in command of the 2nd Battalion. The Rifle Brigade was arguably the most famous of all the elite light infantry regiments, and three weeks later, with Bosville's help, I was training at Tidworth as a second lieutenant.
>
> I was an ex-regular and found not too much had changed over the years and I quickly caught up with the much younger men.
>
> Later, I learned that I'd been earmarked for the 1st Battalion which was on the Belgian border. But at that time my job was to train conscripts.

David underwent three months' training towards the end of February 1940, and was then posted to Tidworth on Salisbury Plain to train the conscripts, most of them from the East End of London. He recalled, 'They whined and whinged a lot, complaining that I was merely a movie star telling them what to do and about what they had left behind, so finally I told them, "Right, you lot, now listen to me. You have only left your factories and butchers' shops. *I* could be with Ginger Rogers." And that shut them up and they were very good chaps after that.'

While at Tidworth, Niven took advantage of his film star status to get girls. 'I could have had a different girl every night,' he told me. 'I didn't mind that they only wanted to go to bed with me because I was in pictures. It was a perk. And I needed something to keep my mind off my life back in Hollywood. I actually resented having to leave it behind, you know. Yes, I volunteered, but I resented the war for messing up my film career, and I didn't have much respect for the politicians who had caused the whole bloody mess in the first place. I hated every minute of [the war], and I am only happy that I managed to get through the whole thing without behaving badly. I always did my best, but it was never better than what I was told to do.'

One politician he did have respect for was Winston Churchill whom he met during the time he was still training. He recalled,

I had a few days' leave [in February 1940] and went to Ditchley for the weekend where Nancy and Ronnie Tree lived. Nancy was a cousin of Nora Flynn, one of Errol's ex-wives. Ronnie Tree was an MP who had voted with Winston Churchill against Chamberlain over Munich. [Tree was also the First Lord of the Admiralty and a personal friend of Churchill's.]

Churchill and his wife were among the guests, as well as Brendan Bracken and Anthony Eden, and when Churchill saw me sitting at the other end of the table, he got up and strode over and shook my hand.

He said, 'Young man, you did a very fine thing to give up a most promising career to fight for your country.'

I said, 'Thank you, sir.'

Then he growled, 'Mind you, had you not done so, it would have been despicable.'

The next day – it was a Sunday – Churchill asked me to stroll in the garden with him, and he talked about the joys of gardening, and then got on to the subject of food rationing. He asked me about the problems a young officer in the Army faced, and he was always most attentive to what I had to say. Ah! To have the ears of the mighty!

Ronnie Tree asked me to arrange for a special screening of a Deanna Durbin film for Churchill so I hired a private cinema in Soho and invited the Edens and the Trees, but Churchill was late. When he eventually arrived, he lit a cigar, drank a brandy and sat down to enjoy the film. Halfway through he got up to leave. I saw him to the door and he thanked me but said that something important had come up and he had to return to the Admiralty.

What I didn't know at the time was that Churchill's business for that evening was ordering HMS *Cossack* to chase the German supply ship *Altmark* into the Jossing Fjord in Norway, board her and free 299 British merchant seamen whose ships were sunk by the *Graf Spee*. The mission was one of Britain's early successes.

The date was 15 February 1940. The 'phoney war' was over and the real war had begun.

In April David was promoted to lieutenant. He was also best man at his brother Max's wedding. Meanwhile, he waited impatiently to be posted to the 1st Battalion in France. 'I wasn't impatient because I wanted to do anything clever or heroic,' he said. 'I just got so bored which happens to soldiers who know they will go into action eventually. You only want to go because you want to get it over and done with.'

Then came the evacuation from Dunkirk in the last days of May and the first few days of June. The 1st Battalion was fighting in Calais with its back to the Channel, protecting the evacuation of the troops from Dunkirk. Eventually Niven received his orders to stand by along with 200 replacements to head for Dunkirk. But by 4 June it was all over and the entire 1st Battalion had either been killed or taken prisoner.

'It could have all ended for me right there, at Dunkirk,' he said, 'but providence kept me out of the thick of it, and then it was all over. I can't pretend that I wasn't relieved. On the other hand, there is a sense of guilt one has about not being there. Hundreds lost their lives on the beaches at Dunkirk.'

I have read some accounts which placed Niven at Dunkirk, but he never reached there; those accounts were probably invented by fan magazines and studio publicity. 'I may have enlarged on various aspects of my life,' he told me, 'but not about the war. That was too serious. Too bleak. Too overwhelming in regards to the consequences to humanity to make up stories about false heroics.'

Secret military organisations were being set up all over Britain, and a call went out for volunteers for a new commando unit under Colonel Dudley Clarke whose primary purpose was to make 'cut and thrust' raids on the enemy coastline. Niven put his name forward and went before Colonel Clarke who revealed little about the unit except that he had some special ideas which he would disclose at a later date. Meanwhile, David was ordered to report to Lochailort Castle in the Western Highlands of Scotland for training.

David never boasted of any great aspirations to perform any acts of courage and derring-do. 'Most of the volunteers were made of much sterner stuff than I,' he said. 'I was there out of boredom. I never was a hero.'

Among his instructors were Lord Lovat, demolition expert 'Mad Mike' Calvert, and numerous other highly decorated and important commando leaders. 'They taught us a variety of methods of silently killing,' he recalled.

In July 1940, Niven and his fellow commandos were put to the test. Germany had bombed the Channel Islands of Jersey and Guernsey on 28 June 1940, and by 30 June Guernsey was under German occupation. It was decided that the commandos would execute a raid on Guernsey, and in preparation they trained on the Isle of Wight.

The raid took place on 15 July. David wrote in *The Moon's a Balloon* that the operation was a success, but in 1978 he said, 'The truth was, it was generally considered a farce. The commanding officer slipped and accidentally fired his revolver, thus alerting the enemy. Three men said they couldn't swim to the pick-up boat and so they were left behind. One team ended up on Sark due to compass failure, while another team landed on undefended points of the island to no purpose. We did manage to take a few bemused prisoners from their beds. But, really, we were undertrained.'

In 1982 he made one change to his account at Sark; 'The truth about the war had to be bent for the sake of morale. When we landed on Sark, we didn't even manage to take any prisoners, but the public were told we had. It's sometimes important to bend the truth when you want to boost morale.'

In September 1940, Niven was promoted. 'I became a captain, and made liaison officer for MO9 which was the War Department responsible for commando operations,' he explained. 'I was installed at the War Office where I shared a desk with Captain Quentin Hogg. But most of the time I was travelling around contacting the various commando units. Because of the very real and imminent threat of invasion, the commandos were switched from being offensive to defensive, and plans were drawn up for us to transform ourselves into an underground movement.'

He again met Churchill at Ditchley.

'He asked me what I was doing at the moment, so I told him about my part in commando operations. "You shouldn't be telling me this," he said. "Your security is very lax." I never knew for sure if he was genuinely angry, but he was probably right.'

There was one particular wartime story that David embellished, but not for the sake of boosting morale. On the night he met Jimmy Bosville at the Café de Paris in London, before he had been sidetracked by Bosville's suggestion he join the Rifle Brigade, he had set eyes upon a beautiful WAAF. David went on to tell me, that by lucky coincidence he spotted the beautiful WAAF one day at the National Gallery in London and introduced himself to her. She was Primula Rollo, a cipher clerk at the

RAF Reconnaissance Squadron at Heston. He said it was love at first sight. They became engaged and were married at the parish church of Huish on the Wiltshire Downs on 21 September. Michael Trubshawe was the best man. Throughout the ceremony, the Battle of Britain raged above in a cloudless sky.

In 1978 Niven told me a different account of how he met Primmie, as he called her. 'I went to the RAF station at Biggin Hill [south of London] and there was an air raid. I jumped into a slit trench and found I was sharing it with Primmie who was a cipher officer. She gave me a telling off for almost crushing her as I jumped in, and I told her I was dreadfully sorry but wasn't making too much of an effort to see what I was landing on and that I just didn't want to get blown up by a German bomb. We started to argue, and she said she outranked me, and I said I outranked her, and then we saw how silly the situation was as bombs went off all over the airfield and we were more concerned about who outranked who. We began laughing, and I honestly think I loved her from that moment.'

Everyone I ever talked to who knew Primmie adored her. Michael Trubshawe said,

> David had told me that he had met the most wonderful girl in the world and that he was going to marry her and was the luckiest man alive. I thought, *Oh, here he goes, falling in love again*, but when I met her I could see that she was finally the perfect girl for him. She was an absolute darling, very radiant. She was what you think an English girl of the 1930s and 40s should have been. She was *it*. That world of rose cottages in the country, well behaved children, the upper class lady, like Mrs Miniver.
>
> I think that she immediately gave David something he needed badly in his life, especially when the war came along – a sense of continuity. A purpose. A reason to come home. The war seemed to make more sense to him when he married Primmie. His life made sense. She *was* his life.

Peter Ustinov said in an interview I did with him in 1984, 'She was perfect for David. She had no ambition to be anything other than Mrs David Niven, which is what he wanted. But she managed to stand out and, in fact, you always felt she was a Very Important Person but without being condescending – a bit like a member of the royal family who smiled a good deal and talked in that very fine almost mincing voice the Queen has – "*My husband and I…*" She always seemed interested in you. She *looked* interested, and that expression was always there when you met. I think she would have done very well if she had been sent to visit factories during the war because she would have at least *looked* very interested in what everyone was doing.'

Mr and Mrs David Niven bought a cottage near Slough. Primmie left the RAF and, determined to contribute to the war effort, cycled each morning to Slough to help build Hurricanes at Hawker's factory while David volunteered for a highly secretive unit called 'Phantom'. He explained,

> It was one of the least known of the wartime special regiments invented by Colonel Hopkinson who had realised during the retreat from Dunkirk that there was a dire need for reliable communication from the front line.
>
> He came up with the simple idea of deploying highly mobile squadrons equipped with radios and dispatch riders among forward units. We even used carrier pigeons. Phantom's commanding officer would remain with the Army Commander, and when situations needed clarifying, the Squadron Commander checked his map to find the Phantom unit in the problem vicinity and then sent a message directly to it.
>
> I was made a major and took over 'A' Squadron. We became involved in the preparations to form underground movements in the event of invasion. My own special disguise was that of a parson.
>
> Actually, I was convinced that Hitler was about to invade us, and I felt that would be the end of everything. I saw it as the end of the world, and I can't deny I was actually quite terrified. I would wake up at night sometimes, having dreamed the Germans had landed, dreaming that I was waking up to find myself staring up at jack booted Nazis with guns. If I was with Primmie, I would look at her, still asleep, and cry because I was so afraid I would lose her. I couldn't bear that thought.
>
> If I awoke in barracks, without Primmie there, I would have this feeling that I would never see her again, and that would also make me cry. So when we were together, I enjoyed every minute, every second. I was never happier in my life than when I was with her. Never.

Despite his incredible happiness, he was unable to stay faithful to her. Laurence Olivier was quite critical of Niven on that score. 'Even when Vivien was at her worst [with mental illness], I never was unfaithful to her though she was to me, but David had the most perfect wife in the world and he could not stay faithful to her. I became a philanderer through necessity. David was born a philanderer.'

If that seems harsh, then here's what John Mills had to say to me in 1985. 'Niv loved Primmie to death, but he loved *all* women, though not in the way he loved Primmie. So he loved as many women as he could – even when he was married to Primmie. I didn't approve, but it's not my place to judge.'

In 1982, David confessed to me that he had been unfaithful to Primmie. 'I was a fool. When we were apart during the war, it was all too easy to have sex with other women who wanted to go to bed with a Hollywood movie star. Some of them no more than 16, but I was insatiable, you see – always have been. It's a terrible flaw in me. I can forgive myself by and large, but to be unfaithful to the best wife a man ever had was unpardonable. I knew it at the time, but my erection was stronger than my spirit, if you'll pardon the vernacular.'

In the late summer of 1941, Niven made a film for the British Government, *The First of the Few*. 'We weren't doing well in the war and the government needed something to inspire the nation during a time of crisis and films were an ideal way to do that, so they persuaded Sam Goldwyn to let me do *The First of the Few*. I was still under contract to Goldwyn and even the British Government had to borrow me from Goldwyn for a suitable sum of money.'

David was released temporarily to civil employment so he could make the film which was backed by the RAF. It was the story of R.J. Mitchell, the aircraft designer who invented the Spitfire. Niven played the fictional role of an ex RAF officer who joins Mitchell as a test pilot. Leslie Howard produced and directed the film, and he and Niven became firm friends. Released in 1942 in Britain, the film found favour with British critics and audiences. 'The film is full of action...and flashes from the Battle of Britain with which, pointing its moral, it begins and ends,' wrote the *Sunday Times*. 'It has moments of pathos and many scenes of agreeable, flippant comedy, contributed for the most part by David Niven who gives one of his best performances.'

The *Observer* noted, 'David Niven's flippant assurance is just right here. The real-life story is the more real for his imagined presence; he gives the rather abstracted film a body.'

The Scotsman, said, 'David Niven's performance as the test pilot is one of the best he has ever done.'

Niven told me, 'It wasn't a difficult role for me to play. Like the character from *Dawn Patrol*, I knew men like him. Things hadn't changed in the military since my days at Sandhurst. I could play an officer. I played many officers. I suppose it took another world war for me to find my niche in pictures. I probably played more military officers than anybody else. It took just four weeks to film. Leslie Howard did a wonderful job of both directing and acting in it, and we became very good friends.

'It didn't do well in America where it was released through Sam Goldwyn who hated the film. He renamed it *Spitfire* which didn't mean much to the Americans, and he cut the film and ruined it.'

During this break from active service, David met with Churchill for another garden stroll, and the Prime Minister confided his fears of an invasion of Britain to Niven who asked Churchill if he thought the Americans would ever enter the war. 'Mark my words,' Churchill told him, 'something cataclysmic will occur.'

It did, on 7 December 1941, when the Japanese attacked Pearl Harbor and effectively brought the United States into the war. Some months later, Niven reminded Churchill of his prediction about America and asked him what made him say it. Churchill replied, 'Because, young man, I study history.'

Pearl Harbor had a positive effect upon David. 'I stopped having nightmares about Britain being invaded. I knew then we could beat the Germans, and I thought that if I could just manage not to get myself killed then when the war was over I'd be completely happy with Primmie for the rest of our lives.'

Although *The First of the Few* was filmed quickly, Niven was given extended leave over the Christmas period and returned to service in Phantom in late January 1942. It proved to be a particularly harsh winter, and in freezing and icy conditions Niven led his men to Wales for a two-month reconnaissance along the coast to plan for a potential German invasion from Ireland.

When he returned home in March, Primmie became pregnant and gave up her work at the aircraft factory. She went with David wherever he was sent, and they lived out of rented rooms but were blissfully happy. 'I don't think David was ever so happy in his life,' John Mills said. 'The war was on and we all hated that, but out of it came moments of extreme bliss, and that was true of David and Primmie. He told me once, "Johnnie, the war took the lives of some wonderful friends, caused untold misery for millions and, although not profoundly important in the scheme of things, it almost wrecked my career. But the war gave me Primmie and my first son and the greatest happiness I ever knew."'

During the early months of 1942, Churchill and the Allied commanders prepared for Operation 'Jubilee', a joint Canadian and British amphibious attack on the French port of Dieppe. The plan was to seize the port, occupy France for about 12 hours, capture enemy documents and prisoners, and generally test the Germans for what would eventually be a complete Allied invasion of France.

'Jubilee' was launched in the early hours of 19 August 1942 – 252 ships loaded with troops and equipment followed mine sweepers in near radio silence, sailing from four south coast ports. There were around 4,000 Canadians, 1,000 British commandos and 50 US Rangers. They arrived 8 miles [13 km] off the coast of Dieppe at 03.00. The whole area to be attacked was divided into nine different sectors: Yellow Beach 1, Yellow Beach 2, Blue Beach, Red Beach, White Beach, Green Beach 1, Green Beach 2, Orange Beach 1 and Orange Beach 2.

Douglas Fairbanks Jnr led a series of small diversionary raids along the French coast by commandos under his command on HMS *Tormentor* from which his landing craft was launched.

It has always been assumed that Niven didn't take part in the actual attack by Lovat's force, but Laurence Olivier, perhaps in revenge for Niven spilling the beans about his SOE operations, told me that David was in 'the midst of the action and was nearly killed, which wouldn't have pleased the Government one bit as there was a general policy of keeping famous film stars away from the action. So the reports of the time said that Niv stayed out of the action. But he was there, amid the carnage and the horror, the blood and the bodies.'

In 1979, I asked Niven if what Olivier said was true about him taking part in the raid, and he said, 'Yes I was there. I came through it. Too many didn't. I can't bear to remember Dieppe. The loss of life was unpardonable.'

Leading 'A' Section of Phantom, Niven accompanied Lord Lovat's No 4 Commandos in an attack on 'Hess' battery at Orange Beach 2, about 1.5 miles (2.5 km) west of Dieppe. They landed on the shore at 04.50. Half the unit of 250 men followed Major Derek Mills-Roberts up a narrow gulley to the clifftop while Lovat took the rest of the unit in a wide arc to attack the battery from the rear.

Niven said, 'I was one of the lucky ones. Those of us with Lord Lovat had comparatively few casualties. Just about anything that could go wrong did go wrong.'

A gunboat leading No. 3 Commando in 20 landing craft to Berneval on Yellow Beach 1 came across five armed German trawlers and a fire-fight ensued. Although the 20 landing craft were able to disperse while the gunboat was destroyed, the sound of battle was heard by the Germans. Nevertheless, one landing craft managed to land and the Goebbels battery was captured before it fired a single shot. It was the one success in what turned into a tragic disaster.

A landing craft carrying men of the Royal Regiment of Canada lined up behind the wrong gunboat and found it was heading for the wrong beach. It took 20 confused minutes in darkness to sort out the problem but by the time the men landed on Blue Beach, the Germans, now aware they were under attack, cut them down with machine gun fire.

Niven recalled, 'There were 27 officers and over 500 men who landed on Blue Beach, and only three officers and less than 60 men survived. It was pretty much the same story all along the coastline, I'm afraid.'

A total of 1,027 Allied men lost their lives, and 2,340 were taken prisoner. David told me he had to write letters to the wives and girlfriends of the men lost in his squadron. 'It was like a scene from *Dawn Patrol* when the Commanding Officer wrote letters of regret. I was struggling to find the words to say, and the adjutant told me, "It doesn't matter how you word it, sir, it'll break her heart just the same."

'You wonder if the cost of the operation in human lives was worth it all. You could say that the mistakes at Dieppe taught us invaluable lessons that ultimately saved lives later during the Normandy invasion.'

Niven was not supposed to have taken part in the raid. He said, 'Because I was considered a popular actor, my safety seemed to be of greater importance than anyone else's. That was not only an insult to me but to the thousands of men who had no choice in the matter. I talked it over with Doug [Fairbanks] and Lord Lovat, and they said that if I really wanted to go then I must. I said, "I don't *want* to go. I'm a soldier, and it's my duty." You see, I was sending men to their deaths because one of my duties had been the assigning of men from Phantom to the mission.'

He had told me in 1978 about what he described as 'the hardest decision of my life. I had to choose between two radio operators who were both excellent at their jobs but the one who was the better was married with three children. I chose the better man – and he didn't come back. I had nightmares about that decision. I still do. In my dreams I see his wife and children asking me, "Why?" I asked myself the same question over and over, but I could only answer that I made what seemed the right decision. I could have chosen the bachelor – I often thought I should have – and those are the kinds of decisions you were making all the time.'

He admitted that he had to make life and death decisions that haunted him all his life, but he hated admitting that he took part in actual action. He said, 'There were men – and women – who were in danger far more, and more often, that I ever was, and they are more scarred than I will ever be. The mental scars of war stay with you. My mental scars are more than I can handle. I leave them alone when I can. The horror of actual battle is more than I can stand. But I can say, today, that I am proud of the part I played.'

He was proud but not to the point of ever wanting to boast about it. 'I was a bighead in Hollywood,' he said, 'but not in the war.'

He disobeyed orders by joining the attack force on Dieppe and risked court-martial, although as Douglas Fairbanks told him, 'If you get killed, old boy, they'll call you a bloody hero instead of a bloody idiot.' Lord Lovat was complicit in the cover-up; officially Niven was never there. That suited David because he didn't want to have to remember being there.

I asked him if he would have been more inclined to admit he was at Dieppe had the mission been a total success. He said, 'Oh no, old bean, I would have been court-martialled for sure. No, the only way to have been officially recognised was to have been found among the dead and I'm very glad that wasn't the case.'

The horror of war gave way to personal joy on 15 December 1942 when Primmie gave birth to David William Graham at the Royal Northern Hospital in London. Niven was given permission by his commanding officer to spend each night with Primmie and their baby, so every evening he got on a motorcycle and rode from Richmond to the hospital through a blacked out and heavily blitzed London to sleep on the floor next to Primmie's bed. Not long after he took her and David Jr home to Dorney, the hospital was hit by a bomb and 12 children were killed.

'David [Jr] had a good thespian start in life,' David Snr once told me. 'His godfather was Nöel Coward and his godmother was Vivien [Leigh].' Larry Olivier was also at the christening and presented young David with a Jacobean drinking mug. Coward's present to the child was a silver cocktail shaker with the inscription,

> Because, my Godson dear, I rather
> Think you'll turn out like your father.

Unable to escape his film star status, David Niven was sent to Glasgow on a recruiting drive, making speeches and shaking countless hands, and in January 1943, he was seconded to the Army's director of PR and became active in discussions with film director Carol Reed in an attempt to come up with an idea for a further morale-boosting picture. The result was *The Way Ahead*, a film about ordinary men recruited into the Army, and of their experiences from their first day in the Army to their first battle. It was based on a short story by Eric Ambler who, with Peter Ustinov, wrote the screenplay.

Ustinov had enjoyed his first success as a playwright with *House of Regrets*, and as a private in the Army he was attached to the Army Kinematograph Service, and in that capacity he became a writer on the film which Niven would star in and which Carol Reed would direct.

Goldwyn was reluctant to allow Niven to make another movie without being properly compensated and demanded that the production company, Two Cities, pay in full for Niven's services. Two Cities told Goldwyn that they would simply order Niven to make the film, and Goldwyn reluctantly agreed to let them 'borrow' David for $100,000.

He still had his 'A' Squadron duties to perform and he led his men on manoeuvres on Dartmoor where he and his men lived off the land without food and water for three days. When German E-boats were sighted off shore, Niven and his men were put into boats with their anti-tank rifles for several nights to try and find the German boats, but the Germans slipped away without a shot being fired.

In April 1943, Niven was again released temporarily from duty so he could work on pre-production on *The Way Ahead*, preparing the film with Carol Reed and working closely on the screenplay with Private Peter Ustinov who, in order to be able to work with officers, had to be seconded to Niven as his 'batman'.

In the film, Niven played a former Territorial Army officer who is recalled to train recruits. A host of British character actors played the recruits, including Stanley Holloway, James Donald, John Laurie, Jimmy Hanley and William Hartnell. Filming began in August on Salisbury Plain with interiors shot at Denham Studios. David and his family moved into a house close to Denham. Many of their friends would often visit, such as the Oliviers, Jack Hawkins and John and Mary Mills. 'There was quite a collection of us,' John Mills told me (on a foggy location for the TV series *Quatermass* in 1978), 'and we would meet in each other's houses.'

Niven recalled such a gathering at the home of Larry Olivier and Vivien; 'I remember that no one could carve a chicken like Larry Olivier.' Niven told me this while we were lunching at Pinewood Studios where he was filming *Candleshoe*. I'd opted for the chicken and had been given thick, generous slices of tender breast, and this provoked a memory Niven had of the days during World War II when he would be home on leave and he and Primmie would be visited by friends who brought their own food and drink with them. 'Sometimes there would be a rather large party, and Larry and Vivien would always come over, and if we had a chicken Larry always did the carving. He'd been raised in a low-budget parsonage and could make a chicken do for as many as 10 people.'

During the summer of 1943, Captain Clark Gable, on leave from the American Army Air Force and based in Britain, went to visit David and Primmie and their baby son at their thatched cottage. Gable had joined up after his wife, Carole Lombard, was killed in an aeroplane crash while on a War Bonds tour. He rose from lieutenant to major and flew several bombing missions over Germany. David told me,

Clark arrived unannounced and I was out so Primmie took care of him. I came home to find Clark Gable in his American uniform sitting in *my* deck chair, playing with *my* son, drinking *my* last bottle of whisky being served to him by *my* wife. At first I hadn't realised it was Gable but thought it was some audacious Yank because he had changed so much, but then he said, 'What's the matter, Nivvy, can't an old friend drop by to take advantage of your wife and whisky?' and I realised it was him, and I was over the moon to see him.

The war had changed his face. The loss of his wife had changed him. He was in complete misery over his loss, and yet even in his deep misery at the loss of Carole, he found it possible to rejoice over the great happiness that had come my way, which was very generous of him and just like him.

We talked a bit about the war and what we'd been through. He admitted that he was always scared stiff during the bombing raids, but the thing that frightened him most was the thought of being captured by the Germans and what Hitler might do to him. He said, 'That sonofabitch'll put me in a case and charge 10 marks a look all over Germany.'

He came to visit us often after that, and I thought he seemed to be gradually getting over Carole's death, but I could see that there were times when he was overwhelmed by my own family happiness, and one evening he disappeared into the garden. Primmie found him sitting on an upturned wheelbarrow with his head in his hands. He was crying. Primmie sat down beside him and held him.

In November the cast and crew of *The Way Ahead* sailed in a troopship to Algeria and Tunisia to film the battle scenes. 'That was a worrying voyage,' Peter Ustinov told me in 1978 when he was making *The Thief of Baghdad* at Shepperton Studios. 'You never knew if you were going to be torpedoed by a U-boat or bombed by the Luftwaffe. My main concern was losing my life but Niven and Reed seemed more concerned over how the end of the film might have to be altered if we were all to be sunk.'

With the final scenes shot, Niven returned to England at the end of November and was promoted to lieutenant-colonel. By this time he had seen enough of the war, as he admitted to me years later. 'I had enjoyed making *The Way Ahead*, and I was sick of the war. Who wasn't? It may have been selfish of me but I reached the point where I just wanted to go back to Hollywood and making films. Goldwyn wanted me back for a film [*Coming Home*] about men returning home from the war, and I was hoping to get a release from the Army, but it took most of the next year for it to decide that it couldn't do without me. I'm sure they could have, but they didn't want to set a precedent, they said. My chums like Larry Olivier and John Mills and Rex Harrison all had an early release so they could make films for the war effort, but I was the one they said couldn't do that.'

I think David underestimated his contribution to the war. Harrison, Mills and Olivier were not ever actually in the thick of it, and ultimately, despite their own intentions of doing their duty, they were undoubtedly able to serve their country better as actors and, in Olivier's case, as a director of the film *Henry V*. But Niven was a real soldier with a Sandhurst background, and he was an excellent officer.

'His men under his command had tremendous respect for him,' said Ustinov in 1984. 'He wasn't a mere prop – a Hollywood film star in uniform. He was a real soldier. An excellent officer. The Army needed him.'

The Way Ahead was released in 1944 to great acclaim and even greater success than *The First of the Few*. The British Press were enthusiastic. *Picturegoer* said, 'The dialogue is completely natural as is the humour and there is nothing forced or phoney in a single foot of a wholly enjoyable and inspiring film.'

The *Sunday Times* praised Reed and the writers who had 'admirably captured the qualities of mingled suspicions, irony and readiness to get on with the job which characterises many recruits to the British Army', and it noted 'the excellent playing of the whole cast', although it did feel that 'it was not until the second half and embarkations for overseas that *The Way Ahead* seemed to show its real quality'.

The film also found favour with some American critics. 'In one scene, wherein [David Niven] dresses down the trainees, he accomplishes a truly heart-disturbing soldier's monologue,' wrote Bosley Crowther in the *New York Times*.

During the spring of 1944, David was ordered to report to General Sir Frederick Morgan in Sunningdale, and he duly arrived at the carefully camouflaged HQ in the middle of a wood where Morgan, as Chief of Staff to the Supreme Allied Commander, had been working on preliminary plans for Operation 'Overlord', the codename for the invasion of Occupied Europe.

David recalled,

The first and most important decision Morgan and his staff had to make was exactly where to land on the French coast. Information was supplied to him that had come from the French Resistance about the German defences, and he had hundreds of photographs taken by the RAF. He ruled out landing in Norway, the Netherlands and the Bay of Biscay, and he had to choose between France and Belgium. The Germans knew that the most obvious landing on the French coast would be at Calais, crossing from Dover, so Morgan knew he had to plan further down the coast and [in June 1943] had arrived at the conclusion that Normandy would be the point of invasion.

The date had originally been set for some day in June 1944, and it was shortly before then that I was summoned to Sir Frederick's headquarters. He told me that because I had spent a great deal of time in America and I liked Americans, he was taking me out of Phantom and promoting me to lieutenant-colonel and assigned me to an American general called Barker with whom he'd worked on the initial invasion plans. I found General Barker's Nissen hut where he told me he had been given the task by Eisenhower of making sure there were no weak links between the various Allied forces.

Barker said, 'From now on you take orders only from me, and when the invasion comes you will be working only with me. We will be liaising between the British and American forces. You're going to be in the thick of it.'

Through his work with General Ray Barker and General Morgan, Niven came into personal contact with General Sir Bernard Montgomery who was to command the Allied landing force in Normandy. The invasion was originally set for 5 June 1944, but the weather was so appalling that Eisenhower and Montgomery postponed it. On 5 June the Allied Command decided the following day would be D-Day.

'The night before the invasion,' Niven recalled, 'Primmie and I clung together miserably. I told her I wouldn't leave until after we'd had breakfast together. It was a kind lie, I'm afraid. She finally fell asleep just before dawn, and I quietly dressed, took one last look at my wife and my baby son who lay in the cot beside the bed, and left.'

Niven and General Barker boarded the *Empire Battleaxe* at Southampton. The first landings had already taken place, and casualties were being ferried back to England. 'Hundreds of wounded GIs were being helped off a tank-landing craft,' David recalled. 'Their eyes wide with shock. Boys who had grown old in just a couple of hours. A GI who was watching from the deck of our ship saw these wounded men and said, "That's a helluva encouraging send-off for us."'

When the *Battleaxe* arrived off the Normandy coast, Niven was ordered into a landing craft and put ashore. 'The beach was marked with white tape to show the paths around the minefields. The dead rolled in the surf and littered the beaches. I try not to remember it now. What I remember is lying in a trench that first night, hearing the nightingales over the gunfire.'

A small bridge at Carentan was the one vital link between US forces who had pushed up from Utah Beach and the British further east. David, in maintaining personal contact between the Americans and the British, used this bridge which came under constant shellfire, as he recalled to me almost 35 years later.

> I had to make the crossing quite frequently, and I was trapped by the shelling on one crossing. There were fox holes either side of the bridge which I had to dive into and cower as the rain just poured down, filling my fox hole until I thought if I wasn't blown to bits I'd probably drown. The rain stopped and I dared a peek over the top. A few yards away in another fox hole I saw a head and to my delight and surprise it was an old friend of mine, John McClaine, who had been a reporter in New York and was a lieutenant in the Navy attached to the OSS.
>
> He pinned an Iron Cross on my chest which he'd acquired when a delivery of the medals had been parachuted to the German soldiers in Cherbourg but had fallen into McClaine's hands instead. Then he gave me a ride in his command car to a small inn in a backwater that was untouched by the war. We became the first Allied combatants the three ladies who ran the inn had ever seen. They gave us a bloody good meal washed down with bottles of Bordeaux. Then we headed back for Carentan and the war.

Shortly after the town of Caen fell to the Allies on 10 July, Niven came across 'B' Squadron of the secret Phantom force, hidden in a wood near Orme River. Among them was the Welsh actor Hugh Williams who had been among the cast of *Wuthering Heights*. 'Hugh told me that the second-in-command of 'A' Squadron, Hugh Kindersley, had been badly wounded by mortar fire. Hugh told me the terrible injuries Kindersley had sustained, and Hugh and I agreed that if we had known about the German Nebelwerfer, which was a six-barrelled mortar, neither of us would have joined the Army. It had to be one of the most devastating instruments of destruction the Germans had thought of. I have never been able to fathom the depths of cruelty and sadism that mankind has sunk to.'

For various strategic and political reasons, it was forbidden for British forces to enter Paris immediately after its liberation on 25 August 1944. The Free French alone had been allowed the privilege of entering the French capital. David claimed he was the first British soldier to enter Paris a few days after it was liberated. It might even be a true story.

Montgomery and Patton just couldn't agree on how to bring the war to its conclusion, and distorted versions of their differences filtered down to the fighting troops. Montgomery wanted to strike at the Ruhr, insisting that that would destroy the enemy's fighting capability. This upset Patton because Montgomery needed reinforcements from the US 1st Army which would have halted Patton's advance on Metz. So General Barker had his work cut out trying to defuse the rumours while General Eisenhower tried to sort out his prima donnas. The problem was not only one of strategy but also egos.

Barker told me to get to Paris with important documents which I had to deliver to an American colonel in the bar of the Hôtel Crillon. I was given a jeep and a driver – an American corporal. We got to Neuilly and got lost, but I had some friends in Neuilly and, finding their apartment, I told the corporal to wait with the jeep. He was busy anyway as the citizens of Neuilly descended on the corporal with kisses and bottles of wine.

I went inside and my old friends fed and watered me and let me bathe, and when I came back out the corporal had disappeared with the jeep, apparently borne off on the crest of hysterical citizenry.

Fortunately I had the documents on my person so, borrowing a woman's bicycle and fixing two Union Jacks to it, I cycled along the Champs Elysées as the people waved and cheered at seeing what was probably the first British soldier they had seen in five years. I arrived at the Hôtel Crillon, went to the bar and there found the colonel and my corporal. I promptly delivered the secret documents and had a drink to celebrate my single-handed British occupation of Paris.

In 1993, Dirk Bogarde told me that he and his Army companion, Chris Greaves, were the first Allied soldiers to enter Paris the day after the liberation, driving into the city by jeep against orders and finding a bar where they drank to the liberation of Paris. It would have been fun to have been able to sit Niven and Bogarde down together and listen to their respective tales.

David returned to England in August but was back in Paris in September and embarked on an affair with French actress Yvette Lebon. I only know this because he carelessly mentioned her name while telling me how there were countless grateful girls to be picked up in Parisian bars following the liberation and that, as well as taking advantage of these, he also met a number of very grateful French actresses including one he said was called Ivette Lebón – she was better known as Yvette Lebon.

In 1982, as he was facing certain death and was regretting his many infidelities during his marriage to Primmie, David said, 'There's nothing I can do to change the clock. But I have changed my heart, and if only Primmie could know that and that she will be waiting for me.'

Back at the front line, there was further disagreement between Patton and Montgomery when Eisenhower agreed to Monty's plan to invade Holland, capturing vital river and canal crossings, especially on the Lower Rhine where one bridge was at the Dutch town of Arnhem. Patton was furious and relations between the Allies began falling apart, so General Barker and Lieutenant Colonel David Niven had to stage-manage attempts to maintain communications between the British and American forces. The operation – codenamed 'Market Garden' – began on 17 September 1944. By the 26th, the bridges at Veghel, Grave and Nijimegen were captured but the battle to capture the bridge at Arnhem was a disaster. Of the 10,000 troops and parachutists dropped, 1,200 had died and 6,642 were taken prisoner.

David recalled, 'The autumn of 1944 was described by historians as a "lull". Not to the British airborne troops who had to fight for their lives at Arnhem. The whole thing was a shambles, but it is true that if we had taken Arnhem, it would have shortened the war. Montgomery thought that instead of tackling the Siegfried Line he would skirt the northern end and aim for Berlin. As it is, the so-called "lull" was the slow progress towards the Ardennes.'

To Patton's delight, Eisenhower now accepted the 'broad front' strategy whereby the Allies attacked in four areas in their advance on the Rhine. It rained throughout the autumn, turning the ground to mud. Niven was sent by Barker into the battle zones and came across 'A' Squadron stationed in waterlogged fields near Geldrop. He spent a few days with them before moving onto Nijimegen where, among the Welsh Guards, he met Anthony Bushell who had been Laurence Olivier's production manager and was now a company commander.

They stood among the tanks, reminiscing, when, said David, 'there was an appalling explosion. I dived under a tank but Bushell remained standing up, laughing. I appeared to be the only one who had bothered to take cover. I said, "What the hell was that?" He said, "The Germans have this bloody great gun, you see, in a railway tunnel across the river, and every hour they wheel it out and fire it. We're used to it." I am constantly amazed at how human beings can become conditioned to the worst of situations and conditions that they face in war time.'

By December 1944 the Allies had made slow progress. The rain had turned to snow. On 15 December, Niven reported to the US 1st Army headquarters at Spa in the Ardennes to liaise with Captain Bob Lowe, a one-time reporter with *Time* who was now working in 1st Army intelligence.

Captain Lowe took Niven to the map room of the intelligence section; David said he never forgot exactly what Lowe said. 'The other side of those hills,' Captain Lowe told him, pointing through the window, 'there is a forest and in that forest they are forming the 6th Panzer Army, and any day now the 6th Panzer Army is going to come right through this room and out the other side, cross the Neuse, then swing right and go north to Antwerp.'

'Have you mentioned this to anyone?' Niven asked him.

'We've been telling them for days, three times a day.'

The next morning, 16 December, David went on to Marche, and the Germans launched their offensive in the Ardennes; the Battle of the Bulge had begun. Although Niven wasn't caught up in the fighting, he was nevertheless in danger, even from the Americans, as he recalled,

> There was an SS colonel called Otto Skorzney who was attached to the 6th Panzer Army. He could speak with an American accent and, with his men in American uniforms, he succeeded in infiltrating American lines and causing various acts of sabotage. They were called the Grief Commandos, and rumours of these commandos in American uniform ran wild and it was assumed they were on a mission to assassinate General Eisenhower at his headquarters in Versailles. This led to the interrogation of many real GIs and anyone else purporting to be an ally.
>
> The GIs used every trick question, like, 'What's the name of the president's dog?' I had quite a few anxious moments in the Ardennes in my British uniform and jeep with 21st Army Group markings. They'd stop me and tell me to put my hands above my head, pointing their guns at me and asking my name.
>
> I told them I was David Niven and said, 'The actor, you must have seen some of my films.'
>
> But they said, 'Anyone can claim to be David Niven. Who won the World Series in 1940?'
>
> I told them I had no idea but I had made a picture with Ginger Rogers. That satisfied them I was the *real* David Niven.

There was some respite for Niven when he was allowed back home again and moved his family to a new house, a 15th-century cottage near Windsor. He was home for Christmas which he, Primmie and the baby spent with the Trees at Ditchley Park.

David always maintained that he was not a hero. He was able to talk about some of his wartime experiences with humour in 1970, but in 1978 he acknowledged that there were times when his nerves where certainly put on edge if not shredded. 'People were dying all around me,' he told me. 'They didn't have to be firing a gun. German planes could zero in on us at any time, or a shell could land among us. There were plenty of times when I wanted to fight back, but I hardly ever saw the enemy to be able to aim at him. I was kept busy trying to keep the British and the Americans from each other's throats, and really, you know, there were times when I could have easily throttled one or two generals on both sides.'

In January 1945 Niven was back in Paris, continuing his affair with Yvette Lebon, and then he headed back to the front line. When he was home on leave in March, Primmie became pregnant again.

After the Battle of the Bulge was won by the Allies, the move to the Rhine was swift, and during the first week of March they reached the Rhine which was about the time Niven caught up with them. The greatest surprise to the Allies was that the bridge at Remagen had not been destroyed by the Germans in their retreat, and this was so unexpected that Montgomery was not ready to cross because he first needed a build-up of strength. David said,

> The depths of idiocy were surely reached when Patton telephoned Bradley and said, 'I want the world to know the Third Army made it before Monty starts across.' So Patton crossed where he was at Oppenheim [on 22 March] and Montgomery waited until the next day at Wesel. I crossed in Monty's wake.
>
> I had never seen such destruction – the smoking town of Wesel had ceased to exist. I really had to say to myself, there but for the grace of God go I. I thought of what could have happened to England, to the house where my wife and child were, if the Germans had ever breached our defences. I wasn't much of a believer in God, but I had to wonder if Good and Evil really did exist side by side, and that Good would always overcome Evil. If the Japanese had not attacked Pearl Harbor – if the Germans had not attacked Russia – we would have lost the war. Was that Good over Evil, or just the complete and utter madness of one man in Berlin who thought he was invincible and could take on the world but in the end the odds were against him?
>
> When we got to Münster, the only thing I saw standing was a bronze statue of a horse. Hanover was also in ruins. The burgomaster there told me that at least 60,000 bodies lay under the rubble.
>
> In each town a handful of Allied soldiers were posted, and I wondered what good they could do now that Germany was on the run. I thought there was no more fight left in them. But when I arrived in a

village outside of Hanover I heard rifle fire. I was told to get down, and I took cover and saw that a group of British soldiers were firing at a building that was still standing but with no roof. From an upstairs window someone was firing. The sergeant said to me, 'We've got a sniper up there,' but it only took me a few seconds to realise that the person inside was firing wide and was unable to hit anything. I said, 'That's no sniper, stop firing and pull back.' The sergeant began to argue with me that someone was trying to kill them and they weren't about to let him get away. Then I finally lost my temper and yelled, 'Pull back and that's an order.'

At that very moment a woman suddenly came running out of a door of the building screaming 'Stop! He's my son. Stop!' The soldiers simply reacted and shot her dead. The boy at the window stood up and called, 'Mama!' and he was shot dead too. I told the sergeant to get the boy's body, and they brought him out and I saw he could only have been no more than 12. He was one of the Hitler Youth and had somehow managed to get hold of a real gun, probably off a dead German soldier.

I just couldn't make sense of it all. None of it. I still can't.

I moved on with the American 1 Unit and on the road to Osnabrück I saw a hastily erected POW camp to house the captured Germans. There must have been a hundred thousand men already inside. The German defences were falling apart quickly now, and you could sense the end wasn't too far off. I thought about how Hitler had begun all this but now that the chickens had come home to roost, I couldn't find it within myself to gloat.

At that point in the war, David felt, he said, as though he had seen 'every horror imaginable'. But worse was to come. He tried to tell me what it was like in the concentration camps he came across. 'You cannot begin to describe the revulsion. The sights and sounds that stay with you, the stench – all those things that you can never forget because they play like a film back in your mind from time to time – were more than even those of us who had seen all the other horrors of the war could stand.

'I was sick. Physically sick. Even now, I sometimes fancy that I can catch a hint of that stench in my nostrils, and my stomach heaves. I feel like it will never leave me.'

At Liebenau, David came across a labour camp. 'The workers were from all over Europe – from Russia, Italy, France, Poland, Holland, Germany. The gates to the camp were open but there was nowhere for them to go. I have never seen such hopelessness. They just wandered about in a trance

around the camp and outside of it. There were prisoners from a concentration camp who shuffled among them, standing gaunt and lifeless, and
barely alive, none of them knowing which way was home, just wandering
aimlessly. It is a memory that comes to me like a snapshot, a scene frozen
in time.'

He told me one particularly harrowing story which he said he had long
repressed. Near the gates of the labour camp he was approached by a man
carrying another in his arms.

> Both men looked as light as feathers, they were so emaciated. But
> somehow, one of them found the strength to carry the other. The man
> walking was saying, 'Tommy, Tommy!' He didn't put the man down.
> He just stood there, holding him, and they were looking at me through
> eyes that barely sat in sunken holes. The man who was carrying the
> other said in French, 'My brother wants to thank you before dying.'
>
> I said, 'Look, old man, we're here now and you won't die.' Then the
> man who was being carried seemed to smile and died. Just like that. At
> that moment his brother seemed to wilt, and I tried to hold him, but
> the best I could do was help him and his dead brother to the ground,
> and he said, 'Thank you, Tommy,' and died too.
>
> I can't forget their eyes. It isn't like in a film where somebody runs a
> hand over a dead man's eyes and they close, because the eyes don't
> close. They stay open, and the memory of those men's eyes haunts me.

After Germany surrendered, David Niven found himself driving along
a road near Brunswick in a jeep. Welded to the jeep's radiator were
sharpened iron stanchions to break through piano wire that had been
stretched across many of the roads by a band of young Nazi zealots known
as 'Werewolves'. David told me,

> Too many of our men had been decapitated by piano wire laid by the
> Werewolves, and so you took what precautions you could. The war was
> over, but your life was still at risk.
>
> On the road to Brunswick I saw two men in typical farm clothes on
> a one-horse wagon. But the man at the reins was wearing field boots. I
> got out of the jeep, drew my revolver and told the corporal with me to
> cover me. I walked over to the wagon and motioned for the men to put
> their hands on their heads and in rather bad German told them to
> produce their papers.
>
> The one who was wearing the field boots said, 'I speak English. This
> man has papers, I do not.' I asked him who he was and he told me his

name and that he was a general. He said they were not armed. I saluted him and told them to lower their hands and said, 'Where are you coming from, sir?'

He said, 'Berlin.' He looked entirely dejected, totally despairing. I asked him where he was going, and he said, 'Home.' He said he was almost there. He looked to the village I had just come through. We just stared at each other for what seemed a long time.

Then I said, 'Go home,' and then I added, rather ridiculously I suppose, 'but cover your bloody boots.' He just closed his eyes, breathed a huge sigh that was almost a sob, covered his face with both hands, and then they drove on.

As far as his own efforts during the war were concerned, Niven said, 'I can't claim to have exerted much pressure on the squabbling field marshals and generals, but I guess that I must have done my job well because that September General Barker pinned the American Legion of Merit on me.'

David's other medals for his excellent war service were the 1939–45 Star, the France and Germany Star, the Defence Medal, and the War Medal 1939–45. But he received no medal for his action at Dieppe. The official records omitted his participation.

As the son of a man who, like millions of others, played his part in the war on Nazism and gave us our freedom, I'd like to say that I feel David Niven played his part well – as well as any part he ever played on screen. He was, as Peter Ustinov said, the real thing and not just a mere prop.

—

CHAPTER 13

The Greatest Tragedy

David finally retuned home from the war on 31 May 1945. He had tactfully maintained contact with Sam Goldwyn throughout the war with letters relating his news and always making sure that Goldwyn knew he was looking forward to coming back and working for him.

'I knew that Goldwyn was my best chance of getting back into films in Hollywood after the war,' he said. 'So I made sure that I never lost touch, and I had some very nice letters back from him. Some of them were quite touching and, I think, sincere. But I could never forget that he was first and foremost a businessman, and he would only use me if I could make him money. And I needed, desperately, to get back to Hollywood.'

Goldwyn wrote to him and told him he wanted to see him back in Hollywood as soon as possible. In August he gave Niven a new five-year contract starting at $3,000 a week but told him he had to stay in England to make *A Matter of Life and Death*. Goldwyn had wasted no time loaning him to Michael Powell and Emeric Pressburger, the successful partners who produced, directed and wrote their films in Britain.

The film kept Niven in England through the summer and early autumn of 1945. 'I really didn't want to do it,' he told me. 'It was actually intended as a bit of propaganda, made on the instructions of the Ministry of Information who wanted Powell and Pressburger to come up with something that bridged the growing divisions between the Americans and the British. I felt I'd done enough bridge building in the war. What I couldn't know at the time was that these two amazing film makers would come up with something absolutely so mind-boggling that at the time it wasn't at all well received.'

In the hands of Powell and Pressburger, this bridge building exercise became a dreamlike fantasy, bold and imaginative, with some scenes in black and white and others in colour, telling of a dying RAF pilot, played by Niven, who finds himself before a heavenly tribunal with a strong anti-British prosecutor, played by Raymond Massey. In both the real world and the imagined world – if, indeed, it is imagined – appears a girl, played by American actress Kim Hunter.

It baffled some critics, delighted others, and gave David a really solid role that he said was, 'by far the most difficult part I'd had up till then. I found myself having to actually *be* an actor. It wasn't enough to fall back on my military background. In this, Michael Powell was very helpful to me. A very fine director.'

The film had the distinction of being chosen to be the first Royal Film Performance, a matter that bewildered the *Daily Graphic* which announced, 'There will be widespread editorial indignation at the choice for our first Royal Film Performance of a picture which might have been made specially to appeal to isolationist and anti-British sentiments in the United States.'

The *Observer* was unable to understand what the producers were trying to do: 'The main trouble with *A Matter of Life and Death* which is original in conception, honestly acted by Mr Niven and Kim Hunter, is that it leaves us in grave doubts whether it is intended to be serious or gay. When they tell me that it is a "stratospheric joke" I reply that a matter of life and death can never be a good joke.'

The *Sunday Express* seemed to get the joke, and it liked Niven's performance: 'David Niven gives the thoughtful whimsical joke a warm and human heart.'

There was more praise for David from the *Daily Telegraph*: 'David Niven has done nothing quite so good as his airman trembling on the brink of a nervous breakdown without ever lapsing into hysteria.'

It also found favour with some American critics. The *Journal-American* thought it 'beautifully written, beautifully acted, beautifully executed. You would think such formidable merits would add up to quite a film – and darned if they don't.'

The film was too abstract to be a commercial success on either side of the Atlantic. Niven said, 'At first I thought that Goldwyn was simply trying to sabotage my career before I could get back to Hollywood when I started on the picture by loaning me out to make this film *I* didn't understand to start with. But I'm glad I did it. I got to find something inside of me as an actor I didn't know was there. Or if I suspected it was there, I hadn't had the opportunity to practise it before.'

While he was still making *A Matter of Life and Death*, the British taxman demanded several thousand pounds he said David owed because he had been a British resident since 1939. He argued that he had only come back to fight in the war, but he was told he still had to pay and was given three years to do so.

In November he was at last discharged from the Army, but he remained a reservist until 1954.

On 6 November, Primmie gave birth to their second son, James Graham – they always called him Jamie – in London. They hired a nurse, Beryl Rogers, who always wore a pink nanny's uniform and so was nicknamed Pinkie by David and Primmie.

In December David sailed back to America, leaving Primmie and the two boys to join him later. He arrived in New York on 10 December and, after being the guest of a party thrown in his honour at the 21 Club, he caught a sleeper train to California and arrived in Pasadena two days before Christmas. A huge banner was hung at the Goldwyn studio – WELCOME HOME, DAVID. A huge press party was thrown by Goldwyn at which he made a speech about David's great courage and solid character. 'It was all bullshit,' said David, 'but I thoroughly enjoyed the bullshit.'

> I felt I was finally back home where I belonged, and I was playing the Hollywood game. Hedda Hopper was there and made a speech about how wonderful I was – so I *knew* it was bullshit – but that was Hollywood, and I loved it. When I made my speech I told them how happy I was to be home among my friends and that I was never, ever, going to talk about the war. All I did say was that I had been asked by some American friends to try and find their son's grave in Belgium. It was in the middle of 27,000 other graves of American soldiers, and I said to myself that here were 27,000 reasons why I should keep my mouth shut. I think they were all very understanding about it.
>
> Goldwyn said to me, 'David, I'm proud of you. A lot of guys come back from Europe having had it quite cushy compared to you, and they sound off about what they accomplished. But you have humility,' and coming from Goldwyn that was a sincere and unforgettable compliment. There were times, you know, when Goldwyn was someone I was really fond of. And I think he was fond of me. But business just got in the way.
>
> Unfortunately, I wasn't feeling too well, and during the last stages of

lunch I began to feel really ill, and ended up with a bronchial pneumonia. I had to take to my bed, and some time later I talked to John Huston about it. He'd really been in the thick of it in Italy, filming combat and really coming under heavy fire, and he shot a film in a hospital where servicemen were suffering terrible trauma which they used to call shell shock. I said, 'I got through the whole war perfectly fit and well, and when I got back to California I came down with pneumonia.' He said it was common for soldiers to hold on physically through the worst times, and when it was safe and there was nothing to threaten them, they often sort of loosened up, and then they were overcome with all kinds of physical and mental illness. He said he had it himself. He had the shakes. He said that I probably had bronchial pneumonia months before but some kind of will power kept me going until I relaxed – and then I got it.

Goldwyn didn't waste time loaning David out again, this time to Hal Wallis who was producing *The Perfect Marriage*. Niven and Loretta Young played a couple whose marriage, on their 10th wedding anniversary, suddenly hits the rocks. As Niven put it, 'It was about married people who in the end don't get divorced.' And that was all there was to it. Loretta Young told me, 'My career had peaked by the time I made that movie with David, but I knew he might find it hard to get work of any quality when he came back – the same happened to a lot of stars; Jimmy Stewart, Clark Gable for instance – and so I asked for David. I knew, as well, that without him the picture would have been a lot worse. I felt he and I had a chemistry that might just pull it off.'

The chemistry didn't. David's first Hollywood film after the war was a disaster. The *Times* felt that the film 'pretends at a sophistication never present in the luxurious sets, and Mr Niven, that most admirable and sophisticated actor, seems to think that if he can keep quiet enough the whole thing will turn out to be a delusion'.

'My prompt regard for David Niven,' wrote the film critic in the *Observer*, 'prompts me to say very little about *The Perfect Marriage*.'

While waiting for Primmie and the boys to arrive, David spent his time fishing, playing golf and tennis, and chasing women. He even attempted a romance with Loretta Young who let that little secret slip when she told me, 'He was lonely when he came home from the war so we spent some time together and I thought for a while he might even want to marry me.'

This might have seemed a delusion of Loretta's, but Ava Gardner, then a starlet who had arrived in Hollywood during Niven's absence and who David would later pursue, told me that Loretta, despite her Catholic

Niven was a supporting player in *Bluebeard's Eighth Wife* in 1938, escorting Claudette Colbert on a European beach built in a Hollywood studio.

Niven finally got a good leading role in a major movie, opposite his dubious friend Errol Flynn in *The Dawn Patrol* in 1938.

Niven co-starred with his sometimes girlfriend Loretta Young in *Eternally Yours* in 1939.

A rare still of David Niven during service in World War Two.

Niv's happiest days, being married to his wife Primmie and carrying aloft his
first son, David Junior.

With his second wife, Swedish model Hjördis (pronounced Yer-dis).

Cutting a dashing figure in *Enchantment* in 1948.

With his friend Stewart Granger in the comedy adventure *Soldiers Three* in 1951.

All at sea with Glynis Johns in *Appointment with Venus* in 1951.

David found his perfect role as Phileas Fogg when he went *Around the World in Eighty Days* in 1956 with Shirley MacLaine and Cantinflas.

A good role for Niven as the playboy father in the controversial (for 1957) *Bonjour Tristesse* with Jean Seberg as his daughter and Deborah Kerr as his old flame.

An Oscar at last for Niven, as the seedy and bogus major befriended by mousey spinster Deborah Kerr in *Separate Tables* in 1958.

June Allyson shows her appreciation to butler David in *My Man Godfrey* in 1957.

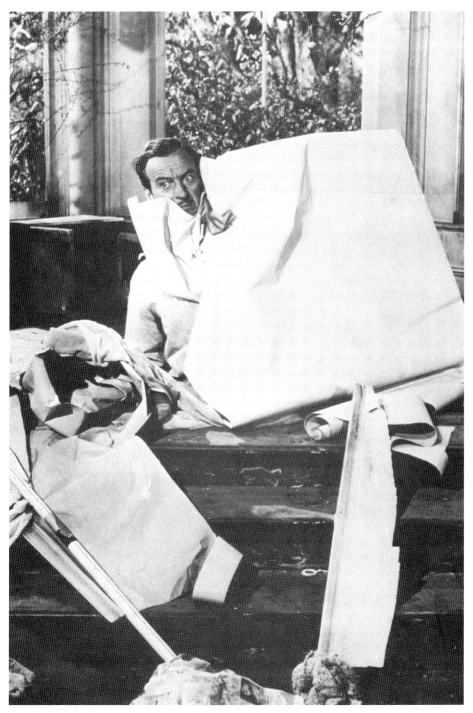

Another fine mess, but a good comedy role for Niven in *Please Don't Eat the Daisies* in 1960.

Sturdy Charlton Heston, stunning Ava Gardner and dependable David Niven all looking composed despite being besieged by thousands of Chinese Boxers in the 1963 epic 55 *Days at Peking*.

Not the usual image of James Bond, but in *Casino Royale* in 1967, Niven as Sir James Bond was sending up 007. He was good, the film was not.

David and Hjördis with Kristina, the secret daughter David had whom the Nivens officially adopted.

Niven, before he was struck by Motor Neurone Disease, still looking dapper in *Paper Tiger*, one last really good performance in 1975.

beliefs, was 'not a saint, although she liked to be portrayed as Saint Loretta, and believe me, she was just as amorous as the rest of us. Nivvy was having his way with her while she was married [to producer Tom Lewis] and he was married [to Primmie]. That was the game everyone played in Hollywood. The only difference was that Loretta thought Nivvy might actually divorce Primmie – as if *that* was ever going to happen. I guess a lot of other men would divorce their wives for Loretta Young.'

David looked for a house to buy and found it on a hill above Sunset Boulevard. He was only able to buy it because Sam Goldwyn loaned him the deposit. It was a rambling old building with a huge garden and a view of the mountains on one side and the sea on the other. It was painted pink which was the colour of Primmie's home when she was a child – so it remained pink and was called the Pink House.

'There was a lot of pink,' David once said rather wistfully when he lunched with Lynne Frederick and I in 1980. 'The house was pink and our nurse was pink.'

He didn't want to move in without Primmie, so while he awaited the arrival of his family he rented himself a house in Beverly Hills. Primmie and the boys finally arrived at the end of March 1946. She fell in love with the Pink House and, rather than move straight in, wanted to furnish it herself so that when it was ready he could carry her over the threshold. She began the adventure of decorating it and buying exactly the kind of furniture she felt would make it her home as well as sending for personal items from England.

The Hollywood social whirl began almost at once for Primmie as she was whisked off to meet David's friends and to attend parties and eat out at swish restaurants. 'He loved showing her off to everyone,' Laurence Olivier recalled, 'and everyone fell in love with her. He needed a car so I sold him one – a black Packard I had left behind when I went back to England and didn't need anymore.'

In April 1946 Niven started work on *Magnificent Doll*, another loan-out which earned Goldwyn $100,000. He did, however, give David a bonus which came to several thousand dollars. 'He was trying to buy me off,' David told me. 'Before the war he had promised me that he would only star me in Goldwyn pictures, but he was reneging on that gentlemen's agreement. I wrote and told him that I would only be truly happy when I was working at my "home" studio. As for the film he stuck me in, it was rather dire, I'm afraid, despite Ginger Rogers.'

Ginger Rogers was given top billing in *Magnificent Doll* and David's name came second. The fact was, Niven wasn't, and would never be, a top rated star in Hollywood. It took a long time for him to accept that, and only in his latter years did he come to terms with the fact that he was never as big a star as he had hoped to be. He recalled,

> I was lacking in something. I don't know what it was, but if anyone knew what it was they would have bottled it and we would have all had some, and that would have done no good to anyone. We needed – we still need – the major stars – superstars they call them these days. The Gables and the Coopers, the Bette Davises and the Crawfords. But even those people could bomb disastrously in the wrong pictures.
>
> After the war the studios had trouble finding the right kind of pictures for me. I think it took time for it to dawn upon them that I had *already* made the right kind of pictures for me during the war. That's why I've worked so much in war films or pictures with a military backdrop. If you want a dependable British officer, call for Niven. I knew I was good at light comedy. But Cary Grant got all the best scripts first.

Magnificent Doll was a period piece set during the early days of American independence. Ginger Rogers played a woman who runs a boarding house and is much admired by Senator Aaron Burr, played by Niven, who is plotting to become the first Emperor of America. David was cast as a villain but, he admitted, he didn't know how to be a villain. 'I tried to be nasty, but it's hard to be nasty to Ginger Rogers' he said. 'So I just read the lines and didn't make much of an attempt to be nasty at all.'

The *Sunday Times* noticed 'David Niven as Aaron Burr looking traitorous in a gentlemanly sort of way'. The *Daily Express* said, 'David Niven plays Aaron Burr as if he were cheering on the boat race.'

David recalled, 'I thought I recognised a political slant to that picture. There was some ill feeling towards the British from the Americans after the war, and since we had been the villains in their war of independence, they decided a smooth talking English actor would make the perfect corrupt American senator. I was beginning to think that being an English actor in America after the war wasn't such a good idea after all.'

He was beginning to have doubts about a future in Hollywood.

He was able to take a week off from filming *Magnificent Doll*, and he and Primmie joined a group of friends – Clark Gable, Nigel Bruce, Ida Lupino and Rex Harrison – on a short vacation in Monterey to fish and play golf. Back at the Pink House, Pinkie the nanny was taking good care of the boys who came to love her, and she them.

I have heard it said, and have read, that Niven didn't like Rex Harrison and that he told Sam Goldwyn that he would never work with James Mason and Rex Harrison because he felt they had shirked their duty by staying out of the war. Actually, Harrison served in the RAF, a fact which had escaped David at the time of his complaint, and he and Harrison became good friends. I did a formal interview with Rex Harrison in 1982 in Norfolk, where he was filming an episode of *Tales of the Unexpected*; we both knew of David's terminal illness then.

'I knew David a little and we got on very well,' Harrison said. 'He'd had a marvellous war record and I suppose I was something of a military lightweight compared to him because he was and had always been a professional solider. I got into the RAF when war broke out, and I was one of those actors the government didn't want getting killed, so I was kept at home. David told me he was envious, that he had often wanted to get out of the war and get back to Hollywood. But he was torn between duty and ambition, and I don't think the Army was prepared to let a professional soldier like him go.'

Back in 1946, Harrison and his wife Lilli Palmer were to play a part in the greatest tragedy of David Niven's life.

At the end of the holiday in Monterey, David and Primmie returned to Hollywood on Sunday 19 May and went to a party at the home of Tyrone and Annabella Power where many of Niven's friends were gathered including Rex Harrison and Lilli Palmer, Bob Coote, Richard Greene and his then wife Patricia Medina.

David never spoke to me about what took place there; he was able to write about it in *The Moon's a Balloon*, but he was never actually able to talk about it to me. I don't think he talked about it to many. But I did get two accounts of what happened, one from Patricia Medina who I met in London in 1980 when I interviewed her husband Joseph Cotton, and the other from Rex Harrison when I interviewed him.

'David loves games, always has,' said Harrison (speaking of Niven in the present tense in 1982). 'Cesar Romero was there and he said he knew of a game called "sardines" where people play hide and seek but in the dark. So it was decided to play this childish game and we turned off all the lights. Nobody could see where they were going and there was a lot of whispering throughout the house.'

Harrison recalled hearing what he described as 'a sickening serious of thuds, and I just knew that someone had fallen down steps. Primmie had gone through the wrong door. It was the door to the cellar, and she had stepped into the dark but there was no floor, just stone steps and as she stepped forward into empty air she went down, all the way. A terrible, ghastly tragedy.'

Patricia Medina recalled, 'I was upstairs with Tyrone Power and we heard a thud. Ty put on the lights and we rushed down stairs and, oh my

God, we found Primmie in the cellar, lying unconscious after falling some 20 feet (6m).'

'She was taken up to the living room,' recalled Harrison, 'and was laid on the floor. David was deathly white – in shock. He was clearly distressed but he somehow remained outwardly calm. Perhaps it was his military training. He said to me, "If anything happens to her, I think it will be the end of me. I really do." I poured him a brandy while Lilli sat on the floor, cradling Primmie's head.'

A doctor was called and Annabella Power mopped Primmie's head with icy water. Pat Medina could remember hearing her say, 'I feel so strange.' Harrison remembers her saying, 'David, darling, we'll never be invited again.'

David went with Primmie and the doctor to St John's Hospital in Santa Monica. The doctors told him she was suffering concussion and was still unconscious but would be fine. 'David was terribly worried, of course, but I think he felt better that the doctors were so reassuring,' said Harrison, 'so the next day he went back to work [on *Magnificent Doll*] and then went to the hospital in the evening, and the doctors were really most optimistic. He told me that while he sat by her bed, holding her hand, she opened her eyes and saw him and then he felt her hand giving his a little gentle squeeze. Then her eyes closed and she went back to sleep.

'He left her there thinking that she would be expecting him the next day but he got a call from the hospital almost as soon as he got home that evening and they told him they would have to operate because she had a blood clot.'

David was kept company by Bob Coote while the operation was in progress. After two agonising hours the head surgeon told David that Primmie had died.

Pat Medina recalled, 'He went into such terrible shock that he wandered around the streets in a daze and turned up at our house in tears, literally screaming.'

Richard Greene remembered that he and Pat tried to comfort him, 'but it was impossible. He'd lost the only woman he truly loved.'

'I believe he was never the same after that,' said Rex Harrison. 'He never got over her. Even when he married again, he always loved Primmie. He said to me once, "Do you believe there is the one very special person for each of us, someone we are destined to be with, and when we find that person, we have to make the most of it because we don't know when we'll be parted?" I said, "David, I think we're lucky if we *ever* find one very special person, and some of us never do, but I don't know that we are *destined* to find her." And he said, "I believe I was destined to find Primmie, and so the very short time we had together is something I will always treasure, and nobody can ever take her place. And perhaps if there is a heaven, she is there waiting for me, and then I'll be with her for eternity." And I think he believed that, and that kept him going.'

When I saw David in 1982, he said pretty much the same thing to me, and I told him that I believed, as I then did, that he would find Primmie waiting for him, and that gave him tremendous comfort. I hope it might actually be true.

CHAPTER 14

—

The Darkest Time

After Primmie was cremated, David flew her ashes back to England and buried them at the church in Huish where they had married six years earlier. The inscription on her tombstone read, 'Here lies Primula, loved wife of David Niven, died at Los Angeles 21st May 1946, aged 28.'

He flew straight back to Los Angeles where there was a memorial service for her on 29 May. Another was held that same day in London at the Grosvenor Chapel, attended by Grizel, Joyce and her husband plus dignitaries and titled people.

David was unable to bring himself to go anywhere near the Pink House so he went to stay with Douglas and Mary Lee Fairbanks for several weeks while Pinkie took care of the two boys. He received many letters of condolence but was unable to answer them so Mary Lee dealt with them; he kept every one of those letters in a shoe box and, over the years, he periodically took them out and read them.

Then a former girlfriend arrived in Hollywood – Ann Todd. Their affair had ended when he went to Hollywood, but she was still fond of him. 'I was in New York and he called me up and wanted me to fly out to Los Angeles to be with him,' she told me. 'So, of course, I did. He was a very different man to the one I had known. He was extremely bitter. There wasn't much more I could do other than listen to whatever he had to say. Then he really took me by surprise by trying to make love to me. He wasn't in his right mind, and I had to yell at him and tell him to pull himself together. He just cried and cried. I thought he would never get over it, and I don't think he ever did. He just learned to live with it.'

His friends all rallied round. Clark Gable, who knew exactly what he was going through, spent a lot of time with him just talking. Others could do little more than try to divert him. 'I went to see him every weekend,' said Rex Harrison, 'and I bought him a Boxer puppy and told him his name was Phantom. Over time David learned to smile again, and some of the old spark started to come back, but he was…different.

'Lilli and Fred [Astaire] cheered up the two lads by painting their nursery walls with Walt Disney characters and while they did that Pinkie and the boys went to stay with Ronnie Colman. Everyone got involved.'

With a lot of help, the Pink House was almost ready to be lived in, and eventually David was persuaded to move in. When the furniture and china that Primmie had chosen arrived from England, almost all of it had been smashed.

One night, after David returned from work, he discovered somebody had broken in and had stolen a case containing Primmie's most precious possessions such as mementos from her childhood, photographs, jewellery and the letters he had written to her during the war.

That night he nearly gave up and tried to take his life.

During the 'angry interview' I did with him in 1979, he said, 'Before Primmie died I remember I had actually asked myself if I had any right to be so happy. Did any man have that right? I had two wonderful sons, many wonderful friends, a life in Hollywood that I loved, and a wife who made my life so complete that – and I remember thinking this – that without her, my life would be incomplete.

'And then I lost her so suddenly, and I lost all sense of reason, and when somebody stole a case with all her most precious mementos, I decided to blow my brains out.'

Hearing those words from him took my breath away, and he fell silent for a few moments.

I asked, 'Did you simply change your mind?'

'Oh no, not at all. I took a gun and put the barrel in my mouth and with barely no thought for my children, which was unforgivable, I pulled the trigger. And the bloody thing didn't fire. I was strangely calm about it all up till then, and then I began to shake. I didn't know why the gun didn't fire. I knew about guns, but I couldn't think why it hadn't fired and I think I may have actually thought that this might be God telling me to carry on living for the sake of my children. I even thought it might be Primmie giving me a message and that she had made the gun fail. I shook and cried, and my friend Bob Coote found me. The poor chap, he turned as white as a ghost when he saw the gun. He took it away and said, "No need to have this now, is there?" My great blessing was to have such good friends around me at the darkest time in my life.'

Almost as soon as David had told me this, he said, 'I've told you, and now I am asking you not to publish this story when you come to write your article.' Although I was working at *Photoplay* at the time, I was long past the stage of being a career journalist, and I promised him I wouldn't write it. When I saw him next, in 1980 for Peter Sellers' memorial service in London, I told him that I hadn't published a word of that whole interview, and he said, 'My dear boy, I don't know another journalist in the world, except perhaps Roddy Mann, who would have done that for me.'

Finally, he felt able to take Pinkie and the boys to live in the Pink House. But he did one very strange thing, according to Patricia Medina. 'He locked the door to the cellar, and kept it locked and never let anybody down there, even though it wasn't the cellar she had her accident in. I think he was always afraid the same thing might happen to someone else. The only person who ever went down there was him.'

He began a routine of rising early every morning and going straight to the studio, throwing himself into whatever work came his way, and then getting home so late that he saw little of the boys. He often walked alone on the beach after dark and had little sleep.

His behaviour became more erratic. He began picking up girls and even prostitutes. He told me, 'I had some bizarre illness. I had to have sex. I think it was my only way of deadening the pain. That, and getting drunk, but I preferred sex. I paid for it when I had to. Often I didn't have to because there were always plenty of starlets willing to sleep with anyone they thought might be able to help them in their careers.

'One girl I met at a party was called Marilyn Monroe. I don't remember anything about how I met her except that it was at a party where I got terribly drunk. I only remember waking up in the morning in a friend's bedroom with the worst hangover, and lying next to me was this starlet called Marilyn Monroe.'

For two years after Primmie died, David left the care of his sons firmly in the hands of Pinkie. She was, he once told me, 'an absolute rock, a brick. What I would have done without her God only knows. She devoted herself to my sons when I was unable to be a real father to them.'

It took time, but slowly – *very* slowly – David began to emerge from the deep dark despair he had been lost in, finding some comfort in sex, work and his family. The work was the most readily available source of much needed diversion, physically but not creatively satisfying. He had managed to finish *Magnificent Doll* after Primmie died, doing his best in a bad film.

Goldwyn realised that David needed to work after his initial grieving, but he seemed unable to find him the perfect part in the perfect film. Niven was an actor out of fashion in Hollywood, and major studios didn't want him, so he found himself working for independent producer David Lewis in *The Other Love* in which he was featured opposite Barbara Stanwyck. It was a would-be tear-jerker in which he played a doctor falling in love with a concert pianist dying from tuberculosis. It wasn't the easiest film for David to make at that time in his life, just three months after losing his real wife.

He recalled, 'Barbara was a sweet lady to work with and she knew I was still grieving, but she was a tough little actress and she said to me, "Come on David, let your emotions do the job for you," which was in some ways rather harsh but also good advice. Most people who lose someone they love can go to work and usually their work has nothing to do with what they have gone through in life, but acting can be a mirror on your life. It was for me, at that time. But I didn't deal with it at all well. I couldn't use the "method". I'm sure Marlon Brando could have done wonders in the same situation, but I was just barely able to remember my lines and hit my marks. Barbara helped me through it, but the film wasn't good, and neither was I.'

I actually found *The Other Love* to be an engaging film, with an excellent performance by Stanwyck and a sympathetic and moving performance from Niven. It was a good B-movie.

Throughout his life, Niven often criticised Goldwyn for pushing him into films that were barely more than good B-movies and taking the loan-out money, but David had to admit that Goldwyn could sometimes be very generous and even paternal. 'Goldwyn gave me a very generous bonus when I made the film with Stanwyck. He didn't have to do that but he wanted to show me that he wasn't just hiring me out for the sake of making money from me. He wanted *me* to make money from me too. I was getting $3,000 a week from Goldwyn and he was paid just $15,000 for my loan-out, so when he then gave me an extra $7,000, he was actually out of pocket.'

David asked Sam Goldwyn to keep him working. He was prepared to do anything to keep his mind busy. It was easy for Goldwyn to loan him out to other studios, but what he wanted to do for David was find him a film that would really be a special picture built specifically around him and he began preparing what was intended to be a star vehicle for David which might actually propel him into the top league of major stars.

Loretta Young recalled, 'Sam Goldwyn had a marvellous film he was getting ready for David called *The Bishop's Wife*. I remember Sam saying to me, "I am really fond of David, and I think he knows it, but I'm also trying to keep everyone under contract to me working. They all deserve my attention. But I do like David very much and sometimes I wish we could just enjoy our relationship without the work getting in the way. Money spoils relationships." Sam meant it. All through the war David wrote to Sam, and Sam wrote back. Not like a father and son but more like an uncle and favourite nephew. Sam was delighted when he came up with *The Bishop's Wife* and David was happy for the first time since losing Primmie.'

The Bishop's Wife was the whimsical tale of a Protestant bishop who prays to God to help him find the money to build a cathedral and also to save his troubled marriage. An angel in a suit and tie turns up but the bishop doesn't recognise him as a celestial being, especially when the bishop's wife begins to fall for him. David was to play the plum role of the angel and Cary Grant the bishop.

Then, suddenly and cruelly, David had the role taken from him. He recalled,

> I loved the story. I thought it was charming and I felt that it would be a quality production. Then one day, before production began, Goldwyn called me to his office and said, 'Look, David, I'm sorry, but Grant is insisting he play the angel.'
>
> I said, 'Oh come on, Sam, you promised the part to me. It's the best part in the picture.'
>
> He said, 'I know, David, but Grant is the bigger star.'
>
> 'Then what the hell am I playing?' I asked, and he said, 'The bishop,' and I swore very badly and said he can stick the bishop where the sun doesn't shine.
>
> I was mad, upset, disappointed, but Goldwyn said, 'The bishop is a wonderful role, David. It's unlike any other part you've played. I think you would be perfect as the angel but I also think you are perfect as the bishop.' And he said all the right things and pressed all the right buttons, and when it came down to it, I was under contract and had no choice in the matter unless I wanted to go on suspension without pay.
>
> I was as mad as hell at Grant for taking my part away from me, and I let him know it. I do love Cary, and he's a lovely man, but he's also given to moments of selfishness – I suppose we actors all are – and he said to me, 'I'm sorry David, but I'm not cut out to be a bishop whereas you could be a bishop *or* an angel. Hell, I bet you could even play the wife,' and he laughed, but I wasn't laughing.
>
> I said, 'Oh come on, Cary, that's bullshit and you know it. You only want the part because it's the best in the picture,' and he sucked on his cheek and then said, 'You're right, it is. That's why I want it.'
>
> I sulked through much of the filming, but that was okay because the

bishop is a pretty miserable old bugger anyway. They even greyed me up for the part to make me look older. They said I didn't look distinguished enough. The director, William Seiter, asked me to remove my moustache. I went to Goldwyn and said, 'Sam, I'll play this bloody bishop and I'll turn up on time every morning and I'll know all my lines, but I won't shave my moustache off for all the tea in China,' and he said, 'That's exactly how I feel, David, and I'm letting William know that the moustache stays.'

There were times when Goldwyn was my biggest ally. But I also thought he could have told Cary Grant he couldn't play the angel. It sounds childish, I know, but I really needed that role, and Cary Grant bullied Goldwyn into giving it to him, and I thought Goldwyn had more backbone than that. And I thought Cary Grant had more humanity.

Loretta Young, who played the bishop's wife, was probably one of David's greatest allies. She said, 'When Cary Grant got the role of the angel, David was deeply upset. I sat him down and said, "Do you believe in God?" He said, "I'm not a religious man. I feel that if there is a God He's let us all down by allowing Germany to kill millions." I said to him, "I do believe in God and I believe in angels and I believe in men of God. But you don't have to play the part as a man of God. You just have to play the part as a man who has asked God for His help and is disappointed when he believes his prayers are unanswered. You can *do* this, David." And he did. It's one of his best performances.'

She also scolded Cary Grant for taking David's role. 'I told him he was selfish, and he said, "Yep, you're right, I am." Then I said, "You're also heartless." He said, "Guilty!" Then I said, "Don't you care about how David feels right now?" and he said, "Of course I do, but we're making movies. We're not doing missionary work in the Congo." And then he said, "Just you wait and you'll see David give a wonderful performance, and the three of us will make this movie the best it can be." And he was right.'

Filming such a modest little story didn't go well. Two weeks into the shoot, Goldwyn fired William Seiter and replaced him with Henry Koster and filming had to start all over again at some cost, but from then on it proceeded smoothly. David, however, was in a bad mood, especially with Cary Grant. Loretta Young recalled, 'In many scenes David had to look daggers at Cary. Oh my, those daggers were very real at times. I said to David, "You really do look at Cary as though you'd like to knock his block off," and he said, "That's because I do." David wasn't happy.'

Niven had another gripe about Grant. 'I went back home to fight for my country,' he told me. 'Grant stayed in Hollywood to get rich and famous. I wasn't too sympathetic towards him when Goldwyn told him he wasn't masculine enough in the part of the angel. He went into a sulk about that. I'm sorry that Cary and I didn't get along on that picture.'

The Bishop's Wife has the reputation of being a failure. It wasn't. It was a huge success when released in 1947 and was nominated for a Best Picture Oscar and selected for the Royal Command Film Performance in Britain. But the critics hated it. The *Daily Herald* complained, 'Mr Niven's jaunty, moustached bishop and Cary Grant as an angel are equally unbelievable.' The *News Chronicle* said, 'It is the Protestant comeback to the deadly successful R.C. propaganda of *Going My Way* and *The Bells of St Mary's*. *The Bishop's Wife* surpasses in tastelessness, equals in whimsy and in technique falls well below those crooning parables. It is really quite a monstrous film.'

Variety liked it. 'While a fantasy, there are no fantastic heavenly manifestations. There's a humanness about the characters, even the angel, that beguiles full attention.' It must have irked David when *Variety* said that Cary Grant 'has never appeared to greater advantage', while it seemed less satisfied with Niven's performance, saying it was 'played straight but his anxieties and jealousy loosen much of the warm humour gracing the plot'.

The film is a fine example of one that succeeds despite the critical backlash. Today it stands up well and, with its Christmas time setting, makes for perfect old fashioned festive film entertainment, a judgement generally reserved for *It's a Wonderful Life* which was, ironically, a box office bomb when released the year before *The Bishop's Wife*.

Around this time, David embarked on a new career – writing monthly reports from Hollywood for the *Daily Express* in Britain. He was known for giving amusing interviews, and he felt he might try his hand at turning his seemingly endless supply of stories into what he described to me as 'a nice little earner. The *Express* was willing to pay for my stories, and I was happy to write them and get paid.' They were written in the form of open letters to Michael Trubshawe. As Sheridan Morley noted, these articles were the start of what would become his second and most successful career, as a writer who chronicled the professional and social life of Hollywood.

He began his articles, 'Dear Trubshawe,' but Trubshawe, reading the articles in England, was irked that David rarely wrote real letters to him. 'I was becoming more of a joke,' Trubshawe told me in 1984. 'I didn't much care for that. I wrote to David and told him how I felt, and I got a letter back saying, "My Dear Trubshawe, you mustn't feel that way." But I did. I felt I was being used. I wouldn't have minded if he made the effort to write to me, or even get me the occasional part in his films.' Trubshawe was hoping to become an actor, and he couldn't understand why Niven didn't help him out. I think Trubshawe was more miffed about that than anything else, and I think David was finding it tiresome getting hints from Trubshawe to help get him acting work when David was, in fact, struggling to rebuild his own career.

After writing several articles, Niven found that his Californian friends were growing tired of having to pass on the studio gossip for his benefit, and he realised he couldn't carry on as a columnist *and* be a Hollywood actor, so just before Christmas 1946 he stopped his series of open letters to Trubshawe and concentrated on his acting career which he felt needed all the help it could get.

At least he halted his sexual rampage when, in March 1947, he settled into what seemed like a very steady and serious relationship with Rita Hayworth.

'Some people were surprised that they seemed to suit each other so well,' Ava Gardner told me, 'but I thought they were perfect for each other. Rita was really a very sweet girl and she had a wonderful sense of humour. She was also on the rebound from her marriage to Orson Welles. I'm not sure you could say David was actually on the rebound as he'd been rebounding all over Hollywood for months.'

I had another dinner with David and Ava in 1979 in the same restaurant in West London as four years earlier, and during this one, the conversation turned briefly to Rita, and also to David's attempts to seduce Ava which occurred during the months immediately following Primmie's death although no mention of that fact was made.

I simply sat and listened as these two wonderful people played verbal ping pong across the restaurant table. They talked of Rita having been a 'star-fuck', which I took to mean she was the sexual target of the men in Hollywood who could make or break her. It was, I understood, an occupational hazard for all female newcomers to Hollywood, and Ava said that she herself had been invited onto every casting couch in town, to which David said, 'And how many did you grace?'

She said, 'None of your goddamn business. Jesus, every actor, director and studio head was trying to get in my pants.'

'They were very popular pants,' said David.

'Well, honey, you were one of those trying to get in them.'

'Yes, I was rather keen,' said David.

'Keen? You were persistent to say the least.' She laughed loudly.

David coughed and said, 'I must admit, it's all a little vague in my memory now. Tell me, did I succeed?'

'*Nooo!*' Ava screamed, getting quite hysterical. 'You wouldn't take no for an answer.'

'Was that at the Coconut Grove?'

'I can't remember where the hell it was, honey, but we were dancing.'

'I think that was the first time we met.'

'Maybe it was,' said Ava, 'but if it was, you weren't wasting time.'

'I'm sure I was the perfect gentleman.' He winked at me and said, 'Of course, perfection is in the eye of the beholder.'

That made Ava laugh even louder and she said, 'You were too damn drunk to be a gentleman.'

'Oh dear, was I?'

'You were trying to ask me to dance, and you kept saying, "Would I care to dance with you, Miss Gardner?"'

'I didn't.'

'You did. I swear. You never said, "Would *you* care to dance with *me*," but "Would *I* care to dance with *you*, Miss Gardner?" I never forgot that.'

'I did that on purpose.'

'Like hell you did, honey.'

'But it worked. You danced with me.'

'Oh yeah, and all the time you were grabbing my ass.'

'I was trying not to tread on your feet.'

That sent Ava into more shrieks of laughter. David told me that he took Ava through a near-perfect tango and was sure he couldn't have been as sloshed as Ava said he was.

'Sloshed or not,' said Ava, 'you kept saying, "How about a little kiss? Just one! On the cheek! I'll even close my eyes."'

'Don't believe a word of it,' David said to me.

'You got a better version of events?' Ava asked him.

'Give me time and I'll think of one. The point is, my darling, is that your face was the most beautiful in Hollywood and any man would want to kiss it.'

'You wanted a little more than that, David.'

'I'm embarrassed to say that the worst thing about all this is that I can't remember what happened next.'

So Ava explained that not only did he not get a kiss from her but he didn't get anything else either.

I didn't say a word through all this, mesmerised, captivated and thoroughly entertained by an amazing double act. Here was a rare moment when David was actually unable to recall many details. But as Ava pointed out to me a few days later, David was drinking hard after Primmie's death, as well as trying to seduce every girl he came across. 'It would be a miracle if he could remember half of what he did during that period of his life,' she said.

She told me that he continued to pursue her but she resisted 'because I knew he was really grieving and not really interested in anything other than a screw to help him through a lousy time'. I asked her if she would have otherwise been interested, and she said, 'Oh, Christ, yes. It was hard to resist him. Not many girls did. He was so funny and so charming.'

David, then, did not have any kind of affair with Ava Gardner – at least, not at that time – and the funny thing was, David couldn't remember whether he'd been successful or not, as was clear in that West London restaurant in 1979, because he asked Ava, 'Tell me truthfully, my darling, did you resist me?'

'Oh God, yes,' she laughed.

'Oh well,' he said, gently stroking his moustache and giving me a knowing look, 'you can't win 'em all.'

'You did okay,' Ava reminded him, 'you got the most beautiful gal in Hollywood – Rita.'

'No, no, Ava,' David protested. '*You* were the most beautiful girl in Hollywood. I settled for the second most beautiful girl in Hollywood which was Rita.'

That just made Ava laugh more and she hit his shoulder and said, 'You can stop the sweet talk now.'

A few weeks after that memorable dinner with David and Ava, I reminded him what he had said about Ava being the most beautiful girl in Hollywood and Rita being the second, and he said, 'I meant it, old bean. Ava was *the* most beautiful girl in Hollywood. And Rita was a close second.'

David always carried a torch for Ava, which didn't surprise me. Even in middle age, when I first knew her, she was still radiantly stunning and at times even breathtaking. When they worked together on a movie in 1962, she and David would share intimate moments. But, as David told me, 'Ava would never have been an ideal wife. No actress would.'

And that went for Rita Hayworth too. David was exceptionally fond of her but, he said, he didn't love her. 'I thought I did, but I didn't know for sure what I was feeling. Often I just felt as though I had no emotion left inside me.'

David was never able to explain exactly why he went on a sexual feast after Primmie died except to say he thinks he was actually ill. I wondered why he found Rita to be a relatively stabilising force because once he began his affair with her, his sexual rampage came to an end. He told me, 'I think I felt that I could have really fallen in love with her, and for a while I wanted to give it a chance. But the problem with Hollywood is that there was a perpetual rumour mill – still is – and suddenly the newspaper columnists were announcing I was going to marry Rita. I was furious. I demanded the newspapers retract their stories. Rita denied it publicly, I denied it publicly, and it wrecked what we had. I don't believe we would have ever married. I didn't want another wife. I had made it clear in the Press that there would never be a Primmie mark 2.'

He thought he could become happy again. But he said he was miserable. 'I was unhappy with everything – so miserable I did what I had never intended to do. I got married.'

CHAPTER 15

—

A Cool Swede

Maybe Sam Goldwyn thought he was doing Niven a favour when he told him he was going to Britain to make *Bonnie Prince Charlie* for Alexander Korda. A year earlier, Niven had told Korda that he wanted to star in a film about Charles Stuart, and so when Korda told Goldwyn that he wanted to make a film about Bonnie Prince Charlie and he wanted Niven to play the title role, Goldwyn agreed.

Korda agreed to pay Goldwyn $15,000 a week for the loan of David who was in turn paid his usual $3,000 a week by Goldwyn. 'It was fair enough,' David told me. 'Those were our terms of agreement, and $3,000 was very good money to be earning.'

But what made Niven so unhappy about the film? 'We were going to be shooting it in the autumn [of 1947] for at least 10 weeks,' he said, 'and I was sure it was going to take longer than that. I just knew I was going to be stuck in Britain making the film for three or four months, and then I would be landed with a heavy tax bill which would mean that I'd be working practically for nothing.'

But it wasn't just money that was on David's mind. 'My family life was just getting settled again. I was living in the Pink House with my boys, and they were settled into a happy Californian life, and the very last thing I wanted was to uproot them. So I refused to go and Goldwyn put me on suspension. Then Goldwyn promised to indemnify me against the extra tax I was going to have to pay, so off I went and made one of the worst films of my life.'

David, the boys and Pinkie sailed to England where Niven rented a small suite at a country hotel close to Shepperton Studios where *Bonnie Prince Charlie* was to be made over the next five months.

To David's distress, his moustache was shaved off and he was put into a blond wig. 'Three directors had a go at trying to finish the film, or even get it started,' he recalled. 'Even Korda directed some of the scenes. I said to him, "This just isn't working, is it?" He said, "Don't worry, we will fix everything." I said, "What with? A miracle, because that's what it's going to need." We didn't even have a script. It was being written as we went along. It amazes me that films can actually get into production without a completed script, but it happens all the time. Sometimes you can fix things, sometimes you can't. This couldn't be fixed. It should have been declared moribund after the first week of filming.'

David was always furious about the fiasco that was *Bonnie Prince Charlie*, although there were compensations. 'I became great friends with Jack Hawkins,' he said. Hawkins was playing Lord George Murray. 'I asked Jack to tell me honestly if, with my blond wig, I looked like a prick. He said, "Yes, and so do I." And he did too. We all looked like pricks. But there was no time for any fun. I was in every shot of the film. I worked every day, all day.'

His evenings were free, and he found time to have a fling with the Duchess of Kent. He also became very friendly with Princess Margaret. Just how friendly, Niven never said, but Michael Trubshawe told me, 'We got together a couple of times when he was making that *Charlie* picture, and he told me he was having a marvellous time with Princess Margaret and then he told me something that she did to him which he enjoyed very much.'

'Like what?' I asked.

'I can't tell you. Not while the Princess is alive.'

I never did find out, but David's second wife Hjördis – whom he was about to meet while filming *Bonnie Prince Charlie* – told me in an interview I did with her in 1986, 'He and Princess Margaret were lovers. But you can't print that.' I think it's okay to print now, after so many years.

At this point, I feel I should say a little something about Hjördis who became the second and last Mrs David Niven.

I have seldom come across any person directly or indirectly connected with Hollywood who has been the victim of such bitter character assassination as Hjördis has. That said, she readily admitted that she behaved unbelievably badly throughout their 35 years of marriage. She became an alcoholic and was beset with mental illness and a terrible secret she harboured from childhood.

Many people who knew the Nivens railed about her as though she was some kind of evil banshee. Much has been said and written about her since her death in 1997. The sad thing is, she would not have disagreed with some of it.

I got to know her a little. The first time I met her was on the second of the three days I spent with David in 1970 at the Connaught Hotel in London. She turned up – where she had been and where she was headed I had no idea – and sat in for a time on the interview and wasn't slow to pick him up on details he got wrong, or had exaggerated, or even invented. Her point, as she put it to me, was, 'I've heard all these stories a thousand times, and they bore me to death.' To which he said, 'Then please go away and die, darling.'

Now this might sound like it was bitter feuding, but it wasn't. It was good natured banter. But that good nature was to fade completely away after David wrote *The Moon's a Balloon* and he went on to make a career out of telling his stories over and over. *Then* Hjördis did grow very tired of hearing them, and when she often commented on how she was bored with them, his friends, always loyal to him and hardly ever to her, came to hate her.

I next saw her in 1979, when I flew to Switzerland to stay with Peter Sellers and his wife Lynne Frederick, an old girlfriend of mine, and I found myself at a dinner party thrown in a restaurant where I saw Hjördis very drunk and very alone. She was, by then, a hopeless alcoholic.

I met up with Hjördis again, in 1986, by which time she had accepted she was an alcoholic and was on the wagon. She seemed to be well on the road to recovering from a long and debilitating mental illness. She was completely sober in mind and body, and full of remorse for the way she had often behaved. I did a formal interview with her, as well as spending some informal time with her, and I think I got to know a very different woman to the one most of David's friends knew because, by then, she was a radically changed person. Perhaps she was more like the woman he knew when he first met her.

She was born Hjördis (pronounced Yerdiss) Paulina Genburg in Sweden and raised at Kiruna, within the Arctic Circle. 'I am a typical Swedish iceberg,' she told me in 1986. She knew she appeared to be cold and distant to many of the Americans she would come to know, but she really did have a wonderful sense of humour which, alas, was lost on David's Hollywood friends.

She was 28 when she met David early in 1948. She had just come out of an 18-month marriage to a rich Swedish businessman, Carl Tersmeden, but remained friends with him. She said, 'We got married after the war, but it was a mistake and we divorced [after 18 months]. But we were still good friends. We weren't enemies, like some divorced people become.'

She was, and remained for a long time, a stunning, very beautiful woman. She was a fashion model and designer in Sweden where she graced many magazine covers. She was the Swedish supermodel of her day, but completely unknown outside of her native country.

She recalled for me how she met David when he was making *Bonnie Prince Charlie*.

I was on holiday in England with a few friends, and they knew the director of a film David was making. I knew that David Niven was in the film but I'd never seen any of his films. I wasn't all that interested in cinema.

I found his chair on the set and sat in it, and when David came along and saw this strange woman sitting in his chair, he was furious. I just smiled at him, and he smiled back. I laughed because he had a blond wig on, and he looked so silly in it. I said 'Oh, I thought you were dark haired,' and he said, 'Yes, I know, horrible, isn't it?'

We talked, and he made me feel like I was the most beautiful woman in the world. He made *every* woman feel like that. He was very, very charming.

He asked me to go for a drink with him, and he took me to a pub by the river and he said, 'Do you play darts?' I said, 'No,' and he said, 'Let me show you.' He threw a few darts and said, 'You have to get the balance right. Don't try to aim the dart like you would a gun, just look at the target and...*throw!*' I said, 'I wouldn't know how to aim a gun.' He said, 'Just watch,' and he hit the dart board and smiled and said, 'See how easy it is?' I said, 'I'm not sure it is so easy,' so he stood behind me, very close, and he held my hand with the dart and he took ages to line it up. He just wanted to huddle close to me, which I thought was charming. I said, 'I can't throw if you hold my hand,' and he said, 'Yes, of course, but do you mind if I stay right here?' He made me laugh, and I threw the dart and hit the board. He said, 'There you go!' It didn't hit the bull's eye but it did hit the board.

He made me laugh so much. I didn't care that he was an actor. I cared nothing about actors. I only liked him because he was charming and he made me laugh and he made me feel special.

The day after he taught me to play darts, he took me for lunch and he was so very charming all the time. It was very easy to fall in love with him. I could see why Hollywood actresses fell in love with him.

I didn't see him over the weekend as I was with friends, but on the Monday he took me to dinner, and we had dinner again on the Tuesday and Wednesday and *every* day.

I went to the studio each day and I met his two sons. I thought they were sweet boys, but it wasn't in my mind that I would ever become their mother. But I was already telling myself that I would marry David if he wanted me.

I think it was the next weekend when I really knew that I loved him. He had some friends in the country who we went to stay with. The two of us sat up very late after his friends had gone to bed, and he said, 'I have to go back to Hollywood in a few more days,' like he was saying, 'Oh, by the way, I have to get my suit cleaned tomorrow.'

I felt suddenly afraid that I would never see him again, and then he said, 'I don't want to leave you behind. Will you marry me?' It was all very sudden, but I already knew that I didn't need time to think about it, and I said that of course I would.

It *was* sudden. Too sudden. David wasn't ready to get married again, and he never was fully able to explain why he married in haste. He tried to once, in 1980, saying, 'I suppose I saw that here was a very beautiful woman who I found exciting and who I was quite besotted with – and the best thing of all, she wasn't an actress. But she looked like she could have been one. It was, as is often, a case of sexual attraction first, and then there was the very important factor essential to a successful relationship with me – I made her laugh.

'But I don't know if I was really in love with her. I did come to love her very much before the bad times came along. But I didn't give it enough time before marrying her. If I had, I don't think we would have married.' After a thoughtful pause, he added, 'I *had* to get married. I needed someone in my life. I was used to having someone special. And my sons needed someone to be a mother to them.' And that was the best reason he could think of for getting married.

Just how long it was between them meeting and getting married, neither of them could say for sure. Hjördis said, 'It didn't seem like much more than a week. But we were in a romantic whirlwind.'

While romancing Hjördis, David still had a film to complete, and he did, with a great feeling of relief and a surety that the film would be so bad that it would bring his career to a tragic conclusion. 'I didn't see how it could be anything but a disaster,' he told me. 'Most of it was filmed on a sound stage at Shepperton Studios. It looked so *fake*, all those scenes set in the cardboard mountains. We looked far too warm. It was a Technicolor fantasy. It should have been a wild historic epic with wind and rain knocking us off real highland mountains.'

The film cost almost a million pounds, an extravagant amount for a

British film of the time, and while it attracted audiences, it couldn't recoup its cost. The critics tore into it. 'The picture is not lacking in moments of unconscious levity,' wrote the *New Yorker*, 'what with David Niven, as Prince Charlie, rallying his hardy Highlanders to his standard in a voice barely large enough to summon a waiter.'

'David Niven disappoints,' said *The Star*, while the *Sunday Graphic* noted that Niven looked, 'as much at home among the Highlanders as a goldfish in a haggis.'

The Times didn't blame Niven for the disaster. 'Mr David Niven has much of the fugitive charm that goes with the part, but the film refuses him the material he needs and only occasionally does his performance blaze up in flame and spirit – the heather is seldom alight and, when it is, the Technicolor fires are crude.'

Today the film is looked upon as a joke, and even in 1978 Niven didn't thank me for reminding him of it. But, as I said to him, 'Surely all actors have to accept that there are going to be disasters as well as the successes,' to which he replied, 'Yes, but the film wasn't just a disaster, it was a humiliation.'

The humiliation was put on hold while David and Hjördis got married at South Kensington register office on Wednesday 14 January 1948. Michael Trubshawe – David's best man for the second time – and Hjördis did not hit it off. Trubshawe gave me his version of events.

> I'm afraid Hjördis and I didn't get on from the start. We met at a party that was given by David's society friend, Audrey Pleydell-Bouverie. I took one look at her and realised she already looked like a Hollywood star and I thought that she was going to marry him just so she could get into movies, so just about the first thing I said to her was, 'Look, if you think that marrying David is a passport to become a Hollywood star, then you're in for a bitter disappointment.' I said that because I knew that David would never want to be married to an actress, and he would stop her before she got started. So we didn't hit it off which upset David, I'm afraid. But he wasn't sure that he should marry her anyway.
>
> That night he told me that he thought everything was happening far too quickly and he wasn't at all sure that he wanted to go through with it. He said, 'It's going to be a disaster, old bean. But what can I do?'
>
> I told him to call the wedding off before it was too late.
>
> He said, 'I can't do that. It's all arranged, and my sons think they are going to have a new mother. How can I deprive them of that?' He said, 'No, I will just have to see it through and we'll see what happens.'
>
> So as far as I was concerned, the marriage was doomed from the start.

I asked Trubshawe to try to tell me exactly what he didn't like about Hjördis, and when he said he just thought she was a gold-digger, I pressed him to comment on her personality, and he said, 'Well, for God's sake, she was a *Swede*. And she wasn't Primmie.' I think that summed up much about how people felt about her.

I didn't tell Hjördis what Trubshawe had told me but simply asked her what she had thought of David's oldest friend. She said, 'I was very upset by Michael Trubshawe. He was David's best man...*again*. He thought I was just a gold-digger and that I wanted to use David to become a star in Hollywood. I had never ever thought about becoming a movie star.'

Although Trubshawe is featured prominently in *The Moon's a Balloon* and was undoubtedly one of David's dearest and oldest friends, Trubshawe accused David of avoiding him in later years. He said Niven seemed embarrassed by his presence, especially when Trubshawe carved out a modest career for himself as an actor and began turning up in bit parts in some of David's films. Trubshawe, a very genial and generally inoffensive chap who I liked immensely, was bitter about the way Niven cold-shouldered him and believed it was because he reminded David too much of the old days and of Primmie. 'I think it was too painful for him to remember all that, and I only reminded him of it all.'

He was wrong. David told me, 'I thought the world of dear old Trubshawe but he let me down when he made himself unpopular with Hjördis. Their friendship was always strained from the day before the wedding. I had to live with Hjördis, not with Trubshawe.'

I think *that* is the reason Niven later avoided Trubshawe. Hjördis thought so too and regretted that she came between two good friends. She said, 'I wanted to be a friend to Trubshawe. I wanted to be friends to *all* of David's friends. But many of them seemed to take an instant dislike to me. I couldn't understand it. I was a *good* person back then. I was faithful to David, I wasn't getting drunk. I did drink a little too much by the time I met David. David drank a little too much. All of his friends drank a little too much. They didn't like me because I wasn't Primmie.'

David was aware that his friends had trouble accepting her. He told me, 'The same thing happened to Sylvia when she married Doug Fairbanks. They had it in for her at the start because she wasn't Mary [Pickford]. I felt very protective of Hjördis. I knew she found it difficult to mix in Hollywood because Swedes have a certain disposition that makes them seem cool and distant, but she was really very warm and funny.'

Among Niven's friends who felt the marriage was a mistake was Peter Ustinov who said to me in 1984, 'Oh, no doubt, David was on the rebound. He should have given himself time to get over Primmie's death.

Mind you, he *never* got over it. No woman would ever be able to compare with her, and that's what Hjördis had to contend with. She had the ghost of Primmie with her the whole time, and I think it wore her down.'

Ava Gardner hit the nail on the head with her theory why David married Hjördis: 'The only reason he married her was because she was the one woman who *looked* like a movie star but *wasn't* one. He could only marry a very glamorous woman, but he couldn't marry an actress. That's why he never married Merle [Oberon] or Rita [Hayworth].'

Ustinov believed that Rita Hayworth wanted to marry David and that he married Hjördis to prevent all further attempts by any actress to become Mrs Niven. 'Rita Hayworth wanted to be the next Mrs Niven. Rita was a great deal of fun and extremely beautiful – all that glorious red hair. David loved her, but not enough to want her for his wife. I don't know if he loved Hjördis, but when she became Mrs David Niven it made him safe from all the others who wanted to be his wife.'

One of the few of David's friends who did approve of Hjördis – or rather, didn't dislike her – was Laurence Olivier who told me, 'It was easy to see why David was attracted to her. She was very funny, very beautiful, and he had two small sons to look after. He thought she would take care of the boys and be a very glamorous wife in the process. I'm afraid it didn't quite work out that way, and I was very sorry it didn't.'

Goldwyn allowed David to take a month's holiday after *Bonnie Prince Charlie* wrapped and expected him back in Hollywood on 2 February to start work immediately on another film, but Niven was exhausted and had come down with the flu. He was also stressed by demands from the Inland Revenue demanding back taxes. He demanded extra time off for a honeymoon.

Goldwyn wasn't sympathetic and ordered him back to Hollywood so just three days after the wedding, David took his two sons, Pinkie and his bride back to California. They had barely settled into the Pink House when David went to work on *Enchantment*, a Goldwyn production which gave David top billing as General Sir Roland Dane, an elderly Englishman who recounts his younger days to one of his young relations, played by his one-time girlfriend Evelyn Keyes.

'It wasn't a difficult part,' David told me. 'I just played the same part I'd played before only this time for a couple of scenes I had to make-up to look old. I think I looked like Mark Twain with a fake white moustache bigger than my own, and a grey-white wig which made my head look large at the top.'

Teresa Wright co-starred as an orphan girl the young Roland falls in love with. Jayne Meadows played Niven's bitter and bitchy sister. It wasn't a bad film and even had some kind words from the critics. 'The little family anecdotes are played with a disarming sincerity and skill by Teresa Wright, David Niven and Evelyn Keyes with some welcome acid by Jane Meadows,' said the *Daily Mail*.

'Little addicted though I am to these four-in-hand romances,' wrote the *Sunday Times* film critic, 'I must give the film credit for sensitive direction and playing capable of extracting emotion from situations that have become clichés of the screen.'

David was becoming more impatient with the way he felt Goldwyn was mishandling his career and underpaying him. He was also trying to cope with introducing his bride to a whole new life. Hjördis recalled,

> When I got to Hollywood, many of the people I met disliked me straight away. I couldn't compete with Primmie so I tried not to. I withdrew quite a lot. I couldn't bear being disliked just for not being Primmie, and so I drank a little more. Then we had to live in the Pink House. It never felt like *my* home. I was glad that Primmie never actually lived in the house because if she had I wouldn't have been able to live in it at all. I found all her towels with her initials on it and I had them all put into the guest house. When David's friends found out, they behaved as if I had committed a crime, but David understood. He felt he needed to stop being reminded of Primmie every day.
>
> It wasn't a happy start to a marriage because David had really been in too much of a hurry, and there was just so much strain on me – on the both of us – but on me because *I* shouldn't have become his wife. I sulked and sulked and everything built up until I needed to quarrel with him to just let it out. David hated quarrels and he went into the cellar and read books and wrote just to escape from me. It was very hard for him. It wasn't his fault. It wasn't mine. It was very bad timing. Maybe another year and we could have got married and been happier.

The most immediate challenge for her was trying to become a part of the two boys' lives. She said, 'I loved the boys, and we laughed and played games, but I wasn't their mother. I was very stupid because I didn't think about what it would mean to marry a man with two sons. I wanted to have children of my own more than anything.'

Some of David's friends in Hollywood made Hjördis welcome. She recalled,

> I did have some good friends but they were the Swedes in Hollywood – Greta Garbo and Anita Ekberg. They understood me. People around

the world are not all the same. Americans are wonderful people, very outgoing. Swedes are more introvert.

Fred and Phyllis Astaire were very nice to me. So was Noël Coward. He used to say to me, 'My dear, you are a delicious Swede. Not everybody enjoys Swede with their steak. They prefer peas and carrots if they are English and ketchup if they are Americans.' That made me laugh. Noël always made me laugh.

We were very good friends with Humphrey Bogart and Betty (Lauren) Bacall as well. They made me feel very welcome, and once I was able to relax David and I became very happy.

The Press took an interest in the new Mrs David Niven and her portrait took up a whole page of London's *Sketch* magazine. In America *Life* followed suit and put her on the cover and featured her in an article that numbered her among the 10 most beautiful women in Hollywood which included Ava Gardner, Jean Simmons, Elizabeth Taylor and Greta Garbo. The difference between Hjördis and the other candidates was that they were all film stars and she wasn't.

She certainly had film star looks and that brought about offers from producers and directors, such as Billy Wilder and David Selznick, to do screen tests. David put his foot down and forbade her to do any.

Stewart Granger remembered the *Life* feature because it included his wife, Jean Simmons, and he was very aware that, after Hjördis appeared on the cover, the Hollywood studios were enthusiastic to turn her into a movie star. 'They thought they had a major new discovery on their hands,' he told me when I talked to him one day on the set of *The Wild Geese* in 1979 (I was an extra in it). 'They didn't care if she could act or not. An actress had to be stunningly beautiful, and if they could act, then that was a bonus. So there were all these producers knocking at her door and telling her she could be big in movies. Oh, David hated that.'

David told me that he was furious at the film producers who, in essence, were trying to wreck his family life. 'I wanted a wife, not another film star in the family.'

There were others apart from Trubshawe who accused Hjördis of trying to use her marriage to become a movie star, but she emphatically denied that this had ever been the case.

I never went to Hollywood hoping to become a movie star. I didn't know anything about acting. I could model. I knew how to look good for a photographer. David Selznick wanted to give me a screen test. He said that I would look marvellous, and any woman would enjoy such flattery. So I thought that maybe I could give it a try. I had no other interest in my life. But David said that *he* should be my interest. And so should his boys. I said that if I had children of my own, I would feel different. So he said we would have children of our own. He was desperate to stop me becoming an actress.

I talked to Greta Garbo about it. She said, 'Become an actress, make a few films, and then when you are bored with it, give it up. It's your life, you must do what you want. If you don't, you will always be just Mrs David Niven.'

But then there were other people telling me I mustn't be an actress as it would upset David. I had people telling me what I should and shouldn't do, even when I wasn't asking them for their advice.

Ava Gardner gave me her opinion: 'I think their marriage began to go wrong when Hjördis was noticed by the Hollywood studios. She was very beautiful. I think David was proud of how beautiful she was, but he was very unhappy when she was named in a list of the most beautiful women in Hollywood.'

It was a bad beginning to their life together. He wanted a stable family life and wanted her to be at home, while she was realising that she was never going to be anything more than Mrs David Niven which began to be a burden because she knew it was impossible to live up to the expectations people had of her. She said, 'I was young and my husband was a widower and a father. That was something I hadn't thought about, but we were married and it was too late. The only thing to do is try your best. But I always felt my best was not good enough. I knew that he thought I was only second to Primmie, and I understand that now, but I couldn't at the time. I think I was like a child who would sulk because I wasn't allowed to be the prettiest girl at the party. Or I should say, the most *popular*. And I couldn't do the things she did. She could cook. I couldn't cook. I didn't know how to relate to the boys. I felt like a bad wife and a bad stepmother. I'm sorry that in time Jamie and David [Junior] came to dislike me so much.'

Some of Niven's friends made hasty judgements about her. Peter Ustinov was one of them. He told me in 1984, 'The problem with Hjördis is that she is such a lazy woman. David was very tidy and also very punctual, but she was always late.'

I put that to Hjördis who said, 'So are many women', which is actually the response I gave to Ustinov who conceded, 'Yes, true. It wasn't so much that she was late but that she couldn't get out of the bed in the mornings.'

I put that to Hjördis too. 'I got out of bed, but not when David did,' she said. 'He was up early every morning. I said to him, "Why don't you have a lie in?" He said he had to get up early ever since he was in the Army. He was conditioned to it. I wasn't a soldier. I didn't *have* to get up and be on parade when the cock crowed. I got up when I woke up.'

Even those who had befriended her when she first arrived in Hollywood began to turn against her. She recognised the problem but was helpless to do anything about it. She said, 'I didn't speak as much English as I do now, so people thought I was being cool and rude to them. Even the two boys thought I was unkind to them. They loved Pinkie, and I was happy that they had someone who could be more like a mother to them. I tried, but I could only do so much. The boys were young but sometimes they would say hurtful things like "We love Pinkie more than we love you." Things like that. It wasn't their fault, they were just children. They needed a mother's love, and while I loved them, I didn't know how to *be* a mother. I told them not to call me *Mummy*. I thought they might like it if they could call me Hjördis. Other people criticised me for *that* too.'

There was another growing problem. Hjördis began to drink more than she normally did. 'I did drink a lot, but so did David,' she told me. 'A woman is not allowed to drink like a man. I always felt second to him. I shouldn't be anything more than his "wife". I shouldn't be an actress, and I shouldn't drink as much as him, or more than him.

'And always producers were asking me to take screen tests. But they wouldn't come to me, they would go to David, as if he was my manager, and he'd say, "No, no, no, she is not going to become an actress." I didn't want him deciding what I could or couldn't be. I felt like I was not in control of my own mind. I hated to be controlled. So, yes, I drank a little more.'

There were other pressures on them outside of Hjördis's control. 'David was in a terrible mood because he was fighting with Samuel Goldwyn. People get upset. It's life. But if I got upset, people told me, "You mustn't upset David. He's having a difficult time." I think I was a good wife to him in the beginning. All these things led to me drinking more. I don't excuse myself. I just say what it was like. I would have been a better person if I hadn't drunk.'

Despite the terrible times that lay ahead, David always maintained that he was as much to blame for the problems as she was. 'I love Hjördis very much, I did from the start,' he said, speaking in 1980 to Lynne Frederick and me, proving that even towards the end of his life and his marriage he hadn't stopped loving Hjördis. 'Sometimes love isn't enough. I've loved other women but didn't want to be married to them. If our marriage didn't work, it was more my fault than hers. In the first few years she was great fun. I didn't care that she couldn't cook. We had someone to cook for us.'

Five months after David married Hjördis, Pinkie left. Some claimed Hjördis got rid of her. Hjördis denied that. 'I would never have fired Pinkie. For a start, David wouldn't have let me, and for another, I couldn't take care of the boys. I needed her. I tried to become a "mother" to them but I wasn't strict with them and let them do what they wanted. David said I was spoiling them. I could do nothing right. The boys loved Pinkie and we needed her, but she felt she wasn't needed any more, or maybe she didn't like me either – I don't know.'

David defended Hjördis, saying, 'She never got rid of Pinkie. She begged Pinkie to stay. But I think dear old Pinkie felt she was getting in the way of the relationship between the boys and Hjördis, so she went off to San Francisco and become someone else's super nanny.' The boys soon had another very fine nanny called Evelyn.

In all the years I knew David, from 1970 to 1983, I never heard him blame Hjördis for the sham their marriage became, and I think that was because he knew that the problems they had, which grew from molehills into towering mountains, were as much his fault as hers. Not even David's closest friends, many of them people I admire and respect and personally like, knew what really went on, or were prepared to accept that David's behaviour was no better than Hjördis's, but they are among those who have castigated Hjördis. David could do no wrong. Hjördis could do nothing right.

Nothing is ever that simple, and the story of the second Niven marriage is complex, baffling, emotional and tragic.

—

CHAPTER 16

Any Old Rubbish

Apart from having to settle into a new and not altogether comfortable marriage, Niven was also making what he knew was a dreadful picture, *A Kiss in the Dark*. 'When I heard the title and that Jack Warner was personally producing it for Warner Brothers and that Delmer Daves was directing, I thought I was going to be in what might be a promising *film noir*,' David told me. 'It turned out very silly indeed.' That was about as much as you could get from David when asking him to comment on his films. But he was right. It *did* sound like a *film noir* but turned out to be a comedy.

Niven played a mild mannered concert pianist who finds himself the unwitting owner of a run-down apartment block peopled by an assortment of odd characters including a disgruntled tenant who punches him, a pretty model (played by Jane Wyman) who treats his injury, and her fiancé who tries to sell him insurance.

The *Observer* complained, 'By far the unhappiest moments of the week were those spent at *A Kiss in the Dark*. Starring David Niven and Jane Wyman it proceeds to waste them both in one of the silliest and trashiest stories seen on the screen for many a day.'

David knew it was a disaster before it was released in 1949, and his spirits were not raised when Goldwyn told him he was going back to Britain to make another costume adventure for Korda, *The Elusive Pimpernel*, a retelling of the Scarlet Pimpernel tale with Niven in the title role. I told him that I thought that he would have been encouraged that this was to be produced for Korda by Emeric Pressburger and directed by Michael Powell, but he said,

Grayson and Mario Lanza singing to each other,' David told me. 'But I got on fine with Mario.'

David was drinking more than usual, according to Hjördis. 'It didn't help that Mario Lanza drank a lot too,' she said, 'so the both of them were getting smashed at lunch time. The difference between them was that Lanza would fall asleep halfway through the afternoon while David appeared cold stone sober. He'd continue to drink at home, and I joined him. We were both drinking, and while he could handle it, I couldn't. I was becoming an alcoholic.'

After the Lanza picture, David didn't work for months, so he began trying his hand at writing a novel which he called *Round the Rugged Rocks*. It was about an English soldier who leaves the Army after World War II and heads for America where he sells liquor in New York, gets involved in indoor horse racing, heads for Bermuda and winds up in Hollywood as a film star. It was clearly semi-autobiographical, and anecdotes that Niven had been telling for years were included.

After a long period of 'resting', he landed a film early in 1950, *Happy Go Lovely*, a British attempt to make a Hollywood musical. In March he rented the Pink House out and sailed with his family on the *Queen Mary* to England to make the movie for A.B.P.C. His co-stars were Vera-Ellen and Cesar Romero. David found a house to rent close to Buckingham Palace and he also bought a huge country pile, Wilcot Manor in Wiltshire, not far from Huish where Primmie's ashes were buried. Hjördis said that it was obvious to her that David couldn't stay away from Primmie 'even in death'. Primmie was, said Hjördis, 'a ghost who would haunt me forever'.

She also thought that there really were ghosts at Wilcot Manor. 'The house was haunted,' she told me. 'There is the ghost of a monk there, and I saw the spirits of two nuns rowing a boat on the lake.'

I asked her if she had been drinking. 'No, no,' she said, 'but I did drink *after* seeing the nuns.' She laughed; she really did have a sense of humour.

David had also talked about the ghosts. 'The poor monk had been driven out of his monastery by Henry VIII and he haunted the bedroom on the top floor,' he said. 'We didn't live there for very long.'

David Jnr went off to boarding school, and David went to numerous London clubs, living as though he were a millionaire. He paid for his expensive lifestyle from his fee for *Happy Go Lovely*. 'I really rather liked doing that picture,' he told me. 'The script wasn't wonderful but I liked working with Vera-Ellen and Romero. We made of it what we could. And we had a good director, Bruce Humberstone, who was also imported from America. It was almost like making an American movie except we shot it at Elstree and had a large British supporting cast.'

I was going to be put into more silly wigs and costumes, and I just look damn silly in all that stuff. But what really made me so mad was that I had only just got my family settled [in Hollywood] and I was going to have to take my boys out of nursery and take my new wife and get them all over to England – at my own cost. So I refused point blank to do it, and Goldwyn put me on suspension. I hoped he would see how desperate I was and be reasonable but he just told me – *again* – how if it wasn't for him I wouldn't have a film career. I tried to hold out, but my agent told me that Goldwyn would never back down, which I knew in my heart of hearts, and so finally, to prevent my family from sinking in poverty, I gave in but made demands. I insisted Goldwyn pay the fare, by sea, for the boys, their new nanny and for Hjördis, there and back. I wanted living expenses for myself and for Hjördis. I wanted a house close to the studio with a housekeeper, a gardener, a cook and a driver, and I wanted a clothing allowance for my sons and their nanny. I also demanded a suite at Claridge's Hotel, tips for the hotel staff, ration books, Scotch to be sent from America, a car – everything I could think of. Goldwyn agreed, although I think he got Korda to cough up half the costs.

I behaved appallingly. I was a spoilt brat. I was conceited. But I believed Goldwyn was wrecking my career and I told him so. We had stand-up rows in his office.

At the end of July 1949, the Nivens sailed for England where David complained that the housing Goldwyn's British representative had found was completely inadequate. Cables went back and forth across the Atlantic and Niven threatened legal action. David also demanded that since his contract allowed him six weeks' holiday a year he was going to take it – straight away – back in California. Alexander Korda offered Niven his own yacht to go anywhere he wanted but David insisted he was going back to America.

'I cannot excuse my behaviour,' David said in 1978. 'It's the only time in my life I was unprofessional.' The family returned to California – at Goldwyn's expense – and then David and Hjördis flew to Bermuda for their delayed honeymoon. All this gave Hjördis an impression of how she thought Hollywood stars behaved. She told me,

I saw a way of life I'd never imagined. Whatever David demanded, he got. I thought that was what everyone did in Hollywood. And I thought it meant that David always got what he wanted. So I decided *I* wanted things and made demands on David who would always say he couldn't afford what I wanted. I couldn't understand how he couldn't afford them since he was getting all this free travel and free accommodation, expenses, everything he wanted from Goldwyn. We would argue and he'd say, 'Have another drink,' so I would drink, and so would he.

Then we had the most wonderful honeymoon in Bermuda. Life was very nice then. We laughed a lot, and we made love and we lived like royalty. I didn't know that David couldn't actually afford our lifestyle. He lived beyond his means, always hoping he could make more money from films. Others made a lot more money, but David wasn't a really big star. His films didn't make big money. I think Samuel Goldwyn was trying to make him into a star with silly costume films.

After six weeks holidaying in Bermuda, the Nivens returned to Los Angeles where Goldwyn refused to see David who, in a sulk, took Hjördis to England and finally began work on *The Elusive Pimpernel* in September, two months behind schedule. Filmed in England and France, it took six months to shoot. David disliked playing the part because, he said, 'it was like being in a musical pantomime without the music.' That wasn't too surprising because originally Goldwyn and Korda had planned to make a musical version of *The Scarlet Pimpernel* but had changed their minds and decided to take out the musical numbers and hoped that Pressburger and Powell could turn it into a film of high adventure. David objected to the script as it was obvious that there were cues for each song left in it, and so there was some hasty rewriting.

He enjoyed working with Jack Hawkins again, and he did manage to get Robert Coote a decent supporting role. But he didn't attempt to get a part for Michael Trubshawe who complained to me that Niven had been 'pretty mean about that'.

Hjördis defended David, telling me, 'He had no idea if Trubshawe could even act and he wasn't going to risk getting him a part and then finding he was an embarrassment.'

David actually began to have high hopes for *The Elusive Pimpernel*, as he explained years later. 'Emeric Pressburger and Michael Powell knew they had a silly script and so they actually made it as a satirical picture. It was a sort of satire on costume pictures, which I thought was wonderful, but nobody got it. They opened it at the Venice Film Festival where nobody understood it, so Korda cut the film and opened it in London in what he thought was a more straightforward and conventional version, and the critics there hated it even more.'

It was finally premiered in Britain on 1 January 1951. David Lewin wrote in the *Daily Express*, 'It must be one of the most expensively dull films

we have made in this country for years. David Niven plays the Scarlet Pimpernel with the sheepish lack of enthusiasm of a tone deaf man called to sing solo in church.'

In *Punch*, Richard Mallett wrote, 'I never thought I should feel inclined to leave a Powell and Pressburger film before the end, but I did here.'

But the British public loved it. Goldwyn hated the picture, calling it 'the worst picture I have ever seen in my life', and he refused to release it. Korda sued Goldwyn who counter-sued. Goldwyn had the film re-edited and released in America in 1955 as *The Fighting Pimpernel* – and it was a success.

But that success came too late to save David from a series of embarrassing co-starring roles, the first opposite 20-year-old former child star Shirley Temple in *A Kiss For Corliss*, a film intended to appeal to a teenage audience. It appealed to no one in particular. 'Poor David Niven!' said the *Sunday Chronicle*. 'Only a really great star could save a picture in which he scarcely appears at all.' *The Star* observed, 'It's a tiny part for David Niven but he provides a few moments of quiet humour in a raucous picture.'

Niven told me, 'Goldwyn loaned me out for a Shirley Temple teenage pot boiler as punishment. The only good thing about it was all my scenes were shot back to back because they had started without me and they had to get all my scenes shot quickly. I'd arrive in the morning and be told which scene we were doing, and I was really rather difficult and told them I wasn't prepared for whatever scene it was. I didn't do myself any favours as I wanted to get the bloody film over with.'

David tried to mend bridges with Goldwyn in early 1948. 'I wrote to Goldwyn and begged his forgiveness because I'd realised I'd behaved so badly but he didn't even reply to my letter. That's when I thought it was time I went freelance. I went to see Goldwyn [on 22 July] and told him that frankly we didn't see eye to eye anymore and asked if I could be released from my contract which still had another two years to run. He simply flicked his intercom button and said, "Give Niven his release as from today. He's through." And that was it. I was unemployed.'

He didn't find going freelance as easy as he had thought. Suddenly there was no work for him, and he was using up his money at an alarming rate. He was convinced that Goldwyn had his PR men put the word out that he was difficult and the result was that producers were unwilling t cast him.

Finally, in 1949, he was offered a part by Metro-Goldwyn-Mayer in Mario Lanza musical, *The Toast of New Orleans*. It was Lanza's first fi although the real star was Kathryn Grayson as an opera singer. David billed below them as Grayson's manager.

'There wasn't much for me to do as the whole film was about Kath

I was going to be put into more silly wigs and costumes, and I just look damn silly in all that stuff. But what really made me so mad was that I had only just got my family settled [in Hollywood] and I was going to have to take my boys out of nursery and take my new wife and get them all over to England – at my own cost. So I refused point blank to do it, and Goldwyn put me on suspension. I hoped he would see how desperate I was and be reasonable but he just told me – *again* – how if it wasn't for him I wouldn't have a film career. I tried to hold out, but my agent told me that Goldwyn would never back down, which I knew in my heart of hearts, and so finally, to prevent my family from sinking in poverty, I gave in but made demands. I insisted Goldwyn pay the fare, by sea, for the boys, their new nanny and for Hjördis, there and back. I wanted living expenses for myself and for Hjördis. I wanted a house close to the studio with a housekeeper, a gardener, a cook and a driver, and I wanted a clothing allowance for my sons and their nanny. I also demanded a suite at Claridge's Hotel, tips for the hotel staff, ration books, Scotch to be sent from America, a car – everything I could think of. Goldwyn agreed, although I think he got Korda to cough up half the costs.

I behaved appallingly. I was a spoilt brat. I was conceited. But I believed Goldwyn was wrecking my career and I told him so. We had stand-up rows in his office.

At the end of July 1949, the Nivens sailed for England where David complained that the housing Goldwyn's British representative had found was completely inadequate. Cables went back and forth across the Atlantic and Niven threatened legal action. David also demanded that since his contract allowed him six weeks' holiday a year he was going to take it – straight away – back in California. Alexander Korda offered Niven his own yacht to go anywhere he wanted but David insisted he was going back to America.

'I cannot excuse my behaviour,' David said in 1978. 'It's the only time in my life I was unprofessional.' The family returned to California – at Goldwyn's expense – and then David and Hjördis flew to Bermuda for their delayed honeymoon. All this gave Hjördis an impression of how she thought Hollywood stars behaved. She told me,

I saw a way of life I'd never imagined. Whatever David demanded, he got. I thought that was what everyone did in Hollywood. And I thought it meant that David always got what he wanted. So I decided *I* wanted things and made demands on David who would always say he couldn't afford what I wanted. I couldn't understand how he couldn't afford them since he was getting all this free travel and free accommodation, expenses, everything he wanted from Goldwyn. We would argue and he'd say, 'Have another drink,' so I would drink, and so would he.

Then we had the most wonderful honeymoon in Bermuda. Life was very nice then. We laughed a lot, and we made love and we lived like royalty. I didn't know that David couldn't actually afford our lifestyle. He lived beyond his means, always hoping he could make more money from films. Others made a lot more money, but David wasn't a really big star. His films didn't make big money. I think Samuel Goldwyn was trying to make him into a star with silly costume films.

After six weeks holidaying in Bermuda, the Nivens returned to Los Angeles where Goldwyn refused to see David who, in a sulk, took Hjördis to England and finally began work on *The Elusive Pimpernel* in September, two months behind schedule. Filmed in England and France, it took six months to shoot. David disliked playing the part because, he said, 'it was like being in a musical pantomime without the music.' That wasn't too surprising because originally Goldwyn and Korda had planned to make a musical version of *The Scarlet Pimpernel* but had changed their minds and decided to take out the musical numbers and hoped that Pressburger and Powell could turn it into a film of high adventure. David objected to the script as it was obvious that there were cues for each song left in it, and so there was some hasty rewriting.

He enjoyed working with Jack Hawkins again, and he did manage to get Robert Coote a decent supporting role. But he didn't attempt to get a part for Michael Trubshawe who complained to me that Niven had been 'pretty mean about that'.

Hjördis defended David, telling me, 'He had no idea if Trubshawe could even act and he wasn't going to risk getting him a part and then finding he was an embarrassment.'

David actually began to have high hopes for *The Elusive Pimpernel*, as he explained years later. 'Emeric Pressburger and Michael Powell knew they had a silly script and so they actually made it as a satirical picture. It was a sort of satire on costume pictures, which I thought was wonderful, but nobody got it. They opened it at the Venice Film Festival where nobody understood it, so Korda cut the film and opened it in London in what he thought was a more straightforward and conventional version, and the critics there hated it even more.'

It was finally premiered in Britain on 1 January 1951. David Lewin wrote in the *Daily Express*, 'It must be one of the most expensively dull films we have made in this country for years. David Niven plays the Scarlet Pimpernel with the sheepish lack of enthusiasm of a tone deaf man called to sing solo in church.'

In *Punch*, Richard Mallett wrote, 'I never thought I should feel inclined to leave a Powell and Pressburger film before the end, but I did here.'

But the British public loved it. Goldwyn hated the picture, calling it 'the worst picture I have ever seen in my life', and he refused to release it. Korda sued Goldwyn who counter-sued. Goldwyn had the film re-edited and released in America in 1955 as *The Fighting Pimpernel* – and it was a success.

But that success came too late to save David from a series of embarrassing co-starring roles, the first opposite 20-year-old former child star Shirley Temple in *A Kiss For Corliss*, a film intended to appeal to a teenage audience. It appealed to no one in particular. 'Poor David Niven!' said the *Sunday Chronicle*. 'Only a really great star could save a picture in which he scarcely appears at all.' *The Star* observed, 'It's a tiny part for David Niven but he provides a few moments of quiet humour in a raucous picture.'

Niven told me, 'Goldwyn loaned me out for a Shirley Temple teenage pot boiler as punishment. The only good thing about it was all my scenes were shot back to back because they had started without me and they had to get all my scenes shot quickly. I'd arrive in the morning and be told which scene we were doing, and I was really rather difficult and told them I wasn't prepared for whatever scene it was. I didn't do myself any favours as I wanted to get the bloody film over with.'

David tried to mend bridges with Goldwyn in early 1948. 'I wrote to Goldwyn and begged his forgiveness because I'd realised I'd behaved so badly but he didn't even reply to my letter. That's when I thought it was time I went freelance. I went to see Goldwyn [on 22 July] and told him that frankly we didn't see eye to eye anymore and asked if I could be released from my contract which still had another two years to run. He simply flicked his intercom button and said, "Give Niven his release as from today. He's through." And that was it. I was unemployed.'

He didn't find going freelance as easy as he had thought. Suddenly there was no work for him, and he was using up his money at an alarming rate. He was convinced that Goldwyn had his PR men put the word out that he was difficult and the result was that producers were unwilling to cast him.

Finally, in 1949, he was offered a part by Metro-Goldwyn-Mayer in a Mario Lanza musical, *The Toast of New Orleans*. It was Lanza's first film although the real star was Kathryn Grayson as an opera singer. David was billed below them as Grayson's manager.

'There wasn't much for me to do as the whole film was about Kathryn

Grayson and Mario Lanza singing to each other,' David told me. 'But I got on fine with Mario.'

David was drinking more than usual, according to Hjördis. 'It didn't help that Mario Lanza drank a lot too,' she said, 'so the both of them were getting smashed at lunch time. The difference between them was that Lanza would fall asleep halfway through the afternoon while David appeared cold stone sober. He'd continue to drink at home, and I joined him. We were both drinking, and while he could handle it, I couldn't. I was becoming an alcoholic.'

After the Lanza picture, David didn't work for months, so he began trying his hand at writing a novel which he called *Round the Rugged Rocks*. It was about an English soldier who leaves the Army after World War II and heads for America where he sells liquor in New York, gets involved in indoor horse racing, heads for Bermuda and winds up in Hollywood as a film star. It was clearly semi-autobiographical, and anecdotes that Niven had been telling for years were included.

After a long period of 'resting', he landed a film early in 1950, *Happy Go Lovely*, a British attempt to make a Hollywood musical. In March he rented the Pink House out and sailed with his family on the *Queen Mary* to England to make the movie for A.B.P.C. His co-stars were Vera-Ellen and Cesar Romero. David found a house to rent close to Buckingham Palace and he also bought a huge country pile, Wilcot Manor in Wiltshire, not far from Huish where Primmie's ashes were buried. Hjördis said that it was obvious to her that David couldn't stay away from Primmie 'even in death'. Primmie was, said Hjördis, 'a ghost who would haunt me forever'.

She also thought that there really were ghosts at Wilcot Manor. 'The house was haunted,' she told me. 'There is the ghost of a monk there, and I saw the spirits of two nuns rowing a boat on the lake.'

I asked her if she had been drinking. 'No, no,' she said, 'but I did drink *after* seeing the nuns.' She laughed; she really did have a sense of humour.

David had also talked about the ghosts. 'The poor monk had been driven out of his monastery by Henry VIII and he haunted the bedroom on the top floor,' he said. 'We didn't live there for very long.'

David Jnr went off to boarding school, and David went to numerous London clubs, living as though he were a millionaire. He paid for his expensive lifestyle from his fee for *Happy Go Lovely*. 'I really rather liked doing that picture,' he told me. 'The script wasn't wonderful but I liked working with Vera-Ellen and Romero. We made of it what we could. And we had a good director, Bruce Humberstone, who was also imported from America. It was almost like making an American movie except we shot it at Elstree and had a large British supporting cast.'

Among the supporting cast was Gordon Jackson who I interviewed a number of times, one of them being in 1983 on the set of the TV series *The Professionals*, shortly after David had died. Jackson said, 'David Niven was a joy. He seemed to be having a good time and was always telling funny stories. He was always after the girls. He could charm the pants off girls – literally. They all fell for him. He had quite a few of the girls working on the film, and an affair with a famous actress.'

Many of David's friends would later accuse Hjördis of being unfaithful to him and of driving him to infidelity. But it was David who was unfaithful to her. The trouble with Niven was that he couldn't stay faithful to one woman for long.

During his long stay in England he looked up an old friend, Jamie Hamilton, who had become a publisher. He told him about the novel he had written, but it was another publisher, Cresset Press, that agreed to publish *Round the Rugged Rocks*, paying Niven a small advance.

The critics didn't care for *Happy Go Lovely* although they almost unanimously agreed that Niven was the best thing about it. The *Daily Mail* had little that was good to say about the film itself but commented, 'Yet Mr Niven, back on top of his form after a series of disappointing pictures, is an excellent light comedian.'

The *Spectator* noted, 'David Niven's charm helps enormously to blind one to the picture's defects.'

The *Daily Mirror* was delighted that Niven was 'rediscovered as a light comedian with a delightful portrayal'.

David returned to Hollywood in October and was delighted to receive a call from MGM. 'I went to see Pandro C. Berman who was one of Metro's top producers, and he said he had this wonderful film for me, *Soldiers Three*, with a wonderful cast – Stewart Granger, Walter Pidgeon, Robert Newton and Cyril Cusack. I read the script and I thought, just a minute, this is *Gunga Din* but without Gunga Din. And it was. So I thought, oh well, the pay is okay, and the cast were nice people.'

Soldiers Three was, as Niven realised, a re-working of the Kipling novel and the movie of *Gunga Din* which he'd lost out on thanks to Errol Flynn. It would be redone again later as a Western, *Sergeants Three* starring Frank Sinatra and his Rat Pack.

David had to accept third billing below Stewart Granger and Walter Pidgeon. Granger had just established himself as a major new star in Hollywood with *King Solomon's Mines*. He and Niven became great friends, and I had the pleasure of dining with them in 1979. They recalled their first film together.

'I thought the script was so terrible I asked Cary Grant to take a look, and he said just to do the best I could and get it over with,' said Granger.

'I've done that on almost all my films,' said Niven.

'Do you remember what you said about it when I complained about it?'

'Take the money and run?'

'Not quite,' said Granger. 'You said, "It may be shit and not very good shit but we have to do it so let's just be cheerful about this shit."'

'That's the best way to deal with shit, I find.'

'Do you remember our director, Tay Garnett?'

'He was the best audience we had,' replied David. 'He laughed at every scene. What a shame the paying audience weren't made up of millions like him.'

'He was convinced it was the funniest comedy script he'd ever read. He laughed at every scene,' said Granger.

'Maybe he was crying.'

When I interviewed Granger in 1980 when he was in London promoting his autobiography, he told me, 'I loved working with David. I thought of him as a big Hollywood star but he was my supporting actor in this, and I couldn't understand why. I asked him what he was doing in it, and he said, "Earning some much needed money, old bean." He was in it just for the money. I didn't know then how hard up he was. I thought he was rich. He always behaved and lived as though he were rich. But by Hollywood standards he was struggling.'

The film is actually quite an enjoyable romp, set in India in the 1890s. The *Daily Mail* called it, 'a knock-about comedy' and added, 'Kipling fans will probably have a fit but my guess is that it will have many people in fits of laughter.'

Variety felt that the comical antics 'enliven the film's footage and save it from missing altogether. Granger is very likeable in his comedy role. Niven also is good as the slightly stuffy aide who leads the pants-losing patrol.'

The film wasn't a huge hit, but I think it's worth taking a look at, if you get the chance.

'In the early 1950s, I was accepting any old rubbish being offered to me,' David told me later. One of the worst, made in 1950, was *The Lady Says No!* in which he was a chauvinist magazine photographer chasing a best selling feminist authoress who gives up her ideals for his love. It was premiered on 6 January 1952 and was slated by the critics and then ignored by the public.

Towards the end of 1950 he accepted another film purely for the money. This was *Appointment with Venus*, filmed in early 1951 in Britain. Niven was actually perfectly cast because he was back in a World War II

British Army uniform with a mission to rescue a pedigree cow from one of the German occupied Channel Islands.

'It was a comedy,' he recalled. 'I'm not sure that it was actually funny.'

The American critics were especially bemused by it. 'The humour sometimes wears a bit thin,' noted *Time*. The *New Yorker* pointed out that it was 'an English film [which] sets out to be a farce and then gets so earnest about itself that it winds up as a kind of blurred melodrama. Since the liberation of a well bred cow struck me as being too elfin a notion I may have missed some of the humour.'

The Times spoke up on behalf of the Brits, observing that the picture combined comedy and adventure, 'always a tricky mixture for a film to handle, but *Appointment with Venus* manages it skilfully enough even if the joke itself is a trifle faded. Still, it is pleasant to see Mr Niven going about his work.'

In the cast was an upcoming English actor called Kenneth More who told me, in one of a number of interviews I did with him, 'I think David is a wonderful chap. He was very nice to everyone. He was a star then, and I was just getting started.'

David was well aware that he was the star of the film and Kenny More wasn't. The film's director, Ralph Thomas, who directed Niven again in 1979 in *A Nightingale Sang in Berkeley Square*, told me, 'David is no trouble to direct, always professional, and when we first worked together on that film about the cow, he was fighting to save his career and to maintain his position as the star of that film. In fact, he thought that Kenny [More] was a little *too* good. He'd watch the rushes and laugh at Kenny's great comedy timing, but it worried him, and he insisted that one of Kenny's best scenes be cut. I said to him, "Look, if you cut Kenny's best scene, he'll be just another supporting actor," and Niven said "Exactly!" So I had to tell Kenny his scene was cut and he was very disappointed and as much as he liked David, after that he was wary of him.'

It seemed that Niven could be just as ruthless as Cary Grant had been. However, he did try to make things up with More by inviting him to Wilcot Manor for the weekend. He got Kenny very drunk and then persuaded him to break a chair which David said was very ugly and should be destroyed, and so Kenny broke the chair and threw it on the fire. In the morning he came downstairs to find Hjördis distraught that her favourite chair was gone. David told her, 'Kenny burned it.' She yelled at More and refused to speak to him for the rest of his stay.

While he was in England making *Appointment with Venus*, David did some painting in his spare time. It was a new hobby which he'd taken up as his film career continued to stall. He even had one of his oil paintings exhibited at the Trafford Gallery in London along with other famous amateur artists.

The prospects of another film coming his way any time soon were bleak, and so Noël Coward got a friend of his, stage producer John Wilson, to offer Niven a play. It hardly seemed the right move for David, who had failed in *Wedding*, his only previous stage play, but with nothing else on offer, he returned to New York to rehearse *Nina* in September 1951. Hjördis went with him, but they left the boys in England – David Jnr to attend boarding school and Jamie to live at Wilcot Manor with Evelyn.

Nina was a French bedroom farce that had been a huge hit in Paris. It had a cast of three; David, former silent screen goddess Gloria Swanson and Alan Webb. Surprisingly, David relaxed into his new role of a stage actor and did well. The play premiered in Hartford, Connecticut in November, then moved on to Boston, Philadelphia and finally Broadway where it ran at the Royale Theatre for 45 performances. Somewhat surprisingly, David Niven had become a successful stage actor, but the stage wasn't where he wanted to be.

He did, however, want to be an author, and his first book, *Round the Rugged Rocks* was published in December 1951. Sheridan Morley told me, 'I think it was the best thing he ever wrote. It's a wonderful light comedy. It's written in something of a jocular journalistic style and although it was all based on his own experiences he insisted it was not an autobiography. It quickly went out of print and he made sure it stayed out of print because so much of it turned up in *The Moon's a Balloon* and *Bring on the Empty Horses*.'

It sold around 5,000 copies, which wasn't bad for a first novel, and it also came out in paperback. But the royalties weren't enough to live on, and stage producers didn't pay much, so what he really needed was a boost to his film career.

He returned to Los Angeles and hoped for the best. He brought the boys back to California and was, said Hjördis, 'an excellent father. He spent time with the boys and they loved him very much. He wouldn't tolerate them telling lies, and he taught them to be polite. He was a more natural parent than I ever could be. I think he made an effort because his own parents had not shown much attention to him.'

The boys grew to dislike Hjördis who showed little interest in them. She became more aloof and friends found her to be growing ever more distant. She tended to suffer from bouts of depression and her drinking had increased. The problem was that while she might have been a poor mother and David was a good father, David was also proving to be less than a fine husband. He was continuing an affair he had begun while filming in England – and Hjördis knew it.

'I was depressed because David was already having affairs,' she said. 'He was never faithful to me. I've been accused of being the one who was unfaithful. Well, yes, later I was unfaithful, but that was because he was going with other women, and I thought, to hell with him, I can do that also. But again, in Hollywood, a man can play around, but a *woman*?

'My depression was not just a sulk. I was really suffering from depression. People told me to snap out of it. But when you are depressed and not just having a sulk, it is hard. It is an illness. I didn't know I was ill, but I was.'

As the crisis in David's career deepened, the more he fooled around. I asked him why he couldn't stay faithful, and he said, 'There are times of crisis when I need the relief.' That may have been part of the reason. And his career was certainly in crisis. But he was about to be thrown a lifeline from a most unexpected source.

CHAPTER 17

—

Four Star

Just as it looked like he would never find success as a screen actor, David landed firmly on both feet in television. It was the medium that Hollywood considered its greatest enemy. Film stars were not supposed to do television; it was only the newcomers, the unestablished actors that did regular television drama. David had done just a couple to start with, *Portrait of Lydia* in 1950 and *Not a Chance* in 1951. But in 1952 he did four – *The Petrified Forest*, *A Moment of Memory*, *The Sheffield Story* and *Sword Play*.

Most of them were aired live, and his stage experience allowed him the confidence to perform well. But he was warned by well meaning friends that he would be blacklisted by the major Hollywood studios for doing too much television. He told then, 'What difference does it make? I'm blacklisted anyway.'

He might never have made another film – at least, not in Hollywood – had it not been for director Otto Preminger who had seen him on stage in *Nina* and was so impressed that he wanted him to be in a movie he was about to make, *The Moon is Blue*, a comedy of romantic errors set in a New York bachelor pad and based on a successful and slightly risqué stage play.

Preminger thought it would be a great idea to put on the play and have David star in it as preparation for the film. United Artists, who were financing the film, told Preminger he was crazy to hire Niven who was washed up in Hollywood. But Preminger stuck to his guns and David had considerable success on stage in *The Moon is Blue* in California.

At the theatre next to his, in San Francisco, Charles Boyer was appearing in *Don Juan in Hell*. Niven and Boyer had dinner together several times, and one time Boyer revealed that he and Dick Powell were forming a TV production company and asked David if he would like to join them. With nothing to lose, David agreed, and so he, Boyer and Powell started Four Star Playhouse. They had hoped to actually find a fourth star to join them in their venture, but every Hollywood star they approached backed quickly away. Many, however, agreed to appear in their productions, such as Merle Oberon, Joan Fontaine, Ronald Colman and Ida Lupino who went on to become a regular with the company acting *and* directing.

Four Star became one of the most successful production companies in television, producing one-off dramas and regular series such as *The Rifleman*, *Zane Grey Theatre* and *Wanted Dead or Alive* which launched the career of Steve McQueen.

'I rather liked being a producer at last,' David told me. 'There was always regular work for me, and I had plenty of acting work in my own productions. I was never going to be out of work again.' *Four Star Playhouse* became a popular series, and David starred in an episode called *The Island* in 1952. Many more episodes would follow.

To Hjördis's surprise and delight, David suddenly offered her a role in one of his productions. This seeming change of heart he had about her being an actress backfired. She recalled,

> After years of telling me I mustn't become an actress, he told me he wanted me to be in one of his television films. He said he needed someone to play a foreign spy and he thought my accent would make me sound like Mata Hari or something.
>
> I found I really enjoyed doing it. And I thought that because David had allowed me to be in his production, he would be happy if I did some films. I was offered a part opposite Robert Taylor. I thought that I could finally become something other than a good wife and a bad mother. But David refused to let me do the film. I understood his concern. He'd known many Hollywood marriages to break up. He said, 'I'll be at one end of the world making a film and you'll be at the other end, and there will be temptation.' He meant one or other of us would have an affair. I felt like I was being accused but *he* was the one not resisting temptation.

Hjördis began to sink further into bouts of black despair and heavy drinking.

On top of his success as a TV producer, David starred in Preminger's film version of *The Moon is Blue*, opposite William Holden, Maggie McNamara and British actress Dawn Addams. It outraged many because the dialogue included words such as 'seduce' and 'virgin' and was condemned by the Catholic Church and banned by the censor in America. United Artists and Preminger defied the censor and were successful in getting local counsils to grant the film distribution to great success; it was the first time the American censor had been bypassed.

Its notoriety caused much publicity and almost guaranteed its success. It also happened to be a good film in which David was excellent, earning him the Golden Globe Award for the best comedy performance of the year. Maggie McNamara was nominated for a Best Actress Oscar, and the critics received it generally well. *Kine Weekly*, the British film trade publication, said, 'David Niven completely disarms', and *Variety* said, 'Niven's middle-aged playboy is mighty fancy play-acting.'

It wasn't all play-acting. I got to know Dawn Addams in 1974 when I worked at Columbia-Warner, and discovered that he was playing the middle-aged playboy very successfully with her. 'I think the film's racy theme had an effect on David,' she told me. I think she may have been the actress he had been having an affair with in England.

I asked Hjördis why she tolerated his affairs. She answered, 'What could I do? I loved him, and I kept thinking he would change. But he was a man who needed sex all the time and he needed it from different women. He couldn't be monogamous. I don't know why. I thought of divorcing him many times.'

She hoped that a holiday they took to Rhode Island in November 1952 would help their ailing marriage. They were supposed to spend a weekend shooting pheasants, but Hjördis had a premonition. 'I am psychic,' she told me. 'That's why I can see ghosts. And I can sometimes see the future. I dreamed that I would be shot and I told David I didn't want to go shooting. He wanted me to go and said I was being silly, so I went. I was shot in the face and neck, and in my chest.'

David was severely shaken by the accident and feared he was about to lose a second wife. But the injuries were not severe. She had been hit by just three pellets, and while the injuries to her face, neck and chest healed easily enough, the marriage didn't. She was suffering more bouts of depression and began to experience panic attacks. He thought she was faking it.

'I didn't recognise that she was really becoming most unwell,' he told me in 1982. 'I'd seen Vivien Leigh suffer from mental illness, and I didn't want to think that my own wife could be mentally ill as well. It wasn't the same. Vivien was a manic depressive which is an actual condition. Hjördis was suffering from...*things* in her life.'

She had experienced a trauma in childhood which affected her for the rest of her life and at some point she shared her secret with David, but he never told me what it was. 'That is not my place,' he told me, which was right and proper.

However, in 1986 she told me what had happened to her. 'I was abused when I was small.'

'Abused sexually?' I asked.

'Yes.'

'Can you tell me what happened?'

'I can't,' she said, and began to cry. 'I can't. I wish I could. I was just a child and he did things.'

She wouldn't say who 'he' was except that he was a member of her family. The trauma of that experience had never left her, and it took a long time before she was able to discover through therapy that this was the cause of her initial depression and anxiety. It was only made worse by David's infidelity. Her desire to break out of the domestic role he had firmly cast her in and become an actress, a career she had not originally sought when she married him, added further despair; it wasn't that she wanted to be an actress but she craved control over her own life. She told me that she felt she had not been in control of her life since being abused.

'I might have failed as an actress, but at least I would have tried,' she told me. 'I can't bear to be controlled. I want to be in control of myself. My memories controlled me, alcohol controlled me, and David controlled me.' In 1986 she felt she was finally in control. But she didn't even begin to start to get better before things got worse.

David's reference to Vivien Leigh's illness was based on first hand experience of seeing her in the grip of what was once called manic depression but it now known as bi-polar disorder. He had to call Stewart Granger one night when Vivien became ill while filming *Elephant Walk*. Granger told me,

> David rang me early one morning and said that he had a problem, that Vivien was very sick and there was a fellow called John Buckmaster who was upsetting her, and he needed my help. Buckmaster was Gladys Cooper's son who had mental problems of his own. I went straight to Vivien's house where David was waiting outside, looking like he was about to have a nervous breakdown. He said he'd been trying to get rid of Buckmaster for hours and he was the last thing Vivien needed, but he wouldn't leave and he wouldn't let David near her.
>
> I went in the house and saw Buckmaster with just a towel around him, standing on the landing, saying he had been sent by a 'higher power' to protect Vivien and we were not going to get past him. I told

him I'd been sent by an even higher power to make sure he got the hell out of there. David thought this was funny and he chuckled nervously, fingering his moustache. He said, 'What are you going to do, Jim?' and I said, 'I have no idea.' That made Niven laugh all the more but he had to try and stifle his laughter.

I advanced on Buckmaster and he suddenly changed his mind and said he would get ready to leave. David gave me the studio doctor's phone number and said that while I got rid of Buckmaster he'd look after Vivien. I had the easy job; I only had to get Buckmaster back to his hotel, and he went very quietly, and then call the doctor who said he would meet me at Schwab's which was an all-night drugstore. He gave me four capsules to sedate her, and he said I should call him to come over with a couple of nurses when she'd taken the first one.

I got back and David said that Vivien was behaving very strangely, and sure enough, she was wearing only a towel and sitting in front of the television looking at just the lines because there was nothing being broadcast. It was as though she were hypnotised by it. It was past midnight and I suggested we all had early breakfast and went to the kitchen to make scrambled eggs and broke one of the capsules and mixed it in to the egg and put some in her coffee. She got very suspicious because I hadn't thought to actually make breakfast for David and myself.

David told her, 'Eat up, Viv, breakfast is the most important meal of the day.' She scooped up a forkful of egg and pointed it at David and said, 'You have some too, David dear.' He said, 'No, no, they are for *you*.' She refused to eat any of it so he took a mouthful of the scrambled egg and drank some of her coffee. I shouldn't have laughed but it was funny; poor David had no idea the sedative was in there and he started to yawn and then said he needed to take a nap. He lay on the couch and went fast to sleep. So then I was trying to deal with her on my own. I couldn't wake him up. So I tried to get Vivien to take a sedative. But she managed to gradually empty the bottle of sedatives into the swimming pool. She stayed awake all night watching television – naked! Finally a nurse came, and I had to hold Vivien down on the bed while the nurse injected her with a sedative.

Laurence Olivier, in England, was called for and he came and collected his sick wife and took her home where she underwent extreme forms of treatment which sickened David when he heard about them. In later years, as he watched his own wife become increasingly sick, he promised himself he wouldn't put her through what Vivien went through.

In early 1953, he received bitter news. His brother Max had died from a heart attack at the age of 50 on his farm in South Africa. David was unable to attend the funeral because of his film commitments; he had accepted to make two films, one in England followed by one in Ireland.

He knew that being a star of British films in the 1950s wasn't a step forward. 'I was a refugee from Hollywood – a has-been – and British studios often hired has-beens to make their modest films look more appealing in America, though God knows why because they didn't seem to like me in America any more,' he said.

In *The Love Lottery*, filmed at Ealing Studios in March and April of 1953, he played a film actor who is the number two star at a studio where the number one star is a dog. It was a good spoof on Hollywood, and Niven came out of it well. 'The cinema seldom goes far wrong when it decides to laugh at itself,' wrote the *Daily Mail*. 'The new Ealing picture does this with gusto. David Niven has his best part for a long time and rises splendidly.'

As soon as he finished on *The Love Lottery* he went straight to Ireland to star in *Happy Ever After* as an ex-General who becomes the squire of an estate in Ireland where he proves so unpopular that the locals attempt to murder him. Irish actor Barry Fitzgerald, who played virtually the same part in this as he did in John Ford's *The Quiet Man*, kept teasing Niven, 'Duke Wayne wouldn't have done it that way,' to which Niven eventually replied, 'Duke Wayne wouldn't have done this bloody silly film in the first place.'

Reviews were mixed: 'Mr Niven who has his limitations outside light comedy, seems most unhappy in this part,' said the London *Evening News*. While the *Daily Mirror* said, 'David Niven has an unusual role – the bad boy. He carries if off surprisingly well.'

It was while he was making *The Love Lottery* and renting Laurence Olivier's house in Chelsea – Olivier was filming in Italy and Vivien Leigh was in hospital – that he heard he had won the Golden Globe for *The Moon is Blue*. It gave him hope that his Hollywood movie career might be revived. But when he returned to America after finishing *Happy Ever After*, there were no film offers waiting for him.

Four Star Playhouse provided him with plenty of work and he appeared in seven episodes in 1953 – *Man on a Train*, *No Identity*, *Night Ride*, *Finale*, *A Matter of Advice*, *For Arti's Sake* and *A Man of the World*. Hollywood became increasingly hostile towards him.

There was a film offer from Britain, *Carrington V.C.*, and he returned to England in September to make the film at Shepperton Studios. He played a British war hero court-martialled for fraud. The film was a hit with British critics and the public. 'Not only has it a great and moving quality but it sends you away feeling proud of Britain's film-makers and actors,' wrote the *News of the World*.

'Mr David Niven is very good in this part, having just the spontaneous decency of reaction and the temperamental mixture of lightness and dash of which heroes are made,' said the *Financial Times*.

It is an excellent film, especially for lovers of courtroom drama, intelligently written and directed, and with a superior performance from Niven. Unfortunately it ran into censorship trouble in America – where it was shown as *Court Martial* – because Niven's character has an adulterous affair with a WRAC officer, played by Margaret Leighton. Nevertheless, America's film trade publication *Variety*, happily conceded, 'David Niven gives one of his best performances in recent years.'

Despite this acclaim and his Golden Globe Award for *The Moon is Blue*, Hollywood was unwilling to forgive and forget, and the best Hollywood had to offer him in early 1954 was the role of a villain in a third-rate MGM swashbuckler, *The King's Thief*. He was ill suited to the part and, embarrassingly, he was billed third below Ann Blyth and Edmund Purdom who played the dashing hero with very little dash.

The only pleasure Niven got from making the film was forming a friendship with a young British actor trying for success in Hollywood, Roger Moore. They remained friends to the very end, and in 1980, when I interviewed Roger Moore when he was promoting *The Sea Wolves*, one of Niven's final films, Moore told me, 'I was in a terrible film called *The King's Thief* but the blessing of making that film was to become friends with David Niven. I thought it was simply a privilege to share the screen with him.'

From what Moore observed, David and Hjördis were happy, although Roger didn't know then the troubles that were simmering in their marriage. 'She was a really glamorous woman,' Moore recalled, 'and people's jaws dropped when they saw her. She'd come to the set and everyone stood there with their mouths open. Personally, I thought she wore too much make-up. But David loved her and they were always hand-in-hand.'

Fortunately for David, he could still do good work in television, and in 1954 he starred in eight Four Star productions, one of which, *The Answer*, earned him an Emmy nomination. But that didn't help him to get good movie parts, and he was offered only a major supporting role in *The Birds and the Bees*, greyed-up to play a crook and former colonel using his daughter, played by Mitzi Gaynor – oh, how the mighty had fallen, to play the *father* of Mitzi Gaynor – to fleece the son of a tycoon.

'I had come to realise that I was not an A-movie star after all,' he told me in 1978, 'but a minus-B-picture star. I had started in B-pictures and I was still making B-pictures, and that's all I was ever going to be.'

Even if, by 1978, he was acutely aware that his star had not so much fallen but had barely failed to rise, in 1970 he had painted a different picture, saying that he 'had a stroke of bad luck. I was making really rotten pictures and I thought it only had to be a matter of time before someone realised how wonderful I really was and give me a wonderful picture.'

In March 1955 he and Hjördis holidayed in Jamaica at Noël Coward's winter home where David suddenly went down with chicken pox and had to be quarantined. Hjördis admitted, 'I was never a good nurse and hopeless at taking care of David when he was sick so Noël made sure he was looked after.'

He recovered and, while Hjördis returned to Hollywood, Niven went to New York to appear in a Four Star production and there had an affair with Grace Kelly. Dawn Addams told me, 'Infidelity seems to be an occupational hazard with many actors. With David it was almost a second career.'

Hjördis believed that his womanising wasn't helped by the friends he kept. From 1941 he had been good pals with Humphrey Bogart and Lauren Bacall around whom a whole circle of friends had sprung up whose main aim was to enjoy a good time. Bacall told me in 1974 on the set of *Murder on the Orient Express*, 'To be a part of that circle one had to be addicted to nonconformity, staying up late, drinking, laughing, and not caring what anyone thought or said about us.'

In 1955 Bogart and their friends turned up in Las Vegas to give support to Noël Coward who, after a slump in his career, was attempting a comeback performance at the Desert Inn. David recalled the event for me,

Noël Coward was appearing in Las Vegas at the Desert Inn. Frank Sinatra invited a few friends to go with him to Las Vegas for the opening. The group consisted of Betty and Bogie, Mike and Gloria Romanoff, Ernie Kovaks and his wife, Swifty Lazar, Sid Luft and Judy Garland, Angie Dickinson, Hjördis and myself.

When Sinatra organises anything, the arrangements are made with legendary efficacy, not to mention generosity. We all boarded a bus outside Bogie's front door. There was caviar and champagne to sustain us during the drive to Union Station, where, with a cry from our leader [Sinatra] of 'Yellow armbands, follow me', we marched on to the train and into a private coach for the overnight trip.

Sinatra provided individual apartments for everyone at the Sands Hotel, as well as a large communal suite with hot and cold running food and drink 24 hours a day. A big bag of silver dollars was presented to each girl in the group.

We watched Noël's triumphant first night and then on the other evenings we visited all the other shows in Las Vegas. We all gambled endlessly, and it all began to get very tiring. After three days of this, Judy Garland slipped me something that she said would keep me going. It was the size of a horse-pill, inside of which were dozens of little energy nuggets which were timed to go off at 40-minute intervals.

After four days and nights of complete self-indulgence, the only one of us who seemed physically untouched by it all was Frank Sinatra, while the rest of us were wrecks. It was then that Betty Bacall surveyed the bedraggled group and said, 'You lot look like a goddam Rat Pack!'

A week later, we returned to Los Angeles and some semblance of normality. The Rat Pack threw a testimonial dinner to Frank in a private room at Romanoff's where we were welcomed with a surprise package, tied with pink ribbons and flown down especially by Jack Entratta who was the entrepreneur of the Sands Hotel. We opened our packages and we each found a while rat. During the unpacking, several escaped and, running throughout the restaurant, created instant alarm among the chic clientele, among who were some eagle-eyed columnists who made a point of finding out what was going on – and this was heralded as the existence of Frank Sinatra's Rat Pack.

David became a very close friend of Sinatra who, Niven wrote in *The Moon's a Balloon*, had once helped him out of a 'very bad spot'. He wrote that 'help was provided instantly and in full measure without a question being asked'. In 1979, over dinner with David and Ava, I asked him if he would elucidate, but he replied, 'I couldn't possibly, dear boy. When Frank helps a friend, it's a precious gift not to take for granted.'

Ava shoved me lightly and said, 'Go on, Mike, tell him.'

'Tell him what?' I asked.

'You know goddamn well what.'

That got David's interest, so we made a pact. I said I'd tell David my secret Sinatra story if he told me his. Ava already knew what mine was. I gave David my story – which doesn't need to be told here – and so he then told me that he had got into a 'difficult situation' regarding a so-called 'agent' who had strong-armed him into signing a contract which would have resulted in Niven having to pay the Mafia half of everything he earned from Four Star. Knowing that Sinatra had friends in the Mob, David asked him for help and Sinatra obliged and succeeded in freeing Niven from the contract. Just how Sinatra did this, Niven never explained. 'Nobody but Frank could have got me out of that spot – except maybe Al Capone,' he said.

By the mid 1950s, David should have been happy with his lot – a family, a successful career as a TV producer, recognition for his work as an actor on television – but he was dissatisfied because what he wanted above all else was success as a movie actor. He finally got what he had long hoped for. 'I got a wonderful picture, *Around the World in 80 Days*, but I didn't get it because *I* was so wonderful. Mike Todd gave me the part because he didn't *need* a big star. The picture was the star. And so was the balloon.'

CHAPTER 18

—

Resurrection

Mike Todd was a 46-year-old showman who had invented a new screen process called Todd-AO which was intended to project a 70mm picture onto a massive curved screen to give a 'you are there' sensation as a rival to Cinerama. The first Todd-AO production was *Oklahoma!* in 1955 but Todd felt it didn't provide the Cinerama type effect he intended, so he personally produced a film that would do just that, a film of Jules Verne's *Around the World in 80 Days*.

'Cary Grant was Todd's first choice [to play Philias Fogg],' David told me. 'I heard about the film and thought it was just what I needed and I thought, as modestly as possible, that I'd be perfect for it. I didn't think Cary was right for it at all. So I got my agent on the case, and after Todd failed to get Grant, he offered me the part. It took some negotiating because I was a TV star but not a major film star, and I was happy to admit that the picture and that balloon were the stars. I had some help also from Evelyn Keyes, an old friend of mine, who was living with Todd, and she put in a good word for me. Finally he gave me the role, and it saved my career. It was my resurrection.'

Todd paid him a handsome fee of $100,000. The production itself was massive, taking six months to film, and not all of it around the world as one might think. Most of it was filmed in California, but there were locations in England, France, Spain, Hong Kong and Japan.

Todd peopled the film with big stars in tiny cameos, including Frank Sinatra, Buster Keaton, George Raft and Marlene Dietrich. More important supporting roles were played by such character actors as

Trevor Howard, Robert Morley and John Gielgud. There was a major supporting role for Robert Newton as the Scotland Yard inspector who tracks Fogg around the world thinking him to be a bank robber, and a prime role for Mexican star Cantinflas as Fogg's faithful valet. Twenty-one-year-old Shirley MacLaine was the film's leading lady – it was only her fourth film.

David told me, 'I didn't think Shirley could do it because she was playing a Hindu princess, and I was very cynical about her to start with, and not very friendly towards her, which I regret. I can be a total bastard, you know. People think I'm always so wonderful. However, I saw how good an actress she was and how seriously she took her work and she was a really nice person as well, and in the end we became very good friends.'

Around the World in 80 Days was one of the three big box office hits of 1956, along with *The King and I* and *The Ten Commandments*. It also received almost unanimous praise from the critics, and Niven received good personal notices. The *Financial Times* said, 'David Niven is superb. His hauteur never varies a fraction but beneath it powerful forces can be seen at work.' The *Sunday Times* claimed, 'David Niven as the imperturbable traveller could hardly be bettered.' *Variety* proclaimed, 'David Niven, as Fogg, is the perfect stereotype of the unruffled English gentleman and quite intentionally, a caricature of the 19th-century British propriety.'

The film won the Oscar for Best Picture, probably because it was pretty sensational in its day, although, unlike other films of the period, it hasn't stood the test of time so well. The film's director, Michael Anderson, shot long travelling scenes – much like in the original Cinerama travelogues – in which the camera was perched on the front of trains or on boats and other forms of public transportation, with relatively little of its 2 hours and 50 minutes devoted to the actual story. Unless viewed on a giant curved screen – and there were few cinemas in the world equipped for Todd-AO as it was originally intended – it quickly becomes wearisome. But that didn't matter in 1956 when it was one of *the* films to go and see.

But before it was a hit, before the reviews glowed about Niven's performance and before the Best Picture Oscar, David, upon finishing the film at the end of 1955, prepared for the next one he had agreed to do, *The Silken Affair*, another British production.

Before he set off for England, Hjördis was hospitalised early in 1956. She had been pregnant, a secret she and David chose to keep because she had fallen pregnant before and each time had miscarried. It had happened again, only this time there were complications and she had to undergo a hysterectomy.

Despite her failings as a stepmother, Hjördis had hoped to have children of her own, and as one pregnancy after another failed, the depression she was prone to became worse. I have read and heard that by this time she wasn't allowing David to have intercourse with her, but the fact that she was pregnant shows that they were obviously having sexual relations. It was only when she was pregnant that she didn't allow him to have intercourse with her, and that depressed David – or rather, it sent him into a sulk and seeking satisfaction elsewhere.

I've also read and heard that she was seeing other men at this time, but this I don't believe. It has been said that she sent him into the arms of other women, but David was responsible for his own actions. I am amazed at how many enemies Hjördis earned and how little consideration was ever given to what she went through.

In 1986, Hjördis told me,

> After my last miscarriage I was very ill and was told I would never have children. When I had my womb taken away I felt like a part of me had been destroyed. I didn't feel complete any more.
>
> I don't show my emotions. That is the Swedish part of me, but losing my babies was shattering. It was for David too. He could show his emotions far more than I could. People thought I didn't care, but I did. I felt like my babies had died and I was mourning for them, but because I didn't show how I felt, people thought I was a bitch. They had no idea how much I was hurting. Only David knew. He understood that Swedish part of me.
>
> I had terrible depression after the miscarriage. People told me I should cheer up. I couldn't cheer up. My soul was in darkness. But when they looked at me all they saw was a cold Swede. They thought I was just down in the mouth.

After six weeks in hospital she was well enough to go with him to England when he made *The Silken Affair* at Elstree Studios. He played a dull accountant who livens up his life by cooking the books of various companies, making a failing silk stocking manufacturer appear to be a success while turning one of that company's successful rivals into a failure, at least on paper.

The film actually begins well but the joke wears thin, although Niven's performance still makes it very watchable, as many of the critics noted. The *Daily Telegraph* thought the film 'agreeable, civilised entertainment with enough style and wit to atone for the bits that don't come off'. The *Financial Times* praised Niven saying he 'remains one of the most accomplished light comedians in the business', and the *Daily Mail* thought that Niven in this film 'has a chance to show that when he is properly suited he has no equal in his own field of precise, polished comedy'.

Like many of Niven's films, it came and went and was rarely heard of or seen again.

He took time off from filming *The Silken Affair* so he and Hjördis could fly to Monaco to attend the wedding of Grace Kelly and Prince Rainier on 19 April. Hjördis took to Prince Rainier and they stayed friends for many years but they did not, as far as I know, have an affair.

In May the Nivens returned to Hollywood for a five week break and then set off in June for Rome where David was to film *The Little Hut* for MGM at Cinecittà Studios. It was the rather saucy story of three people stranded on a desert island. Based on a rather risqué play, it revolved around a *ménage à trois* as the husband allows his best friend to share his wife. Stewart Granger was the husband, Ava Gardner the wife and Niven the best friend. The film suffered because it had to be toned down. But it is an engaging film, and all three stars are excellent in it.

Stewart Granger, however, hated doing the film.

> I *had* to do *The Little Hut* because I was under contract. David wasn't, but he accepted anything that was offered to him. Ava Gardner had to be in it too because she was under contract to Metro.
>
> I couldn't bare the thought of trying to do comedy opposite David Niven's moustache because he only has to play with it or twitch it while somebody else is talking and he steals the whole scene with no effort. That's the genius of David. He wasn't given credit for being a good comedian, but he knew exactly how to get the laughs. No, he *stole* the laughs, and I don't blame him.
>
> But I was pretty inconsolable about the prospect of making that film, because of Niven's moustache, and because it was to be shot in Rome which was a separation from Jean [Simmons] that I didn't need right then because she was pregnant.
>
> It was fun to make, even if the film didn't turn out well. Ava was very happy because she was in love with Walter Chiari who was an Italian comedian who had a part in the film. And David is always great to work with because he never lets your spirits drop. He is funny and never missed an opportunity to make you laugh.
>
> One day I was in a furious temper, and he said, 'Whatever's up, old bean?'
>
> I said, 'This film is taking forever to make. I asked Mark Robson [the director] when we were going to finish because I had to get back to Jean before the baby comes, and you know what he said?'

David said, 'I can't begin to guess.'

I said, 'He told me that he was going as quickly as he could and the baby would just have to wait. He said the baby had to *wait*, for God's sake.'

And David, very dryly said, 'Then simply cable Jean and say, *Will be home late. If I'm not there start without me.*'

For a moment I was so mad at *him* that I wanted to knock him on his arse, but two seconds later I burst into laughter.

I got home just in time for the baby to be born. I sent a cable to David and said, 'Have a beautiful baby girl. Jean did wait after all.' He replied, 'Congratulations Dad. Trust a woman not to be early.'

David and Hjördis returned to England in the late summer of 1956 where he made the effort to see Trubshawe. 'It wasn't quite the same,' Trubshawe told me. 'He wasn't talking about the old days any more and I was.'

In September the Nivens took a brief holiday in Sweden but were back in Los Angeles in October for the premiere of *Around the World in 80 Days*. The film suddenly made Niven into a major star. His reputation on television was further enhanced in December by another Emmy nomination for one of his Four Star productions.

But there was sadness on 14 January 1957 when Humphrey Bogart, who had been suffering from lung cancer, died. David went to the funeral, ushering and throwing out newspaper photographers. He spent a lot of time with Lauren Bacall to help her through the grief. That was one of his great gifts; helping people through times of grief. He did the same for me when I lost my grandfather.

He went to work on a good film, *Oh Men! Oh Women!*, a comedy in which he played a psychiatrist who has a client, played by his old friend Ginger Rogers, who pours out her troubles over her husband, leading him to crack up. The *Financial Times* loved it, calling it a 'shrewd and wicked farce'. The critic at the *Sunday Despatch* said, 'I haven't laughed so much for a long time.' But the *Observer* called it 'a dull consulting room comedy. The ugliest sort of fun.'

Like almost all of Niven's films, this one has generally dimmed into near obscurity even though it was relatively successful. The same is true of his next film, *My Man Godfrey*, an entertaining remake of a very good 1936 comedy about a tramp who becomes a butler. William Powell originally had Niven's role, and Carole Lombard, as the butler's socialite boss, had the role June Allyson now took. Somehow it didn't quite work. As the *New York Times* said, 'Maybe June Allyson and David Niven are just not Miss Lombard and Mr Powell.'

There were further TV productions, but not so many, and he was now getting more film work coming his way. He was eager to accept his next assignment, *Bonjour Tristesse*, filmed in the south of France, and directed by Otto Preminger who once again was pushing the boundaries of censorship. Niven played a middle-aged playboy with a taste for pretty young girls and has a particularly close almost incestuous relationship with his teenage daughter, played by Jean Seberg. Deborah Kerr played a former flame of Niven's who tries to steer him away from his philandering ways. This unorthodox tale ends tragically with Kerr driving her car into the sea.

The problem with the film is that people expected it to be another Niven comedy, but it had an edge to it, and so did Niven's performance. The critics didn't know what to make of it, and neither did the public which stayed away. It's actually a film worth watching; uneven but quite absorbing, largely due to the performances of Niven, Seberg and Kerr.

While making the film David and Deborah Kerr became firm friends – it was a friendship to last the rest of David's life. There were suggestions that the two had an affair, but I don't believe they did. It was just a very happy and healthy friendship.

Hjördis initially felt threatened by the friendship, thinking in the beginning that there was more to it. But there were other reasons to be jealous. 'After my miscarriage David said he was going to stay faithful,' she said, 'but it wasn't long before he was chasing after girls again. I never knew if he was having an affair with Deborah Kerr. He swore that they were not. I think that time I believed him. But he was always having affairs with other women. I felt as though I was not desirable to him any more. I wasn't allowed to have a career, I couldn't have babies, and I couldn't have him to myself. Yes, I was very unhappy.'

The final scenes of *Bonjour Tristesse* were shot in England at Shepperton Studios where, as soon as the Preminger film was finished, David began work on *Separate Tables* in November. That film was adapted from the marvellous play by Terence Rattigan who worked with screenwriter John Gay on transforming what was essentially two plays set in the same location – a hotel at Bournemouth – into one story.

Niven played Major Pollock who turns out not to be a major at all but a seedy character arrested for molesting women. He strikes up a friendship with a plain spinster, played by Deborah Kerr; both stars, cast against type, produced impressive performances. Niven managed to make the bogus major sympathetic and was nominated for a Best Actor Oscar.

Most critics were ecstatic about him. 'David Niven acts out the finest role of his career,' said the *Daily Sketch*.

'David Niven crowns his considerably successful career with a shining performance,' said the London *Evening News*.

'David Niven gives one of the best performances of his career,' said *Variety*.

Filming on *Separate Tables* finished the first week of January 1958. In March he and Hjördis attempted to heal their ailing marriage. She said,

> We tried to fix our marriage again by having a holiday. He wanted to go around the world in 180 days, which I thought was a wonderful idea. Shirley MacLaine and her husband [Steve Parker] came with us some of the way. We had a wonderful time sailing around the Greek Islands. The boys flew out to meet us there. It was a very happy time for a while.
>
> But everywhere we went people knew David and they kept wanting to talk to him. We could never be left on our own. He loved it. He loved talking to people. I said to him that we were on a holiday to fix our marriage and he said that he couldn't be rude to people who were his fans. There were a lot of female fans. I could tell they would all sleep with him if they had the chance. Of course that made me jealous. I worried that he would meet someone much younger – he loved the younger girls – and then he would leave me. I couldn't help my moods. I had depression and I drank to ease the dark feelings.
>
> I don't say these things now that David is dead to make him into a monster. He was never a monster. He was a wonderful man, and there were times when we were wonderfully happy. People didn't always see the happy times we had because they were private times.
>
> When I wasn't feeling depressed I would feel extremely happy. I would laugh and joke, and that's when his friends liked me. My moods swung one way and then the other. When I was depressed I drank because I was so sad. When I was happy I drank just because I was so happy.

After *Separate Tables* David made *Ask Any Girl*, a good light comedy that has long been forgotten. It featured a fine performance by Shirley MacLaine as a kooky girl who arrives in New York and goes to work at an ad agency run by a surprisingly prissy David Niven. She falls for his brother, played by the ever excellent Gig Young, to whom she is just another girl, but, of course, it is really Niven that she wants.

Over dinner one evening with Gig Young in 1970, when I was still a junior publicist, he told me that when they were making the film Niven got Jim Backus, the voice of Mr Magoo, to call Young on the telephone and tell him, in Magoo's voice, that he was from the Government and was calling to ask why he wasn't in school. Young thought he recognised the voice but couldn't place it, and then Backus said, 'Oh, I'm terribly sorry, I see your name is Gig Young. I thought it said young Gig. In that case, you owe us 10 years' back tax.'

Shirley MacLaine won an award for her performance as Best Foreign Actress at the 1959 Berlin Film Festival in February, and she also won the British Film Academy Award. Niven didn't win any awards but he did get good personal notices. 'Mr Niven has certainly taken on a new lease of life since about four films ago,' observed the *Daily Mail*. 'This latest effort seems to confirm him as a captain and *chef du protocol* of Hollywood's British colony for the next 20 years or so.'

There was suddenly no shortage of films being offered to him, but his next was a mistake. *Happy Anniversary* featured him and Mitzi Gaynor – who once played his daughter – as a couple celebrating their 13th wedding anniversary which erupts into a moral storm when he confesses to his in-laws that they had been cohabitating a year before the wedding.

'One wonders how players as charming as David Niven and Mitzi Gaynor ever came to be mixed up with it,' said the *Daily Telegraph*. The *Daily Mail's* film critic wrote, 'David Niven has been choosing himself such good parts lately that I am surprised that he should consent to do *Happy Anniversary*.'

It was just a blip in his career but there was worse happening in his marriage. Hjördis finally had enough of his philandering. She was supposed to go with him to the Berlin Film Festival but she chose to remain in California to be with a lover she had taken. She said to me, 'I just thought, oh well, if it was okay for him to have affairs then it was okay for me also. His friends thought he could do no wrong. They thought it was great fun when he had affairs. One of the women I thought was a friend called me a bitch.'

But Hjördis was with him at the Academy Awards on 6 April 1959. He was up for the Best Actor Oscar against Tony Curtis and Sidney Poitier, both for *The Defiant Ones*, Paul Newman for *Cat on a Hot Tin Roof* and Spencer Tracy for *The Old Man and the Sea*. When David's name was called out, he kissed Hjördis, ran down the aisle of the Pantages Theatre, tripped up the steps of the stage onto his hands and knees, recovered and took the Oscar from Irene Dunne. Arriving at the microphone, he said, 'The reason I fell down was because I was so loaded…' He had intended to say, 'loaded down with good luck charms,' but it didn't matter because he got the night's biggest laugh.

He received 230 telegrams of congratulations the next day. Among them was one from Sam and Frances Goldwyn. He hadn't seen them for 10 years. They invited him to come and have dinner, and a few days later he did.

Everyone was delighted for David – except for Hjördis. 'When he won his Oscar,' she said, 'I felt that I had finally lost him. He was this amazing movie star, and I was just his wife. I was no one. I was not Primmie. That made me less than the best.'

Forty years old and still very beautiful but looking thin and drawn, she decided the time had come to leave him in the summer of 1959. She said,

I decided I *had* to leave him. I was miserable. I was depressed. I felt he was not in love with me, and he said to me, 'You're such a cold fish at times, it's no wonder I look to find love and warmth in other women.' He said, 'So you go right ahead and sleep with other men.' That isn't what I wanted. I wanted to feel loved. I didn't know who or what I was any more. I was just Mrs David Niven, the bitch.

David blamed me for having an affair and wrecking our marriage. There was a terrible argument. I think it was an argument we should have had years before. Things might have been better then. He said, 'I'm sick of seeing you flirting with every man.' I said that I didn't flirt with every man. He accused me of flirting with my eyes, and I said, 'How can I help the way my eyes look?'

Oh, we were yelling and shouting. I felt it was good for us. He said, 'You're sleeping with your doctor.' I said, 'You're sleeping with *every* actress you work with. Every air hostess. Every waitress.' He stopped shouting then. I know now that the boys think I was a terrible mother to them, and a terrible wife to their father. They hate me because I had affairs. But nobody minded that David was having affairs. I was faithful to him in the beginning, but he wasn't faithful to me.

So I left him and hoped I would find happiness. I fell in love with a doctor. I thought I would be happy with him, but I missed David.

In 1982, David told me he was prepared to take responsibility for the marriage failure. 'After I won the Oscar, Hjördis left me, you know. I couldn't really blame her because I took her so much for granted. And my head got too big when I won the Oscar. I thought that finally I was a *wonderful* actor and a really *big* star.

'I knew I had to save the marriage somehow, if not for my sake then for the boys. I don't think they thanked me for saving the marriage. They didn't like their stepmother too much. When we separated, I reached the point where I really missed her. I tried the old fashioned way of sending her flowers. But I didn't think it would work and I found someone I felt I could be happy with.'

I asked him who that someone was, and all he would say was, 'She was a beautiful English model.' He is known to have fallen for a model from a good English family at the time. Her name was Caroline Kirkwood. I asked him why he didn't divorce Hjördis and marry his girlfriend. He said, 'She was very young. I didn't want to be an old man with a young wife.' Caroline was 27. David was 49. He always liked the younger women, but he seemed to think that he couldn't be married to one.

David took the two boys on a holiday to Honolulu to stay in a house owned by Frank Sinatra. According to Ava Gardner, David wasted no time bedding every girl who was willing, 'and they were *all* willing', she said.

Back in California, Hjördis continued her affair with the doctor. 'I'm drawn to doctors,' she told me. 'Almost all my lovers have been doctors.'

I asked her why she thought that was. She said, 'I suppose it was because I think I need someone who can help me be well again. I spent much of my life trying to be well again.'

Patricia Medina remembered visiting Hjördis during the time she was separated from David. 'She had friends round who were *all* drinking heavily. I didn't like the look of them at all.'

Hjördis admitted that, having lost so many friends who were really David's friends, she was looking for friends of her own. 'But sadly the people I thought were my friends were just like me. They drank too much. They were destructive for me, but I didn't know that at the time.

'I was friends with Pat Medina, but we had some rows. She saw what a mess I was in, and when I was living apart from David she came to my house, and she saw all these people I thought were my friends, and she hated them, and she told me she wanted to leave.'

Back in Hollywood, David made *Please Don't Eat The Daises*, a comedy in which he played a professor who decides to become a theatre critic in New York. Doris Day played his wife who convinces him to give up reviewing plays and write them instead. It received a critical lashing at the time but it is actually a very funny film today. Maybe the film critics of the time didn't like the way Niven portrayed theatre critics as the 'butchers of Broadway'.

After three months apart, David and Hjördis got back together. Patricia Medina said that she only went back to him because he was making a lot of money from Four Star and she wanted some of it.

Hjördis denied that. She said,

When I went back to David I had an argument with Pat. I didn't explain myself at all well, but I made it seem like all I was interested in was his money. I was trying to say a joke – that I missed him *and* his money.

I knew that if our marriage was to work the second time he had to stop sleeping with women, and he promised he would. I promised not to sleep with other men, but I said, 'I can't promise not to flirt because my eyes just flirt on their own,' and that made him laugh.

The biggest problem, though, was my drinking. I was getting drunk too much, too often. David said to me, 'You're damaged, and I don't know how to mend you.'

I said, 'Just love me and we'll try and find a way.'

Many of David's friends disapproved of the reunion, but he had come to realise how sick she was, and I think that is partly why he tried to mend the marriage. He said, 'I tried to protect her when we got back together. I tried to be gentle with her because she had become very fragile. Some of our friends were a bit rough on her because they didn't understand what was really going on inside of her head. And they were always *my* pals and so they tolerated her, but they didn't like her much. Peter Ustinov, a great pal, told me that he was very sorry but he didn't like her at all. I said, "You have to understand, Peter, that she's been through hell, and she's very ill." He said, "If she's ill have her committed." I never heard Peter say such a cruel thing before.'

David believed their marriage stood a better chance of survival if they got away from Hollywood. He was also considering how he could keep more of the money he earned instead of giving so much of it away to the IRS. He was making around $200,000 a film and making good money from Four Star, but he was landed with a huge tax bill and that helped him make up his mind to move to Europe.

Deborah Kerr and her husband Peter Vietrel encouraged him to live in Switzerland where they were living and where tax was much lighter. Early in 1960 David and Hjördis flew to Switzerland to house hunt and to search for a new future.

CHAPTER 19

—

Europe

.

David had to leave Hjördis to hunt for houses on her own for a time while he went to Athens to start work on *The Guns of Navarone*, a huge World War II epic written and produced by Carl Foreman and directed by J. Lee Thompson. David was part of a starry cast – Gregory Peck, Anthony Quinn, Stanley Baker, Anthony Quayle and singer James Darren – playing a group of saboteurs with a mission to destroy the powerful guns on the island of Navarone.

This has always been the kind of film I've loved since I was a kid, and over the years working as a film publicist, journalist, behind the scenes, in the scenes, I've always sought out the actors and directors who made those kinds of movies. From *The Guns of Navarone* I've been lucky to interview Stanley Baker in Wales when he was filming *How Green Was My Valley* in 1975, Gregory Peck when he was making *The Omen* in London in 1978, Anthony Quinn when he was making *The Greek Tycoon* at Elstree Studios in 1977, Anthony Quayle on the set of *Murder by Decree* in 1978 and J. Lee Thompson when he was in London promoting a mediocre Charles Bronson flick called *St Ives* in 1976, as well as talking informally to most of them on film sets, on location, in offices, in their homes or hotel suites and at premieres. And David Niven, of course.

J. Lee Thompson remembered the tension among the cast when they first all met up in Athens, before they set off for the bulk of the location filming on the island of Rhodes:

There was a certain amount of rivalry on the set between Gregory Peck, David Niven and Anthony Quinn – friendly rivalry. The first night we all met on the location in Athens, David Niven was very cheery but he felt anxious that he was just going to be left standing around a lot with nothing to do while the other stars got on with the action. It was true that his character was not as well developed as some of the others and he felt, rightly, that all the characters had been written as supermen without much depth to them. He thought he would be forgotten among all those stars like Peck and Quinn. But he had only just won an Oscar and was insecure that Gregory Peck and Anthony Quinn would get all the best acting moments. And there was Peck convinced Tony Quinn would try to out-act him, and Quinn was aware that Niven had won an Oscar, and so they were all eyeing each other warily. Nothing unpleasant, but I felt the tension. Then Tony Quinn brought out little portable chess sets and they all got hooked on playing chess and took out all the rivalry on the chessboards instead of before the cameras.

Anthony Quinn remembered the chess games: 'I thought that playing chess would reveal everyone's character. There was David Niven, the Errol Flynn of the chessboard, charging around with his queen, crying, "Idiotic move, what, eh? Well, never mind, on we go. Charge!" Then there was Peck – calm – like Lincoln – contemplating every move – deep in thought – you couldn't rush him. Stanley Baker was a competitive spirit who displayed terrible fury when defeated but great joy when victorious. Tony Quayle moved his pieces like a general, planning his strategy, studying the board and knowing what his moves would be way ahead. Carl Foreman played too. When he lost, you could see centuries of persecution in his face. And there was me. When I lost I just threw the board at them!'

Anthony Quayle told me, 'Tony Quinn was not always easy to get on with. Because Gregory Peck was a big Hollywood star you felt he was in charge and you could trust him. But for me the delight of the film was working with David Niven,' he said. 'He never failed to say "Hello, old bean, how are you?"'

Stanley Baker remembered Niven's story-telling as something everyone else competed with, like the chess games. 'We were *all* good story-tellers, and some of us had better stories to tell. That's what actors do. In the end we were all competing to tell the best stories, but there's something about David that makes you feel as though you *ought* to pay attention. He'd tell us about a time he'd supposedly fought of Mexican bandits, and Tony Quinn would huff and say, "I was *born* under the sound of gunfire in Mexico," and he talk about Pancho Villa.

'Niv also *listened*. He wanted to know what it was like to be brought up in the Welsh valleys. He was *interested*. But no matter what you said, he always managed to say, "That reminds me of a time I…" and he'd launch into another anecdote.'

Niven told me, 'I had no problem with any of the cast. They were all professional, all very likeable. Tony Quinn was the only one who could throw a tantrum. He got very angry one time and I said, "What on earth's the problem?" and he said, "I have to shoot all these Germans with one gun and I would run out of bullets if this were for real."

'I said, "But, Tony, this is only pretend. There's nothing real about this film. It's a big cartoon." He said, "Don't you need to find what your motivation is?" I said, "Yes, indeed, my motivation is the big fat fee they're paying me." So he laughed and shouted to the director, "Okay, let's shoot the scene and I'll kill 'em all with my one gun."'

Out of the production grew a friendship between Gregory Peck and Niven that lasted for the rest of David's life. Peck told me, 'David was always so incredibly cheerful that when you asked him why he was, he'd just say, "Well, old bean, life is really so bloody awful that I feel it's my absolute duty to be chirpy and try and make everybody else happy too."'

While David was on Rhodes, Hjördis found a chalet, complete with tennis court and spectacular views, in the Alpine valley village Château d'Oex near Gstaad. When David saw it, he agreed it was perfect for them and they bought it. When location work on *Guns of Navarone* was finished, and while waiting to shoot interiors at Shepperton Studios in England, David and Hjördis moved into their new home.

He quickly discovered a nearby hotel he liked, the Olden, where he would lunch and dine often. Many other famous people dined there including Princess Grace and Prince Rainier. Later, Richard Burton and Elizabeth Taylor would become regulars, as would Peter Sellers.

David might have hoped the new home in a new land would solve his and Hjördis's problems, but her problems were not easily fixable. 'I got worse, and drank more,' she said. 'I'd drink all morning and was drunk by lunch time. We used to have lunch at the Olden Hotel almost every day, but I was always drunk by lunch time, and whenever we saw our friends coming in, I gave them loud greetings which embarrassed David.'

It might seem that David would have done better to have left Hjördis at home and gone to the Olden alone, but he had good reason to get her out of the house. She was suffering from agoraphobia and it was becoming increasingly hard for her just to step outside. There were those who thought she was just being difficult and obstinate but agoraphobia is a terrifying disease. Indoors she was also suffering severe anxiety and panic attacks, and she numbed it all with alcohol.

Not all of David's and Hjördis's friends turned against her. A regular visitor to Château d'Oex was Noël Coward who Hjördis dearly loved. She told me,

> He was a dear, dear man. I liked him because he didn't judge me, and he made me feel welcome in his company and made me laugh. I think I felt more comfortable with him than with any of David's other friends. I said to him, 'You actually like me, and that makes me very happy.'
>
> He said, 'Of course I like you, Hjördis. You see, men – *straight* men – find you threatening because they think you are going to get in their pants, and women find you threatening because they think you're going to seduce their men. But your flirty eyes have no effect on me, and Cole isn't afraid I'm going to jump into bed with you.' [Cole Lesley was Coward's partner.]
>
> I asked him how I can stop having what he called 'flirty eyes', and he said, 'Stop taking all those pills, don't wear so much make-up and for God's sake *laugh* at David's stories.'
>
> I took his advice, but it was hard to go without sedatives because I was having panic attacks, so I started taking them again. And I tried laughing at David's jokes, but when I was back on the pills, they were made worse by the booze, and I was back to the way I was.
>
> There were times I just wanted to die. I told David I wanted to die, and he begged, 'Please don't die.' He said, 'Primmie died. I couldn't bear it if you died too.' I think that was the sweetest thing he ever said to me.

She was right about the way many felt about her. Richard Burton once told me, 'Hjördis was the worst kind of wife, I would imagine. She and David would have lunch at the Olden, and she would be drunk every time, but David never complained. And she seemed to try it on with all the men. Even me, even when I was with Elizabeth [Taylor]. I told David he should leave her at home but he said it was good for her to get out.'

I suspect Burton was experiencing those 'flirty eyes' Coward told Hjördis the sedatives gave her.

In November 1960 David returned to England to film interiors of *The Guns of Navarone* at Shepperton. Hjördis went with him to London and began to suspect him of having an affair. She told me, 'David had a "new friend" called Sally [Croker Poole, then married to Lord James Crichton-Stuart]. He took me to her house [in Cromwell Gardens] and she was young and very pretty and that made me think that David would rather have her than me. I wouldn't blame him now, but I did blame him at the time. She laughed at his stories. I never laughed at them. I had heard them so many times before, and always they were different versions. I was having medication at the time and I felt separate from everything. People thought I was strange. Well, I *was* strange, but it was due to the medication, the alcohol, the depression. I was afraid of going anywhere. So I took sedatives to calm me down.'

David admitted to me in 1982 that he did have an affair when in London at that time, but never revealed who it was with. He said, 'I wrecked the marriage. I broke my promise not to have any flings. I think I wanted to wreck the marriage, so I had an affair in England when I was making *Guns of Navarone* and I was so happy that I started thinking about divorcing Hjördis.'

He didn't divorce her because, he said, 'I was desperate not to ever divorce. Call it an insane quirk, but that's how I felt about divorce.'

Despite Hjördis's agoraphobia, David was able to get her sedated enough so they could go to the horse races at Ascot with Greg Peck and his wife Véronique.

Filming the shipwreck scene in Shepperton's large tank was a miserable experience for the whole cast. 'The water was freezing,' said David, 'so Lee Thompson allowed us to drink copious amounts of brandy so we were all slightly pissed except for Greg Peck. He could match us drink for drink, yet he never so much as staggered or slurred his words. It was really quite disgusting to see a man able to handle his liquor like that.'

The scene proved hazardous to film as the actors were thrown about the tank in water stirred up by a wave machine. Peck received a head injury and, worse, Niven cut his lip which turned septic and landed him in hospital. He was gravely ill for two weeks.

The only scene still to be shot was of Niven and Peck rigging the guns to explode. 'While I was dying in hospital,' David told me, 'some Columbia executives flew in from the States to meet Carl Foreman and Lee Thompson to discuss what they would do if and when I died. When I heard this I discharged myself against doctor's orders and we shot the scene in three days. I just about made it through and then I was ill for another seven weeks. The studio brass didn't so much as send me a grape.'

Way down in the cast list of *The Guns of Navarone* was Michael Trubshawe who had one scene but not with Niven. Trubshawe recalled, 'When David saw me on the set, he ignored me. I couldn't understand it. He seemed embarrassed by my presence. He only wanted to be with the bigger stars.' I don't believe David cold-shouldered Trubshawe for that reason. And I was never convinced by Trubshawe's theory that it was because he reminded Niven too much of the past, because Niven was *always* talking about the past. I think it had more to do with the way Trubshawe helped David's marriage to Hjördis get off to a bad start; perhaps he somehow blamed Trubshawe for setting off the almost immediate deterioration.

The Guns of Navarone was a smashing success, the biggest David had since *Around the World in 80 Days*. It would be his last really massive box office hit.

When he finished his final scene, he hastily returned to Château d'Oex to convalesce from his infection. By this time Hjördis was completely incapable of taking care of him. 'When David had been ill and we got home, I didn't sleep with him because he needed to convalesce,' said Hjördis. 'I slept in another room. When he wanted to come to my room, I wouldn't let him in. By then I had lost interest in being intimate.'

David spoke about that time to me:

> It was such a difficult time because I had been ill and then I recovered, but Hjördis was ill *all* the time. People thought she was a hypochondriac – that she only *thought* she was ill. But she was very sick. I'm afraid I got very frustrated and before long I lost patience with her, which was terrible of me. She couldn't help the way she was.
>
> She became ever more crazy, I'm afraid to say. Her behaviour was most erratic. I kept thinking she was a manic depressive, and I had visions of Vivien [Leigh].
>
> I loved the outdoors and went cross country skiing, but she preferred to stay indoors because she was afraid to go out. She liked to sit in the Palace Hotel with some of her friends and play cards all afternoon.

When he recovered from the infection he began a daily exercise regime, walking across country, swimming and skiing. In the town he was welcomed by the locals, often without Hjördis who usually remained at home. When she did go to the Palace Hotel to play gin rummy, she relied on people to pick her up at the front door of her house and get her to the front door of the hotel.

She recalled, 'I would play gin rummy with the few friends I had, but I embarrassed them and everyone because I would suddenly see someone I had never met before, and I'd throw myself at them and kiss them. I was out of my head. David's friends told him I was trying to make him jealous. Maybe I was. I was angry at him. I should have dealt with it much better. I was overcome by compulsions to do these crazy things.'

David now chose to accept films made in Europe because they were so easy to get to and from, and in early 1961 he went to Italy to make *The Best of Enemies*, a World War II tale about an uneasy alliance between a British patrol, led by Niven, and an Italian group of soldiers, led by Alberto Sordi, in the Ethiopian desert. It was a comedy of sorts, directed by Guy Hamilton. Michael Trubshawe had a tiny part, and when he fell ill from the heat, David moved him into his own air-conditioned hotel suite. Niven was always there for a friend when the chips were down.

The film came and went without much fuss or attention. The critics agreed that Niven was perfect for the role. 'Sandhurst-trained David Niven never lets down the light comedy side of officership,' said *Time*. The *Sunday Times* described Alberto Sordi as 'the jewel of the piece' but added, 'One should never underestimate David Niven. He is still one of the most durable of polished comedians.'

When filming was over he returned to Château d'Oex and spent his free time painting and collecting works of art. He hired a butler, an Italian called Bernado who always wore a long white jacket. 'He looked like a milkman,' David told me. 'I thought he looked so funny that I bought him several coats just like that so he would always have one to wear.'

On 18 March 1961 Sir Thomas Comyn-Platt died at the age of 92. David had had little contact with Sir Thomas in recent years and he chose not to go to the funeral, although Grizel and Joyce both went to the memorial service at St James's in Piccadilly. In 1970 David told me, 'When Uncle Tommy died I felt nothing at all. He had never really been a part of my life.'

But in 1982 he said, 'I didn't realise how hard it would hit me when he died. I couldn't let anyone know how I felt, but it was like losing my father all over again. I hardly knew either of my fathers. I think losing him – my *real* father – made me sadder than when the man I had thought was my father died. I wasn't devastated, you understand, but suddenly I was aware that the man who had, frankly, brought me into the world had gone, and it made me think about him and what could have been. It made me think a lot about life and death, family and friends. I knew I had to learn to appreciate more of what I had.'

I think that David regretted that he had never been closer to his real father. Although he dismissed him as his Uncle Tommy and a rather unloving stepfather in his autobiography, David had helped Sir Thomas protect his secret and I think he might well have done that on purpose. There was also, undoubtedly, some bitterness David felt at never being allowed to have a genuine, loving father in his life.

During the summer of 1961, the Nivens, including the boys, went for a holiday to the Côte d'Azur in the South of France. David rented a house there called Lo Scoglietto which was perched on a small peninsula jutting into the Mediterranean. He and Hjördis loved it so much they bought it. She seemed to improve when she was there. She said, 'I felt happier than I had in years. I thought I would get well again, but then David had an affair with a local girl.'

David just couldn't resist the pretty girls and this time the affair had serious consequences.

CHAPTER 20

The Secret Child

In 1970 David told me, 'I thought it would make Hjördis happy if we adopted a child. We talked to friends about the idea and they thought it would be marvellous. Hjördis said she'd love to adopt a Swedish girl, so we did. Her name was Kristina.'

For many years David and Hjördis kept a dark secret. I learned of it in 1982 when David told me, 'She was my own daughter. I want to tell the truth, but I have to do it by writing it as a novel. I couldn't resist a pretty girl. And I was no longer having relations with Hjördis. That part of our marriage was over.'

His novel told the story of a divorced author living in Switzerland who has an affair with an 18-year-old schoolgirl. 'I was going to write how this girl had the author's baby. It was my way of releasing the guilt I have over Kristina. But I can't do it. I can't finish it.'

He allowed me to read some of it. It was based on his own affair with an 18-year-old girl in Château d'Oex who had a baby by him – a little girl. David didn't want the baby to grow up as an unwanted, illegitimate child, but neither did he want to risk a scandal, so he came up with the idea of having Kristina formally adopted by himself and Hjördis. I think the fact that he chose not to shirk his responsibility as a father, even by subterfuge, is admirable. It also reflects his own experience, being brought up as a stepson to someone who was his actual biological father. And I'd like to think, knowing David as I did, that he felt the pull of his own bloodline in that baby which made it impossible for him to reject her. He didn't want to do what Clark Gable had done to his daughter, Judy, by Loretta Young, or what his father had done – he didn't want to deny his own child's existence.

He told me that for some time, he and Hjördis had discussed adopting after it became impossible for her to bear children of her own. Suddenly the need to adopt was very urgent when the girl David had an affair with became pregnant. David knew he had to tell Hjördis the truth and he made her promise never to tell anyone – not even Kristina. The effect upon her was devastating, but she said she felt she had no choice but to go along with the ruse.

> I felt so miserable when I learned the truth. Nobody knew what I was feeling. They all thought I was just a drunken bitch. I *became* a drunken bitch. I had to pretend that I was happy to adopt Kristina. But she was his child by another woman. But, you know, I can look back and realise that he was trying to do the right thing for everyone. He wanted to help the mother of our baby girl, and he wanted me to have a child to raise. His intentions were good. But it all came from his infidelity.
>
> He was so afraid that somebody would know the truth that we kept the adoption a big secret. We wanted Kristina to have a normal life, as normal as is possible when you are David Niven's daughter. Wherever we went in the world, we made sure we were never photographed with her. At airports, she never walked through customs with us. She was always behind us with friends.
>
> When we broke the news that we had adopted her, we said that we were just trying to protect her from the paparazzi. But we were trying to hide the truth.
>
> I tried to cope with everything – all the secrets and the lies. The stress was incredible. I had a hard time dealing with it, and I drank more and more to try and cope, but it didn't make the problem go away. It just turned me into a hopeless drunk again. I was an alcoholic.

Kristina had been born in Geneva on 4 June 1961 and was only a few weeks old when David and Hjördis adopted her. Kristina may not have been Hjördis's very own child, but she came to love her very much.

Because of the success of *The Guns of Navarone*, David was in demand. There were fewer television appearances now and after playing a small gag cameo in the last Bing Crosby/Bob Hope film, *The Road to Hong Kong*, as a Tibetan monk, he made a good drama, *The Guns of Darkness*, set in a South American republic where, as a British planter, he tries to help the ex-president escape from the rebels. His leading lady was Leslie Caron who he didn't get on with, but he worked hard to give director Anthony Asquith a good solid performance. 'I didn't want to be thought of all the time as a light comedy actor,' he told me. 'I had the confidence to try other kinds of roles.'

The *Financial Times* noted, 'David Niven seems continually to improve as an actor.' The *Daily Mail* said, 'The planter is such a convincing figure, a man in agony because he sees and asks too much, that you never think of him as David Niven until the film ends.'

Christmas 1961 started a tradition of spending the winter in Château d'Oex and having Noël Coward and his partner Cole Lesley and their friend Graham Payn over for Boxing Day. Hjördis remembered, 'The best times were Christmas when Noël and Cole and Graham came. Noël always gave me good advice. He helped me get off the pills and to cut down on my drinking, but it would never last.'

The summers were spent at Lo Scoglietto which, over time, became David's favourite of his two homes. 'I miss England,' he told me, 'but I can't afford to live here. The Hollywood I knew has gone. My home is on the Côte d'Azur and in Switzerland.'

Early in 1962 he filmed *The Captive City*, playing a British officer who becomes trapped in a hotel in British liberated Athens when Greek partisan groups attack the city. It's one of Niven's many forgotten films, but not a bad one.

In April Hjördis suffered a horrendous skiing accident. She said it happened because a strange man had been staring at her, and as she skied passed him he whispered 'I love you'. She turned to look over her shoulder to see if he was following and hit a tree. She was knocked unconscious and broke her leg in 15 places.

I asked her how, as an agoraphobic, she was able to go out skiing. She said, 'I was on medication to calm me down which helped, and I was in one of my better times when I could go out. There were days when I felt quite well, and others when I couldn't step out of the door or even get out of bed. I had my niece staying with us and she wanted to go skiing and I wanted to make the effort.'

Despite their crumbling marriage, David was beside himself with worry that she might die and had her flown to Nuffield Orthopaedic Hospital in Oxford in England where she remained for nine months.

In June 1962 he flew alone to Madrid, Spain, to start work on Samuel Bronston's epic about the Chinese Boxer rebellion of 1900, *55 Days at Peking*. It starred Charlton Heston as an American Marine Major, and Ava Gardner as a Russian Countess. David had the role of the British envoy in Peking. It was perfect casting all round – Heston had to be believably heroic, Ava believably beautiful and Niven believably British.

Bronston had spared no costs, building a massive reproduction of Peking on the Spanish plains of Las Matas. The sight of it impressed Niven the moment he saw it. 'It was staggering,' he told me. 'It had everything – the streets, a river, the compound, the Empress's palace. You could get lost in that place. I'd never seen such a realistic set before, or one so huge. It was like the real thing must have been in 1900.'

He remembered touring the Chinese streets with Ava. 'You could go in and out of shops and houses. And everywhere there were real Chinese people. Bronston had emptied every Chinese restaurant in Spain for his Chinese extras. Ava and I managed to get lost and so I thought I'd ask one of the Chinese extras for directions. I knew some very basic Chinese and thought I did a fine job but he didn't understand a word I said. So Ava spoke to him in very good Spanish and he was very happy to show us the way. These were, of course, Spanish-speaking Chinese.'

Although the sets were up, the script was far from ready when they began filming. 'Some of the dialogue was unspeakable – I mean, literally,' David told me. 'Chuck [Heston] and I were rewriting most of our lines to make them sound like real dialogue.'

The responsibility of trying to get his actors to work from a script that was still coming out of the typewriter each day was director Nicholas Ray. 'It was an impossible task for him,' David told me. 'So impossible that he got his wife Betty to write the script. She was a marvellous choreographer but scripts she simply couldn't write. I left it to Chuck Heston to demand that Betty Ray leave the script alone which Nick Ray was rather upset about, but not as upset as Betty was when Chuck told her that her dialogue was complete shit. I have always admired Chuck for that.'

Heston said that working with David was one of the few undiluted pleasures of making *55 Days at Peking*. 'He's a different animal to me. I bury myself in the history of a film like this while David plays the part as written and does it very well. I would say that in that kind of a part he was as good as Alec Guinness and maybe even better than Laurence Olivier could have been, which is saying something.

'We were at a Press gathering – we had a lot of those – at the Bronston studio, and I was earnestly explaining at great length the politics of the Boxer Rebellion to some weary journalist, and I overheard David at the next table talking to his journalist who was roaring with laughter, and I heard David say, "Of course, if we get involved in the politics, we're lost." I thought to myself, why can't I just do that? He's a lovely, funny man.'

Niven, as usual, took it upon himself to keep everyone's spirits up with plenty of laughter. He recalled,

It was a brute of a production. I was lucky. Most of my stuff was indoors, speaking diplomatically while Chuck fought the Chinese Boxers on the walls. But I did insist that I have one good action scene and I convinced Nicholas Ray to let me be a part of a scene where we blow up an armoury.

He looked at me and said, 'David this is tough stuff to do. You could get hurt. Chuck knows how to do this kind of thing.'

I said, 'If I have this right, all I have to do is run like hell before the whole thing explodes, yes?'

So he said, 'Okay, you're in the scene.' We shot it at night, and I was standing with Chuck as we waited for the moment when we lit the fuse and then ran like hell, and I said to him, 'Look, Chuck, I'm getting a bit too old for this sort of thing so don't run too fast or I'll just get left behind.'

He said, 'Don't worry, David, I'll make sure I don't get ahead of you.' We were given the signal for action and I took off and left Heston standing. When he caught up with me, he said, 'I thought you said you couldn't run fast.'

I said, 'My dear Chuck, I said I'm getting a bit too old. I didn't say I couldn't run fast.' He looked bemused for a few moments then laughed loudly and said, 'Let's do it again but this time I'm racing you.' So we did it again and the scene looked splendid.

Without Hjördis in tow, David should have been able to enjoy the comforts of the local Spanish girls, and he may well have, but what I do know for sure is, he spent a lot of personal time with Ava. I know this because she told me. 'David was lonely in Madrid, and so was I. He was worried about Hjördis in hospital and he flew back to England every Sunday to see her. I said to him, "David, you can have any girl in Spain. What's stopping you?" and he said, "I'd feel guilty knowing Hjördis is in a hospital bed." So I said, "How about spending time with me then? Would that make you feel guilty?" He said "Just a little bit."'

I later told David what Ava had said – over lunch in 1980 with him and Lynne Frederick – and he admitted, 'Well, we were old friends and despite many years of trying I had never had any luck with her, and all of a sudden she was inviting me into her bed so I couldn't say no, could I?'

To his astonishment, I replied, 'You could have?' That was the one time David got irritated with me. He expected all his male companions to see his sexual adventures as great sport.

I recall that he frowned and said rather sternly, 'The trouble with you, Mike, is you're so bloody virtuous.' Then, looking slightly embarrassed and, I think, looking for a way out of the hole he had just dug for himself, he took Lynne by the hand and said, 'I know you're only just widowed, my dear, but see what you can do about seducing him, for God's sake,' to which she replied, 'I have and he won't.'

He looked at me, shocked, and asked, 'What's stopping you?'

'Being married,' I said. He just didn't understand that.

Back in 1962 while making *55 Days at Peking*, David and Ava needed each other for more than a romp in bed. They were both shocked when they heard the news that Marilyn Monroe had been found dead. Frank Sinatra had telephoned Ava with the news and had told her he was launching his own investigation because he wasn't convinced it was the suicide the police were dismissing it as.

Ava once told me that David said he felt terrible because he had used Monroe like so many other men in Hollywood had, and he was shocked to think she might have killed herself because of the way she had been treated in Hollywood.

As for Ava, she was fearful for Sinatra, and she became anxious, tearful and at times irrational on the set. Many, especially Charlton Heston, saw this as unprofessional behaviour, and he and Nicholas Ray grew impatient with her. Then, on 11 September, with more than a month still to go on production, Ray had a heart attack. It wasn't fatal but he was unable to finish the picture. Second unit director Andrew Marton concentrated on the battle scenes, of which there were many and didn't involve Niven, and Guy Green arrived to take over the film. David helped Ava pull herself together and she surprised Heston by behaving more professionally. He thought she was feeling guilty about Nick Ray's heart attack, but her change in behaviour was due in large part to David's patience and kindness to her, given in private, even in bed.

55 Days at Peking was generally derided by the critics at the time it was released in 1963 but, like many of the super productions of the 1960s, today it stands up as a fine example of epic film making that has become a lost craft; many of today's critics who are used to computer generated images that create explosions and extras in their thousands, are impressed at what the film makers of the past were capable of achieving.

His next film, *The Pink Panther*, oddly enough, doesn't stand up so well. It is, of course, the film that introduced bumbling Inspector Clouseau created by Peter Sellers. But Clouseau was only a supporting character. David Niven was the star, as jewel thief Sir Charles Lytton, known as 'The Phantom'. Niven began work on it, in Italy, as soon as he had finished helping to defend Peking for 55 days.

The Pink Panther wasn't as funny as it might have seemed on paper and its saving grace was Sellers as Clouseau. It is Peter Sellers' contribution to the film that made it a success which both pleased and irritated David. He told me, 'I thought this was going to be an improvement on the Raffles idea, and I was going to get to play a Raffles character in a major film made by a good director. We had beautiful Capucine and Claudia Cardinale, and we had Robert Wagner who became one of my very best friends, and we had Peter Sellers. But as I watched him on the set and saw how Blake Edwards [the director] would go into uncontrollable laughter on every take, I knew I was not going to win. It was Peter Sellers' film. So I took the money, bent over and took it like man. The film was a hit and I was in it which counted.'

Over the lunch I had with David and Sellers' widow Lynne Frederick in 1980, David told us, 'I remember Peter coming to me and saying, "Look here David, this idiot I'm playing is going to ruin this picture and I don't know what to do about it." So I said, "Are you mad, Peter? You're the best thing in this film." He said, "But maybe I should do it differently. I should get Blake to reshoot all my scenes." I said, "Don't you dare. I need a hit film. I'm counting on you." He wasn't at all sure I was right. But look what happened.'

The film was a huge hit and David was right about Sellers. As the film critic in the *News of the World* observed, 'I never thought someone would steal a picture from that old professional David Niven, but it's happened, so help me.'

The film spawned several sequels featuring Peter Sellers as Inspector Clouseau, all of them an improvement on the original, concentrating on Sellers' genius as the bumbling French detective. For David, alas, it was his last success for a while as he made a series of mediocre films that could have brought his career to a premature end if it wasn't for one thing – his tremendous success with his first autobiography.

—

CHAPTER 21

A Sham Marriage

Hjördis returned home from hospital early in 1963. It had been a long stay but she had been treated for more than just her physical injuries. David told me, 'She needed help with her drinking and anxiety problems. She was getting through so much vodka but then she started on that awful Fernet Branca. The place would smell of Fernet Branca. She loved that terrible stuff.'

I had no idea what Fernet Branca was until Hjördis told me in 1986. 'It's a very strong alcoholic drink. I was told it would help to clean my system, like some kind of drain cleaner.' She laughed and said, 'What a fool I was.'

Her long stay in hospital did do her some good. 'I was getting some very good help then, not just for my broken leg,' she said. 'I was getting help for my depression and anxiety. So I was there for many months, and David came to see me every Sunday, but I was on my own the rest of the time while he was spending the summer playing around again, having flings with young pretty girls.'

I don't believe she ever knew about David's affair with Ava in Spain but she was well aware that he was seeing other women. 'I got my revenge,' she said. 'Jack Kennedy wanted a quickie, and I gave him a quickie.' This happened, apparently, when the Nivens went to the White House in Washington to join in the celebrations for President Kennedy's 46th birthday. Hjördis said, 'He gave me a disease. Chlamydia. It taught me that revenge is not the solution. After that I just got worse. Drinking more, rejecting David. I felt like I was tumbling downward and didn't know how to get back up. Sometimes I was able to pull myself together and behave when we were with other people.

'I tried to behave with the boys. I tried to get on with them. The best times were when David was away filming. But when he came home for the weekends, we quarrelled. I think I had become so suspicious and jealous of what he would have been getting up to that whenever I saw him come home something inside me just made me want to be angry at him. But I think I got on well with the boys when he wasn't there.'

JFK had his birthday bash and a quickie from Hjördis during the time David was making his first film in America since *Please Don't Eat the Daises*. *Bedtime Story* teamed Niven with Marlon Brando. The off-beat casting generated a great deal of publicity and the two actors got on remarkably well. Niven kept Brando laughing throughout production and David said he enjoyed making the film. 'People think Marlon has no sense of humour,' he told me. 'He has a *wonderful* sense of humour. He told the funniest stories and was never anything but pleasant and friendly.'

They played conmen preying on attractive women. The critics hated it. The *Daily Express* called it 'the most vulgar and embarrassing film of the year'. The *Observer* noted, 'The film was shot, unfortunately not fatally, by Clifford Stine.'

In September David joined Charles Boyer, Robert Coote, Gladys Cooper and Gig Young in New York to launch a new Four Star series called *The Rogues*. They each played members of an international organisation of conmen preying on the rich all over the world. It was a tremendously successful series in which David appeared in seven episodes. 'I thoroughly enjoyed doing it,' he said, 'because I was able to play a part that was both Raffles and The Phantom from *The Pink Panther*, and this time I was able to do a good job of it.'

The Rogues was the last TV drama Niven did for 10 years as he spent the rest of the 1960s going through a series of films that ranged from mediocre to downright awful. In *Where the Spies Are* in 1965 he played a British secret agent called Dr Jason Love. It was made when producers were cashing in on the success of the James Bond films but this was a poor imitation, although Alexander Walker of the London *Evening Standard* liked it; 'A vintage star as engagingly witty and implausibility-proof as Mr Niven is worth any Bond-man's arsenal of booby-trapped accessories and machine-made death traps. I welcome him like a flesh-and-blood transfusion in a kind of film that is now tottering under the weight of its own gimmickry.' The film wasn't successful enough to spawn sequels.

Lady L starred Sophia Loren as a woman who goes from being a poor laundress to a rich widow. David played one of her numerous lovers, and his friend Peter Ustinov wrote and directed the film. It proved to be an expensive flop.

The films got worse. *Eye of the Devil* in 1966, co-starring Deborah Kerr, was a horror film which the *Sunday Times* said was 'hilariously bad'.

Worst of all was *Casino Royale*, an unofficial James Bond movie made as a comedy which nobody understood. John Huston, who directed some of it, never understood it, neither did Peter Sellers, nor George Raft or Orson Welles who were among the cast members I personally knew, and neither did Deborah Kerr and David Niven. It was, said the *Guardian*, 'a big colour-ful, noisy, star-studded, plot-less junk pile of a mess'.

There followed *The Extraordinary Seaman* in 1968, an anti-war satire. Marjorie Bilbow writing in *Today's Cinema* said, 'Anyone looking forward to David Niven, Faye Dunaway and Mickey Rooney will be sadly disappointed.'

David co-starred with Deborah Kerr again, in *Prudence and the Pill* in 1968. *Time* called it a 'cretinous comedy', and the *New York Times* said of the stars, 'because their parts are unendurable they give the worst, worst performances of their lives.'

Niven was accepting anything offered to him just for the money. *The Impossible Years* in 1968 was about the generation gap which the *Times* thought to be 'of a dreariness which not even the usually saving presence of David Niven and Lola Albright, as the troubled parents, can alleviate'.

Before Winter Comes in 1969 saw him as a British officer running a refugee camp in Austria in the spring of 1945. *Time* was unimpressed by what it considered to be 'vague plot, conventional camera-work and a feeble scenario'.

He went to France to make *Le Cerveau*, known in America and Britain as *The Brain*. Niven played a gentleman master criminal and the brain behind the British Great Train Robbery.

David had no excuse for making such bad films other than for the money. 'I needed to pay for the lifestyle I enjoyed,' he said to me. He particularly enjoyed lavishly entertaining people at Château d'Oex and also on the Côte d'Azur. He was at his happiest when friends came to visit, but despite Hjördis's long stay in hospital, she had deteriorated again and was becoming an embarrassment.

'I have always enjoyed entertaining guests,' he said. 'I like to have lunch parties at home. She started leaving the table before anyone else and going to her room. She hardly ever ate. I don't understand how she hasn't starved herself to death. Eventually she stopped coming down to join me and our guests.'

Hjördis denied that she starved herself, although she did grow thinner. She didn't know it at the time but she had an eating disorder. 'Of course I ate,' she said in 1986. 'I had a good breakfast every morning, but not much else in the day. Food would make me feel sick.'

She was paranoid about eating in front of other people. 'I couldn't face people. I couldn't face eating. I'd stay in my room, drinking, making telephone calls. I hardly went out. Going out was sometimes the most terrifying thing for me. I had panic attacks going outside. I had panic attacks in the night. I was on Valium, and when you take that you shouldn't drink because it can kill you. It is a wonder I am still alive.'

David found it increasingly difficult to cope with her. He told me in 1980, 'I wanted to love her, and I did, and I still do, but often I just want to get out of the house and get away from her. She isn't good company, and she can't do anything. What she can do is make herself look very good, and she can arrange flowers. But that's all.'

One person who did like Hjördis was Princess Grace who became most concerned about her and wanted to help. David recalled, 'Grace said to me, "I'll talk *men* with her. Just girl talk." I said, "*Any* kind of talk. Please, Grace, just do *something*."'

Hjördis told me, 'One of my best friends was Grace. I felt comfortable with her. We talked a lot about men. She was a very naughty girl, you know. She had a lot of affairs in Hollywood. She had an affair with David.'

But David admitted to me that he had to take the blame for many of Hjördis's troubles, although he was not to blame for the childhood trauma that was the root cause of all her problems. He said he was the one who strayed long before she started taking lovers. He was even unfaithful to Primmie. That was his fatal character flaw.

But he didn't give up on Hjördis. She told me, 'David asked me what would make me happy. I said I couldn't just *be* happy. But I thought that adopting another girl would help. We found a beautiful little baby girl, just four months old, and an orphan. We called her Fiona.

'I had really grown to love Kristina. It was hard at first because of the circumstances, but it wasn't her fault, and I really loved her, and I loved Fiona right from the start. I wasn't a good mother. I had no real idea what a mother does, but I made sure they were always dressed very nicely. The best French clothes. I was so proud of them. Having the girls helped me a lot. Things were better between David and I, and we started to laugh together a lot more.'

Fiona was adopted in December 1963. She was four months old. By this time David's sons were living in America. David Jnr was working in New York at the William Morris Agency, and Jamie, 18 years of age, was about to go to Harvard University. David saw very little of his sons as he was so busy making films in Europe.

In 1966 David started to write his autobiography. What he really wanted to do was write a novel but his friend Jamie Hamilton encouraged him to write his own life story and said he was enthusiastic to publish it. Writing *The Moon's a Balloon* was to prove to be a long and difficult process for David who, despite wanting desperately to be a successful author, found the process of writing harder than acting. He was almost relieved to set aside work on his book every time he took off to make another film. Two years after he started writing his memoir, Hamilton wrote to him asking how the book was coming along and Niven admitted it was not coming on at all well.

His friends, his two daughters, his painting and his films – as bad as many of those films were – were the things that made Niven happy but Hjördis was bringing him nothing but misery. 'I had been thinking again about divorcing her but things improved when we had the girls,' he said in 1980. 'Friends have often said I should just leave her, but they don't know how fragile she is. I wanted to leave her often but I thought that if I did it would not only destroy her but perhaps the girls as well. There was no way out. Now, I think it's till death do us part.'

Hjördis's health deteriorated further. She said,

> I had blackouts. I was told they were epileptic fits. I was so scared of having a fit that I preferred to just stay at home. I could swim and I liked to paint. But I was in fear of blacking out. People thought I blacked out because I drank heavily, but one of the reasons I drank so much was to *stop* the fits. Richard Burton had fits and he told me that alcohol helped to stop them. So I drank more.
>
> I took lovers. I was sick and tired of David's infidelity. I didn't want him to make love to me, but I needed to have intimacy. I shut him out. We were our own worse enemies to each other.
>
> I have to say, though, he was a wonderful father. Not perfect, no father is perfect. What he did for the children was buy them presents, make them laugh when he was with them. But he was away a lot making movies.

David admitted that he had once harboured thoughts that Hjördis might actually solve all their problems for them both by dying. 'I was convinced that she would kill herself, and then I wouldn't have to divorce her. Isn't that terrible, to think that? But you do think terrible things when life is so bad.'

She made an attempt to be a good mother to her girls. She said she knew she fell far short, but she tried. 'I played games with my girls. I played gin rummy and canasta with Kristina. I think I made them laugh. Kristina understands my sense of humour.

'I used to wear a little disc around my neck that said I was allergic to penicillin. So I had it engraved, "I am always allergic to penicillin and sometimes also to my husband." It was a joke. Some laughed. Some gasped in horror.'

She gladly credited David as being the parent who successfully raised the girls, and she had accepted, by 1986, that her daughters may even have grown to hate her.

> I can understand if they feel I wasn't a good mother. I tried not to let my illness concern them. I had trouble showing my love to my girls. I had trouble being intimate with them. David was able to hug and kiss them. I had trouble being intimate with my own children.
>
> When the girls went to school, David took them and collected them. I wanted to, but I couldn't get out of the house. When Kristina was older she tried to get me to go out with her. Just to get out of the house. To go and have lunch. But I got more and more frightened of leaving the house.
>
> I know you shouldn't play favourites, and I do love both my girls. But I think Kristina understood me more, and perhaps I felt that because she had David's blood she was almost my own. It's very painful now for me to think how I could have done everything better. I just have to accept things. I'm a recovering alcoholic and I have forgiven David for all he did – and I'm trying to forgive myself.

In March 1969 David made a concerted effort to concentrate on his book by taking a break from films. Jamie Hamilton was delighted with the first two chapters but progress was slow and there was little more to read by November when David flew to England to make a film that ended up being cancelled because of industrial unrest at the British film studios. Convinced his film career was at an end, he spent the winter at Château d'Oex writing.

In April 1970 he flew to Rome to film *The Statue*. He played a professor whose wife, a sculptress, produces a huge statue of him but with genitals which are not his, and so he sets about trying to find out who they belong to. 'Not for prudes, but a fast-moving package of fun,' wrote William Hall in London's *Evening News*. The *Daily Express* disagreed; 'I am happy to say that David Niven looks thoroughly uncomfortable about the whole sorry business.'

He wasn't uncomfortable at all. He told me, 'I had fun making it. I *always* try to have fun, otherwise what would be the point? If people go to see it and enjoy it, that's a bonus.'

Throughout 1970 Jamie Hamilton urged him to finish the book, but he still hadn't completed it when he came to London later in the year, which was when I first met him. He didn't even mention the book to me and when I reminded him of that some years later, he said, 'I didn't think it was worth mentioning because I wasn't at all sure I would ever finish it.'

I did find out about it, however, when my managing director Ron Lee read the transcript of the lengthy interview I had done with him and thought it could be the basis of a book. In reply to Ron Lee's letter asking if he would object if I wrote his biography, David very kindly wrote, 'I would have been delighted to give my permission if it wasn't for the fact that someone far less creative and yet infuriatingly lazy is already at it as we speak. To be frank, me!'

David later told me that he was convinced that his autobiography was doomed because he thought it was incredibly dull. Jamie Hamilton didn't think so; he wrote to David to tell him that everyone in his office who had read the finished chapters thought it was hilarious and entertaining. Showbiz columnist Roddy Mann even convinced his own literary agent, George Greenfield, to take Niven on as a client. David, who had once been insecure as an actor, was now highly insecure as an author.

George Greenfield discovered that Cresset Press, who published *Round the Rugged Rocks*, had the first option to buy his next book. Greenfield wrote to Cresset, telling them he was Niven's agent and that Niven had written a very long manuscript, written by hand, full of rambling reminiscences, and asked if Cresset wanted to read it. They said they didn't, leaving the way open for Jamie Hamilton to publish it.

David finished the book at the end of February 1971 and was rewarded with a cheque for £7,500 as an advance on royalties. Although the book was very entertaining, it needed a lot of editorial work. Whole chunks were cut, which David objected to, but several years later, David told me that if it hadn't been for a man called Roger Machell who edited the book, 'it would never have been the success it is.'

The book's title, *The Moon's a Balloon*, had no relevance to anything in the book but was simply a line from a poem by E.E. Cummings which begins, 'Who knows if the moon's a balloon?' It simply appealed to him.

He got back to his main career, acting, and starred with Gina Lollobrigida in *King, Queen, Knave* as a husband and wife who take in his teenage nephew, played by John Moulder Brown. The young man and his stepmother become lovers and together they plan to murder the uncle. The film, directed by Jerzy Skolimowski, was admired by some critics. 'It would have been hard to predict that David Niven, Gina Lollobrigida and John Moulder Brown would have teamed so brilliantly in Skolimowski's idiosyncratic style of farce,' said the *Times*. The *Observer* thought it was 'made with grace and style'. But it didn't appeal to the public and became another of Niven's obscure films.

The Moon's a Balloon was published in October 1971 at which time Niven attended a launch party for book critics, columnists and booksellers but spent most of his time talking to the booksellers because he knew they were the ones he needed to impress the most. He had them roaring with laughter at his stories and they went away determined the book would be a best seller.

The reviews were literally raves, but it was his TV appearance on the *Michael Parkinson Show*, which I went to, that sealed the book's success. The next day sales rocketed and the book was reprinted. It stayed at number one on the bestseller lists for weeks and was reprinted again.

He was eager to write another book but he was adamant that it would be a novel. However, G.P. Putnam, who published *The Moon's a Balloon* in America, urged him to write a second memoir, detailing the golden age of Hollywood. They offered him a large advance to do so which he accepted and so began writing *Bring on the Empty Horses*. He told me he only accepted Putnam's offer because he wanted the money.

Now he was a successful author and told me when we met up in 1971, 'I think being an author has brought me more satisfaction than being an actor ever did.'

While he had great joy as an author, he had great misery in his marriage. After I first met Hjördis on the second day I spent with David in 1970, he told me, quite casually, 'Hjördis has a boyfriend. She's had a lover for years.'

She made no apology about taking a lover. She said, 'What was the point of not having a lover? Our marriage was a sham. Our marriage was a mistake. It didn't work well from the start. David suffocated me. He couldn't help being who he was. He couldn't help it if girls threw themselves at him.'

'But he could have resisted,' I said. 'There are some Hollywood stars who have stayed faithful.'

She laughed and said, 'Tell me who they are. I will marry them.'

David was now earning more money than he had ever done. The royalties from *The Moon's a Balloon* were rolling in, he had a good advance for *Bring on the Empty Horses*, and he earned £40,000 in 1972 for making a series of TV commercials for a Japanese deodorant. His usual fee to make a film was around $200,000.

He was also much in demand as a speaker and gave a series of lectures in America in October 1972 which not only earned him good money but also continued to boost sales of his book.

Christmas of 1972 was a sad one. Noël Coward had died on 26 March that year, and the joy he brought to the Nivens each Boxing Day was gone forever. Said Hjördis, 'We were so fond of Noël. His wit and charm made each Boxing Day special. Without him, it was empty.'

The next time I saw David was in April 1973, when he came to London to promote the paperback edition of *The Moon's a Balloon* with a second appearance on the *Michael Parkinson Show*. I was again fortunate to be in the audience, and I met David the next day for lunch. I was still a publicist at Cinerama with aspirations to do greater things, and he encouraged me, 'Be a writer. There's nothing to it.' I told him I was, having worked with Sheridan Morley on a script for John Huston. That impressed David no end, and I think from then he had a high regard for me.

I saw him again in London in July of that year when he was making *Vampira*, a horror spoof in which he played Count Dracula. I hung around the set for a few days at David's invitation, watching him for the first time at work as an actor. He was always smiling, making people laugh, and generally enjoying the whole experience. He would arrive each morning and say good morning to everyone – not just actors but all the crew. That impressed me.

On the set David found a use for me. He nearly always rewrote his dialogue simply to make his lines more suited to his style of delivery – something a lot of actors do – but he was having trouble with some lines so he asked me to help. I made some suggestions and he was delighted with them. He got me to do the same for him later on *Candleshoe*, *A Man Called Intrepid* and *A Nightingale Sang in Berkeley Square* because he came to trust me as someone with an ear for his style of delivery.

In between takes on the *Vampira* set, he talked to me about his children whom he had not really mentioned much before. Kristina was then 12 and at a Swiss boarding school, Le Rosey. Fiona was eight and at school, of course. David Jnr was 30 and now an executive of Columbia Films in London, which may be why Columbia picked up the distribution rights for *Vampira*, a film nobody else wanted to release. Jamie was 22 and finding success at an investment company in New York. 'So far David is the only one who's gone into this awful business,' Niven said.

'The girls still might,' I suggested.

'I hope to God not.'

'Why?'

'Because I know the kind of men they'd meet in this business. Men like *me*.'

I worked on the publicity of *Vampira* because when it finally got a release in 1974, I was at Columbia-Warner which was distributing the film in the UK. The director of publicity for Columbia asked me if I could pull some strings and get Niven to come and promote the film. I tried but David said, 'The film is a dud, of course, like all of them are now. I'm really too busy writing.' And I couldn't blame him.

I suggested to the publicity director he try talking to David Jnr but it turned out he had moved on to Paramount by then.

For Christmas 1973 David took the family on a holiday to Kenya. It was, Hjördis later told me, an effort to get her into a totally different environment where she might stop, or cut down, drinking, and get over her agoraphobia. But neither illness is that easy to overcome.

In January 1974, Sam Goldwyn died, aged 91. The news hit David hard, despite the many battles he had had with him. It also made David acutely aware of his own mortality. Hjördis recalled, 'Noël Coward died and then Sam Goldwyn died. It scared David. He said he couldn't even bear to think about dying. He said, "I've more years behind me than I have ahead."'

In July he returned to England to appear in a television production of *The Canterville Ghost* by Oscar Wilde. It was recorded in Bristol for Harlech Television. Then he went straight to Malaysia to make a film, *Paper Tiger*, playing a teacher of English on a Pacific island whose only pupil is the young son of the Japanese ambassador. Niven's character claims to have had a distinguished military past which has resulted in a damaged leg. But when he and the boy are kidnapped by a guerrilla group, he proves to be a fake. He does, however, summon up the courage in the end to save the boy in what turns out to be the one true heroic moment in his life.

Paper Tiger was filmed in Kuala Lumpur, in the Genting Highlands of Malaysia, and Malacca over a long and tiring 10 week schedule. He arrived in Kuala Lumpur accompanying a beautiful Swedish air stewardess whom he had gallantly rescued from a groping passenger on board the aeroplane. Apparently, David actually hit the man, or maybe he just pushed him back into his seat. Whatever the actual truth, the stewardess accepted her hero's invitation to join him in his suite at the Hilton Hotel.

The film was directed by Ken Annakin who I interviewed in London when *Paper Tiger* opened in 1975. He told me, 'David Niven was the very first choice for the role of the teacher. It's very much the sort of character that he played in *Separate Tables*, and the moment he read the script he jumped at it. I personally think he's a marvellous actor. We were very lucky in having one of the nicest and most co-operative actors in the world today, and that set the standard so that everybody behaved well.'

Annakin was also lucky to get the great Japanese star Toshiro Mifune to play the ambassador, and he found a small Japanese boy, Ando, to play the pupil who hero-worships his English teacher. Annakin said, 'Every evening at around seven o'clock, David spent an hour with Ando, who couldn't speak a word of English at the start, teaching him to play games which helped Ando to learn some English and to be comfortable with David. I don't know of any other actor who would have bothered to do that, and Ando became devoted to David, and you can see that in the film.'

David spent some of his free time working on his new book. When he went off to film in the jungle of the Genting Highlands he left all his notes and diaries he was using for the book in the production office at the Holiday Inn in Kuala Lumpur. A fire broke out, the production office burned down and David lost all his notes and diaries. He hadn't enjoyed the location at all, but this was the last straw. He told me, 'It was the most miserable two months I can remember ever making a picture.'

There were compensations, though. He was paid $250,000 to make the film, and he enjoyed the company of a number of young ladies. Ken Annakin told me, 'About two days before we were due to finish filming, his back went and he collapsed in agony. When he got home he told Hjördis that he had hurt his back when I made him climb up mountains. We never made him climb any mountains. I know why his back went!'

David turned in one of his very best performances. He said, 'It was an easy part for me. All my life I've been pretending to be other people.' The critics were divided in their opinion. Patrick Gibbs wrote in the *Daily Telegraph*, 'I was left feeling strongly that of all the cards Mr Niven holds, pathos is not one of them.'

In the *Daily Mail* Margaret Hinxman wrote, 'Niven's elegance and style make you feel the character is not a nonsense, but a man at odds with a conscience the existence of which he had long forgotten.'

Tom Hutchinson of the *Sunday Telegraph* didn't like the film but did like Niven. 'What saves it all from absolute tepidity is David Niven's portrayal as Bradbury with a quotation for every situation and an excuse for every possible danger. The wary eye beneath the forehead's corrugations tells us the man has lived life at second-hand but would hate to be thought as second-rate. It is a satisfying example of combined star-quality and acting skill.'

It's a film worth catching solely because of Niven's performance, and if not taken as anything more than a simple-minded adventure yarn suitable for a family audience, the movie works well.

David came back to London in October 1974 with Hjördis, and I was invited for lunch. Hjördis said she remembered me from our first brief meeting in 1970 and tried making a joke: 'I'm glad to see that David's friends are getting younger and are not always girls.'

David said to me later, 'She meant that most of my friends are old or dying or dead.'

I said, 'Yes, I realised.'

'She has trouble sometimes making herself understood because she thinks in Swedish and when it comes out in English the words are not always quite right. It's her jokes, mainly. They go down like lead balloons with some people.'

When we had some time alone, David asked me, 'Did you notice her eyes?'

'In what way?'

'She was flirting with you.'

'She was?'

'Didn't you notice?'

I said, 'I thought her eyes made her look like she was stoned.'

'She probably was. Sedatives, old bean. I think she looks at men and flirts but she says it's the pills that make her do that.'

I couldn't honestly say if she was flirting with me – I certainly hadn't felt that she was – but I had noticed that she looked sedated.

From London they went to Leeds to attend a charity ball organised by Roger Moore. Hjördis remembered it as an example of how her sense of humour generally bombed. 'The MC was on stage, and he said, "We are all very grateful to David Niven who has come all this way even though he is so busy. So I said, "What about me? I've come too." Some laughed. Some gasped. I could never win.'

Many of David's friends were urging him to leave her but he had made up his mind that was not an option. He told me, 'If I left her, she'd be a drunk in the gutter. I used to leave leaflets from Alcoholics Anonymous around the house. I hoped she'd get the message. She didn't.'

He continued to have numerous love affairs and rented a flat in London to carry them out. I went there in 1975 and met a beautiful woman in her 20s. David tried to encourage me to have affairs also, even though I had been married for only two years. I told him it was out of the question. He said, 'But it's essential. You'll see. In time it will get boring and you'll need to find a little adventure with other girls.'

I didn't share his philosophy but I never criticised him for it. With David, you just accepted that's what he was like. I thought it was terribly sad to see his marriage in such a state but, frankly, it was now completely unfixable.

In March 1975 he finally finished *Bring on the Empty Horses* which was less a memoir and more of a book of insights and anecdotes about stars from the Golden Age of Hollywood. It was written as he would have spoken it, like a superb raconteur who was an insider rather than an observer.

Roger Machell at Hamilton did a great deal of work editing the manuscript before it was published. David had resisted changes to *The Moon's a Balloon* and he resisted even harder with this book. He talked about his frustration over the editing of the book when I interviewed him in 1979. 'I sweated blood writing the damn thing. You invest so much into it, and then they tell you that they need to change things. It's soul destroying at times, it really is. They make you feel as though you're a terrible writer and that they have to make you look better than you are.'

Unwilling to wait for film work that might never come, David went to Africa, Mexico and Nepal to make two documentaries, *Around the World* and one for the *Survival* TV series. He also provided his voice talents for a cartoon, *The Remarkable Rocket*.

In July 1975, just as he must have been thinking that there wouldn't be another film to follow *Paper Tiger*, he went to Hollywood to make a Disney production, *No Deposit, No Return*, a comedy thriller in which he played a millionaire whose two grandchildren are kidnapped.

He didn't much enjoy working for Disney and told me four years later, 'The ghost of Walt must haunt the place. Everyone is still afraid of him even though he's been dead for years. Every time I made a suggestion to the director, he said, "Oh no, Walt wouldn't have liked that." It was impossible.'

The director, Norman Tokar, might have done well to listen to Niven's suggestion. Like most of Disney's live action films of the 1970s, it was tedious and, at 112 minutes, overlong. Philip French, writing in *The Times*, said, 'Once again one is left wondering why there should be such an unbridgeable gulf between the brilliant professionalism and sometimes innovative genius of the Disney animated films, and the dull artlessness of the majority of their live-action pictures.'

David was glad to get home in time to see Fiona join Kristina at Le Rosey in September. Later that month he flew to England to promote *Bring on the Empty Horses* and again appeared on the *Michael Parkinson Show* which again I watched live – it was an hysterical show and was much talked about. David was now better known as a raconteur and an author than he was for his films. I don't think he minded that too much, but he was hurt by one review of *Paper Tiger* from Russell Davies of the *Observer* who wrote, 'David Niven's recent book has saved him from relegation to the battered figurine department, making his shabby-genteel presence about as well known now as it ever has been.'

He was further hurt by poor reviews of the new book in Britain. It was, said Graham Lord in the *Sunday Express* 'something of a disappointment'. He was better served by the American critics. Bill Buckely of the *New York Times* wrote, 'This might easily be the best book ever written about Hollywood.' The book sold a million and a half copies in two weeks and was at the top of the *New York Times* bestseller list for 18 weeks.

Hjördis came in for a lot of criticism from David's friends because she never read his books. She told me, 'Why did I need to? I knew all the stories. I'd heard them all a hundred times.'

I told her that I knew David had felt terribly rejected.

'I know,' she said. 'I should have read them. But when you live with a man who tells everyone the same stories, and you have become bored hearing them, you can't *read* them as well. But I should have read his books because I was his wife. But there again, that is the thing – I was *just* his wife. I think people like Jack Hawkins and Roger Moore were very lucky because their wives were happy to be who they were. That is good for them. It wasn't good for me.

'But, oh God, I *should* have read his books. It would have been no great sacrifice.'

CHAPTER 22

No Reprieve

At the end of September David flew to Hollywood to appear with a starry cast in *Murder by Death*, a really good crime spoof written by Neil Simon. Niven, Peter Sellers, Maggie Smith and Peter Falk played characters all based on famous literary crime fighters such as Miss Marple, Philip Marlow and Hercule Poirot. I liked it, but not many critics did. Dilys Powell wrote in the *Sunday Times*, 'It seems to me that if you haven't watched the real Thin Man and the real Bogie in the real *Maltese Falcon* you won't see the joke; and if you have watched them, the joke is not good enough.'

The public disagreed with the critics and the film made a nice profit of $27 million.

Despite his displeasure with his first Disney film, David made another for that company, *Candleshoe*, shot in England at Pinewood Studios in 1976 where I interviewed him. He seemed a lot happier on his second Disney film and was able to make changes to some of his dialogue, some of it with my help. He also enthused about one of his co-stars: 'We have this wonderful young actress called Jodie Foster [then 14 years old]. She told me that she really prefers to work with adults rather than children but only if they remember their lines.'

He also enjoyed the challenge of playing several parts – a butler, an Irish chauffeur, a Scottish gardener, a cook called Miss Oglethorpe and an old colonel. He hoped it would be likened to *Kind Hearts and Coronets*. It wasn't even close.

In October he finished *Candleshoe* and went to Lo Scoglietto on the

Côte d'Azur and began work on his next book; this time he was determined it would be a novel.

He hit the promotional rounds again in England in February 1977 with the paperback publication of *Bring on the Empty Horses*. He was still doubting his abilities as a writer, and said, 'I've done so well so far but what if the next book is a disaster?'

He admitted that he had come to hate the promotional tours. In fact, I noticed he was a lot less jovial than usual. It might be that he was getting old and was feeling his age and resenting it. There was definitely a loss of the old Niven sparkle.

Much of it was, of course, to do with Hjördis. His friends continued to blame her for all their troubles. David knew that he had to bear much of the responsibility and he tried, periodically, to do something about it, but Hjördis, by her own admission, was out of reach. 'By the late 70s I was so withdrawn from everything,' she said. 'I felt lost. I felt empty. If I had been brave enough I would have killed myself. And I didn't want David to be a widower a second time. I did love him. I think he loved me. But we couldn't reach each other. No, he couldn't reach *me*. I was out of reach. It would have been better if he had left me. I wouldn't have blamed him.'

Life had become so intolerable that David actually considered killing her. He told me in 1980, 'I came home one night and found her drunk in the bath, unable to get out. I thought she would drown. I thought about pushing her down. Oh God, I wanted her to die.'

'Are you glad you didn't do it?' I asked.

'Oh God, yes! How could I live with *that*?'

David finally made up his mind to leave her. He told me, 'There was someone I thought I could be happy with.' He said he postponed telling her he was leaving until after he had finished his next film, *Death on the Nile*. He flew to Egypt in October 1977 to make the first film in which Peter Ustinov, Niven's old friend, played Hercule Poirot.

'Egypt can be a wonderful, beautiful and fascinating country,' he said. 'But what was so awful were the flies. They are everywhere…all the time. You had to stay out of the sun because it got to around 130 degrees. Everyone was coming down with tummy trouble. I'd been prepared for that and ordered hampers from Fortnum's to be flown to Cairo. It didn't help. I was riding a camel when I felt suddenly very ill. A very inconvenient place to be when you suddenly need to rush to the nearest toilet – on a camel.'

While he was in Egypt, Kristina, aged 16, drove her boyfriend's BMW along an icy road and crashed into a tree. The boyfriend was unhurt but Kristina suffered a smashed skull, a broken leg and a punctured lung. She was taken by helicopter to Lausanne General Hospital where she slipped into a coma which lasted eight days.

As soon as David heard the news, he flew home. Hjördis recalled,

> I had never seen David so distressed. He was terrified she would die. He would have felt the same if it had happened to Fiona, but Kristina was his blood daughter. In just a week he lost much weight. He wasn't the same man for a while. He didn't tell jokes. He didn't tell stories. Normally, if there was a crisis, he'd have the old British stiff upper lip. But this was different.
>
> I too was afraid she would die. My only way to deal with it was to withdraw ever more into myself, wherever that was – it was a dark, lonely place; I hated it there. And I drank and drank.
>
> We stayed at the Beau Rivage Hotel in Lausanne. Some friends came over to be with us. I'm afraid I was too drunk to hardly notice them.
>
> David wanted to hold me. Or he wanted me to hold him. I couldn't. I was unable to hold him and give him the comfort he needed. I needed comfort too but I was out of reach.
>
> From the distance I put myself, I saw him become a frail old man. When he knew she would live, there was then the fear she would be crippled.

After Kristina came out of the coma, she was operated on to relieve the pressure of blood on her brain. She also received treatment from an English physiotherapist, David Bolton, who was practising in Gstaad.

David still had to finish *Death on the Nile* and returned to Egypt. Peter Ustinov recalled in 1984 that when he saw David 'he was suddenly very frail. I'd never seen him like that. He always looked so healthy and strong, even as he got older. But Kristina's dreadful accident made him age 10 years and he lost so much weight.'

When filming was over, David flew Kristina to the London Clinic in December for further treatment, and he returned to her every weekend. He just sat with her and talked and listened to her. She had difficulty speaking at times, often repeating herself, and her memory played tricks on her. She became impatient with herself but he remained calm and unendingly patient.

Kristina did recover, but to reconstruct her face she underwent 22 further operations over the next few years.

David had been set to leave Hjördis after finishing *Death on the Nile*, but he found he couldn't do it. 'When Kristina was badly injured, that stopped me leaving her,' he told me.

Kristina's accident had a positive effect on Hjördis. She said, 'After Kristina's accident I managed to pull myself together for a while.'

David Niven Jnr had become a film producer and had a hit with *The Eagle Has Landed*. Roger Moore said, 'I told David Jnr to stop being a ponce and to give me and his father a job.' Moore didn't really need a job. He was doing very well as James Bond, but I think he felt Niven Snr could do with the work to help him get over Kristina's accident.

The film David Jnr produced was *Escape to Athena*, a comedy action World War II film in which Moore played the German – or rather Austrian – commandant of a Nazi prison camp in occupied Greece, and Niven was an archaeologist keen to investigate local treasures.

It was filmed on Rhodes early in 1978. Telly Savalas, Elliott Gould, Richard Roundtree, Stefanie Powers, Claudia Cardinale and Sonny Bono were also in the film, but all to no avail. As Martyn Auty wrote in the *Monthly Film Bulletin*, 'Performing as though they had met up by chance on holiday, the clutch of box office stars do what they can in a situation where they are the stand-ins and the stuntmen (especially the motorcyclists) dominate the screen.' The film was a flop.

In June David and Hjördis threw a big social event, and Hjördis really had to make a huge effort to be a hostess and not get drunk. She recalled,

> We had a big party for Princess Caroline [of Monaco] the day before her marriage to her boyfriend [Philippe Junot]. I was friends with Grace and I knew she and [Prince] Rainier detested their son in law.
>
> So many people came to the party. They were all David's friends.
>
> Cary Grant was interested in a bronze statue of my head which was at the end of our garden. He said, 'I see you have been immortalised.' I said, 'It's just a small thing but maybe it's the only thing that will remind people of me.' He said that I would be remembered as Mrs David Niven. I said, 'Do you think that is enough?' He said, 'No, frankly I don't. But you and David have been married a long time now. I don't know many in Hollywood who have stayed happy for so long. God knows *I* haven't.'
>
> So I said that if he thought our marriage was a happy marriage, then he didn't see what everyone else saw. Then he said he did, but he didn't wish to appear rude. He was trying to be considerate, and I knew he was. He said that I had everything and what more was there? I said, 'I just want to be happy all the time. I want to be well, I want to be unafraid, I want to be someone else. So, as you can see darling, I can never have what I really want.'

Among the many guests there that day were Ava Gardner, Gregory Peck and Frank Sinatra. I asked Ava what she thought of Hjördis. She said,

> I don't know Hjördis that well, but I could see that she was unhappy. A lot of David's friends hate her. I don't hate her. I don't have any great feeling one way or the other for her. Frank was a little cruel about her. He said, 'I can't stand a dame who can't hold her liquor.'
>
> I tried to talk to her at the party she and David had for Princess Caroline. I think she put up a barrier. I said to her, 'Look, honey, why don't you just tell me, girl to girl, what your problem is.' She said, 'Why would you care?' I said, 'Do I look like someone who has the right to judge you? I've screwed up plenty and, honey, you looked like you're screwing up. I'm a screwed up expert.'
>
> She laughed, and she started to talk to me. She didn't sleep with David any more, and she no longer dressed to excite him. She said she was afraid of getting old and ugly, that she was an alcoholic. She hardly ate. I think she had an eating disorder. She certainly was slim then. *Too* thin. And she wore heavy make-up. She complained about giving him the best years of her life and she hadn't even been able to have a child of her own or a career. She had nothing that was her very own, she said. I didn't have any advice for her. I just thought it was important to listen.
>
> She said to me, 'You've known David for years. Could you be married to him?' I said, 'Honey, I can't be married to *anyone*.'
>
> I thought she tried hard to be a good hostess. She talked to a lot of people. She showed them her gardens. David told me that he thought she was a manic depressive. I think she might have been. She wasn't manic that day. Maybe she was on pills, and she was certainly drinking. But she wasn't drunk.

In September, Kristina was well enough to go back to school, and David flew to London to start work on a TV mini series, *A Man Called Intrepid*. It was about Sir William Stephenson who headed the joint Anglo-American intelligence agency British Security Coordination in New York during World War II. He was given the code name Intrepid.

Over dinner with him one night back at the Connaught Hotel, he talked about Kristina and about the progress she had made. He had changed dramatically from the self-assured actor full of bonhomie I had met in 1970. His hands shook just a little and he certainly looked physically diminished. While the film was being made, he flew to Geneva each Friday to be with Kristina. He was devoted to her.

I think it was during the filming of A Man Called Intrepid that Lynne Frederick persuaded me to fly over with her to the house she and Peter Sellers had bought in Switzerland. We went to eat out with a number of well known personalities and I saw Hjördis sitting on her own in a corner. Peter Sellers suggested I ignore her, but I went over and sat with her. I think she realised who I was, but I couldn't guarantee it. She took my hand and kept hold of it, and she talked about nothing and everything, all garbled nonsense. But I stayed with her for about half an hour until Lynne prised me away, telling me that Mrs Niven was drunkenly flirting with me. I don't think she was flirting at all. She just seemed very sad and desperate.

When I met Hjördis again in 1986, she remembered me as the young man who held her hand and listened to what she had to say. 'I must have been very drugged,' she said. 'People would think I was drunk, but sometimes I just dosed up on sedatives and tranquillisers.'

I asked her if she could remember what she was doing there all alone, and she said, 'I don't know. I just remember you were there, and that meant a lot to me.'

Filming of A Man Called Intrepid was completed in Canada, and then Niven returned to Château d'Oex to try to continue writing his novel which he had stopped work on during Kristina's crisis.

The following year, 1979, he complained of getting continual cramps in his right calf and consulted physiotherapist David Bolton who had treated Kristina. Niven began a strict daily exercise regime, often walked vast distances, and was optimistic that the cramps would subside.

Just as he was again convinced that his acting career was over, he landed a leading role in a British film, A Nightingale Sang in Berkeley Square, filmed in London in April and May. I spent time with him, doing a couple of interviews with him – including the 'angry interview' – and just watching him at work.

He played the mastermind behind a gang of bank robbers. I told him the title sounded more like something Anna Neagle would have made for Herbert Wilcox in 1950s. That made him laugh.

Later in 1979 he was back in England to make Rough Cut for director Don Siegel. He played a Scotland Yard detective, while Burt Reynolds played a jewel thief. I knew Don Siegel a little, having spent time with him during pre-production so I could interview him at length about his career, and he allowed me down on the set to watch some of the filming. I thought everything seemed to be going along well enough and David and Burt Reynolds were getting along. But after the film was finished David discovered much of his part had been cut, and he received only third billing below Burt Reynolds and the leading lady Lesley-Anne

Down. He sued the producer, David Merrick, for breach of contract and it was settled out of court for $125,000. 'Not bad money for being shafted,' David told me.

Niven's next film job was almost something of a favour to him. *The Sea Wolves* was an attempt to follow up on the success of *The Wild Geese* by producer Euan Lloyd and director Andrew V. McLaglen. They wanted Richard Burton and Roger Moore from *The Wild Geese* to star together again, but Burton turned the film down, so Lloyd and McLaglen cast Gregory Peck in his place. Peck wanted Niven in the film, but David wasn't having any of it. 'I didn't fancy the idea of going to India where they were going to shoot much of it,' he told me. 'So I said "No." Roger, bless him, told Euan Lloyd to make me a better offer. Roger knows I can't resist money, and they came back with a much better deal and I said, "Okay, but if I get sick, I'm suing you."'

He was paid $500,000 plus $1,500 a week expenses. And he got sick. They all did. 'The whole cast came down with bloody stomach troubles,' I was told by Brook Williams who was in the film.

The Sea Wolves was based on the true story of a group of ex-soldiers on a mission to blow up German ships in Goa, India, in 1943. It was November when they began filming in Goa, but it still got unbelievably hot, often reaching 140°F (60°C).

I interviewed Roger Moore when he was promoting the film, and he said, 'It was enormous fun to do. We were all great friends. There was Greg and Niv, and Trevor Howard, Patrick Macnee, and me and a dozen or so other great character actors.'

But fun was not had by all. David hated Goa and begged to be allowed to return home for Christmas. Euan Lloyd gave him permission provided he did no skiing. After Christmas, Niven returned to Goa and took to taking long walks along the beach to strengthen his legs which were becoming increasingly weak.

Filming ended in February 1980 and he hurried back to Château d'Oex and immediately went skiing but found that he was so out of breath he had to lie down and rest.

On 1 March he turned 70 and threw himself a birthday bash at the Eagle Club to which he invited many guests. Hjördis didn't join them. She remained at home, scared to go anywhere and probably too drunk to care. She had not only gone back to her old ways, she was worse than ever.

In desperation David sought outside help. 'I asked the advice of the wife of an old army friend because she had had a problem with alcohol. The trouble is, Hjördis won't admit she has a problem, so she can't be helped.'

In April 1980, Niven sent his unfinished novel to his publisher, Doubleday. The book wasn't good but Doubleday hoped it could be improved with editing. They met Niven's demand of an advance of a million and one dollars. David explained that the extra dollar was so he could tell everyone that the deal was for more than a million. Doubleday expected the name of David Niven alone to ensure it sold well. The deal included a second book.

On 24 July 1980 Peter Sellers died of a heart attack. He and Niven had remained friends and so his widow, Lynne Frederick, asked David to deliver the eulogy at the memorial service in London at St Martin-in-the-Fields in September.

Kristina, now 19, left school and started a year-long fine-arts course at Sotheby's in London. David went with her to London to help find her a flat, and then he flew back to the Côte d'Azur.

On a trip to New York that year to see the editors at Doubleday, he was struck by a terrible pain in his leg as he walked along Fifth Avenue. He underwent various tests in London but nothing wrong was found, so he returned to Switzerland and there discovered that although he could still ski he couldn't raise his right heel.

In January 1981 he flew out to Los Angeles to speak at a ceremony at the American Film Institute which was giving a Life Achievement Award to Fred Astaire. David's voice was slurred and he apologised to the audience but he couldn't understand what was wrong. He knew he wasn't drunk.

He finally finished his book in February 1981 which he called *Go Slowly, Come Back Quickly*; it is something a little girl once said to him as he left the West Indies. It was set during World War II and told of a young Polish American who joins the RAF, goes to Hollywood and becomes a film star. It was semi-autobiographical and very crude. David was not a good novelist, but he was a good story-teller.

In May he flew to New York to consult an orthopaedic surgeon who said that he might have muscle problems due to a pinched nerve from a very old back injury. He underwent an extensive physiotherapy course in England.

David Jnr produced another film in which his father starred, *Ménage à Trois* which was retitled *Better Late Than Never*. It was a good comedy about an elderly cabaret star, played by David, now trying to make a living in a strip club in the South of France. It was filmed close to Lo Scoglietto, but somehow David managed to get a living allowance on top of his fee of $150,000.

When the studio saw the rushes and heard how slurred Niven's voice had become, they told the film's director, Bryan Forbes, to have it dubbed. To Forbes' eternal credit, he refused, knowing it would be a humiliation to David.

In October David went to London for the publication of *Go Slowly, Come Back Quickly*. He again appeared on the *Michael Parkinson Show* – this time I wasn't in the audience but I remember watching it on TV and being shocked at how slurred his voice had become. I knew he wasn't drunk because he never got noticeably drunk.

Jamie also saw the programme and became concerned that something was seriously wrong with his father and called him by telephone, urging him to go to the Mayo Clinic in Minneapolis for a thorough medial examination. David flew to the States and checked himself in. He was there for several days.

His PR people at Theo Cowan's office called me to let me know he was due back in London and asked if I'd like to interview him. Of course, I said yes. The day before the interview was due to take place, I got a call to say it had been cancelled and I was confidentially tipped off that David was actually unwell. That was enough for me to call the Connaught Hotel and speak directly to him, and he said to come on over in the morning. I did, and there he told me the grim news.

He had been diagnosed with Motor Neurone Disease. 'It's going to kill me, Mike,' he said. His voice was quavering as well as slurred.

'I'm so sorry,' I said.

'Don't be too nice,' he said.

We sat in silence for a few minutes while he collected himself. Then he ordered coffee which I had to decline because I had by then become a Mormon and couldn't drink coffee. He knew a bit about Mormons. He had been to Salt Lake City and was welcomed by the Mormon President there. 'Nice people,' he said. And then he talked a bit about the old days, and about his problems with Hjördis. Then he asked me, 'Any chance you could convert Hjördis? Maybe that would stop her drinking.'

I tried to say the right things but it's difficult when a friend has just told you he has a death sentence from which there seems no reprieve.

However, I'd brought him a present. It was a copy of my first book – about epic films. I'd even signed it. He said how wonderful that I'd become a published author and that we were both 'in the same club'. He flicked through the pages. It really wasn't well written but fortunately it was highly illustrated and he loved looking at the photographs. He would say, 'Ah, Gable as Rhett Butler. Nobody else could have played that part. Lots of Chuck Heston I see. Well, he was Moses and Ben-Hur, wasn't he? Nobody else could ever be. And here's me in *Around the World In 80 Days*.

God, I've got a bit older since then. Here's Larry Olivier in a Roman toga. What wonderful memories of Hollywood.' He thought *my* book was full of wonderful memories? He was the one who virtually invented the Hollywood memoir.

As I was about to leave, he asked me to keep his secret. It was one all his journalist friends kept. The public didn't know for another year.

—

CHAPTER 23

A Life Given Up

David returned to Switzerland and told Hjördis the terrible news. She recalled, 'When David told me, I couldn't speak. I don't know how it seemed to him. I probably just seemed like I always did. But I was so stunned. It's hard to remember everything clearly. I had become so drunk most of the time that much of it is a haze.'

On 18 November 1981 David's sister Joyce died, aged 81. Every Christmas for many years, David had sent Joyce and Grizel generous cheques. He'd never forgotten to take care of his sisters. Now there was only he and Grizel left from the family.

Two weeks later he heard the news that Natalie Wood had drowned at sea off Santa Catalina. He had remained friends with Natalie's husband Robert Wagner, and he called Wagner every day, desperate to help him through the tragedy. He told Wagner to come to Switzerland as soon as he could. Wagner arrived with his children in a snow storm to be greeted personally by David who had organised a chalet for them to stay in.

In February 1982 he sent his old friend Trubshawe a cheque for £2,000. Trubshawe told me, 'My wife had Alzheimer's Disease and I was struggling to care for her. Money wasn't too good. I wasn't trying to get David to send me money. I just let him know my wife was ill, and he said he would send me some money. I told him not to, but he insisted. I said I'd think about it, and a week later, knowing I was in trouble, I accepted his offer. It was wonderful of him. That's when you know you have true friends, even if there has been a great distance between you – physically and emotionally.'

David's new novel didn't sell well, and since his deal with Doubleday was actually for two novels, he had to start thinking about what his next book would be. He decided it would be another novel, this time about a young man who goes to Sandhurst and is sent to serve in Northern Ireland. He wrote by hand and gave up after little more than 40 pages.

That's when he decided he would write about the story of an author living in Switzerland who has an affair with a schoolgirl. He managed to write 200 pages but when he abandoned that idea, he came up with the story about an author who does an exhausting tour of America, checks into the Mayo Clinic in Minneapolis, is diagnosed with Motor Neurone Disease, and returns to his home on the Côte d'Azur.

In March 1982 he started to make his last two films, shot back to back. They were *Trail of the Pink Panther* and *Curse of the Pink Panther*. For the first film, Blake Edwards had come up with the dreadful idea of utilising out takes from the previous Clouseau films and bringing back actors such as Niven, Robert Wagner and Capucine to fill in the blanks.

David was barely able to work at all but he'd promised Blake he would do the films. I didn't care for either film, and neither did Lynne Frederick who successfully sued Blake Edwards and the producers for using Peter Sellers' image in the first of the two films without her consent, winning over a million dollars.

Because David's voice had deteriorated so much, impressionist Rich Little dubbed his lines. No one thought to tell David this and he found out only when Rich Little spoke about it to the Press.

I received a letter from David early in 1982 in which he said that he would love it if I could come to visit him, or if not, he would see me the next time he came to London. I hadn't realised how desperate he was to see me, or why, and I neglected to try to overcome my fear of flying and get over to see him.

But he did come to London in July and I met with him at his Mayfair flat, recording, at his request, his confessions.

Regarding everything he said about Hjördis, he told me, 'I wish you could talk to her. I'm prepared to take responsibility for my part in this disastrous marriage, but I'm sure she could give you a better insight. Of course, my dear chap, she's never going to be in a fit state to have her say. I think that's a terrible shame because she is entitled to put her side of the story forward. But she never will, you know. She's a lost soul and I don't think she'll live much longer. Really I don't.'

As if I hadn't had enough shocks, he then said something that came like a bolt out of the blue. 'Look, old bean, I don't want to die in agony and without dignity,' he said. 'I'm doing everything I can to beat this thing, but none of it is working. I can't save my own life, but I can take it. And I think I will.'

He was very matter of fact, very unemotional, and there was even a certain twinkle in his faded eye that, for a moment, made me think he was pulling my leg. I said, 'You *are* joking, aren't you?'

'Not in the least, Mike. I'm in deadly earnest. I nearly did it before.' He said he wasn't going to try and blow his brains out again. 'Awfully messy if it works, but also damned inconvenient when the bloody thing doesn't work.'

The he told me his plan. 'I have a doctor in Switzerland who will give me an injection that will put me gently to sleep. So when I know that I can't stand any more, when life becomes too unbearable, I'll exit this world under my own steam. I want control over my life and death. I don't want this bloody disease to take me. I want it to be *my* decision.'

He fell silent. The air in the room was very still. There didn't even seem to be any traffic noise from outside. I no longer have the religious beliefs I had then, but I do believe that human beings have the capacity to be spiritual, and I am convinced that David was experiencing something very spiritual. He was struggling to defeat something dark and destructive inside of him, battling it with his own incredible will.

I could see that he wanted to cry but he was holding it in.

'Do you want to pray with me?' I asked him.

'Yes. Very much.'

'Would you like me to give you a blessing?'

'Yes,' he said. Then he added, 'What is that?'

'I'll place my hands on your head and say a prayer.'

'Is it a healing?' he asked.

'It might be,' I said. 'Just stay sitting in your chair.'

'Oh, thank you. You know, I wasn't looking forward to getting on my knees. Awfully hard to get down, and when I'm down, damn near impossible to get up again.'

I stood behind his chair, lay my hands upon his head, and began to pray that he would find the strength to overcome his fears and that, in time, he might have power over his own life, to be able to give it up when he was ready to do so, as Jesus Christ gave up his life on the cross, and as I said that, David lifted one hand and placed it on top of my hands.

When it was over, he sat quietly for several minutes, and then said, 'That was one of the most beautiful moments of my life, and I shall never forget it.'

When it was time for me to leave, we shook hands and he said, 'I doubt we shall meet again, unless you can come to Switzerland.' I said I would try to come over. 'Write to me,' he said, 'and I'll drop a line to you while I can still write.'

A month later, in August 1982, I read in the newspapers that David was seriously ill; the news had finally broken but it was inaccurate. Princess Grace, in an effort to protect him, had been quoted as saying he had suffered a mild stroke. The public still didn't know the truth about his disease. I had one tabloid newspaper call me asking for information and I told them I was unaware that David had suffered a stroke. Asked what I thought might be wrong with him, I said, 'I expect he's sick and tired of being asked what's wrong with him.'

On 14 September Princess Grace died when her car left the road in Monte Carlo and plunged from the Grande Corniche. David desperately wanted to attend her funeral but was afraid that his emotions, now highly fragile, would cause a scene, and so he stayed away.

Another of his closest friends, Robert Coote, died in New York on 26 November. That month he wrote to me from Château d'Oex and told me about a wonderful Irish nurse, Katherine Matthewson, who was now taking care of him. He had met her while in a London hospital during the late autumn; she was an agency nurse and he decided to hire her. She returned with him to Switzerland and stayed with him to the very end. I think she may have actually been the greatest blessing in his life in his last months. Hjördis was incapable of looking after him. 'The time when he needed me the most, I wasn't there for him,' she told me. 'When David was ill I had a blackout. It may have been a fit. I fell and broke my leg.'

Peter Ustinov had nothing but contempt for Hjördis. 'I think she hated him. Some people aren't capable of hatred. She was.'

I said, 'That doesn't mean she hated him.'

'She gave a good impression of hatred. She said that here was a man who couldn't even make himself understood any more. That's such a cruel thing to say.'

It was. And she knew it. 'I said some terrible things,' she told me. 'I don't expect to be forgiven for any of them. I was cruel to David. But that wasn't who I really was. I had become something else.'

In December 1982 Hjördis issued a short press release to announce that David was suffering 'a muscular disorder, but it is not cancer or a heart attack as many people have supposed'.

David wrote one last time to me to say he had written a letter to Hjördis because he had come to the decision he wanted a divorce and was taking the girls away with him. He said that in his letter he had told her how much he loved her and would to the day he died. But he never gave her the letter because he realised it was a folly to get a divorce now and would accomplish nothing. 'Besides,' he said, 'I would like to be remembered as one Hollywood actor who never got divorced.' That meant a lot to him; he never wanted to be a divorcee.

When I asked Hjördis if she had known of the letter, she said, 'I had no idea. Oh my God!' She was shocked and ashamed.

There was something else he said in his letter to me. 'You won't believe this, but I kneel every night to say my prayers. I pray with Katherine who helps me to kneel and then helps me to get up. She has a beautiful faith. You would like her.'

He continued to work on his novel, but he knew he was failing both because of a lack of inspiration and his growing inability to hold a pen. He managed to complete 50,000 words. He no longer wrote his own letters but dictated them.

A campaign began among David's friends to get him a knighthood. At the time, very few actors were knighted, and those that were knighted were usually the giants of British theatre. Niven himself had little regard for honours in the acting world. He once told me, 'Of course Gielgud, Olivier and Richardson deserved them, but who else can match them?'

In the event, no knighthood was considered for David, perhaps because he was a tax exile. In more recent years that hasn't prevented other British actors from getting knighthoods, and today such honours seem to be handed out far less exclusively than they once were. I don't know if David Niven should have been knighted or if he would have even welcomed it.

He returned to London one more time in February 1983 for further treatment at the Wellington Hospital at St John's Wood. I was able to get in to see him simply by putting on an official badge that identified me as 'Elder Michael Munn of the Church of Jesus Christ of Latter Day Saints', giving me church minister status that allowed me into any hospital at any time.

I found him in a private room under the name of David Snook. He didn't say very much – he was very ill and needed rest, so I just sat with him and talked about mundane things; he particularly enjoyed hearing about my three children, one of whom was named after Tony Curtis and another after Natalie Wood. 'Do you think you'll name one after me, if you have another boy?' he asked.

'I can't,' I said, 'I have a nephew called David and my parents would never forgive me if there were two Davids in the family.'

He smiled and said, 'Just don't name him after Errol. He'd never forgive you being stuck with a name like that.'

He asked me to tell him about some of the people we both knew and liked – Richard Burton, Laurence Olivier, Charlton Heston, George Raft,

Ava Gardner. He loved hearing gossip and he said, 'You've got some good stories. I'll use them in my next memoir and say they happened to me.' I told him he was welcome to.

He wanted to know who my lovers had been, and while there wasn't much to tell him on that score, I was able to give him a tale or two that had him pointing to my Elder's badge and saying, 'You weren't always such a saint, were you?' I took that as a compliment from David Niven.

Then I told him a favourite story of mine, known as *Footprints in the Sand*. Paraphrased, as I told it, a man walks along the beach with the Lord, and as he does so, he always sees two sets of footprints in the sand. But when life became difficult he could see only one set of footprints, and he asked the Lord, 'Why, when you had told me that you would always walk with me, could I only see one set of footprints?' The Lord told him, 'My precious child, I love you and would never leave you. During the times when you were suffering and were in desperation and you saw only one set of footprints, that, my son, was when I was carrying you.'

David listened. He said nothing but looked very peaceful and then fell asleep. That was my last memory of him.

He returned to Lo Scoglietto but was no longer able to go to his favourite public places to eat because he had difficulty swallowing. He swam with difficulty every day, and Katherine swam with him. 'She was wonderful to him,' Hjördis told me. 'He would have to wear a rubber ring, and she was with him the whole time in the water.'

As for her own contribution to his welfare, Hjördis admitted she made none. And her own behaviour towards him was, she said, 'despicable'. She was fond of a doctor she had met at the Wellington Hospital, and he came to the Niven house in the summer. 'He was there to help David,' she said, 'but he was also there for me. I was selfish. I had a romance with the doctor, and my girls were there in the house, and I don't think they ever forgave me. I thought that his nurse could do everything for him.'

During the summer, I received one last and very brief letter from David who surprisingly wrote it by hand so it must have been a painful ordeal for him. He said that he had been blessed to have Katherine and that he was saying his prayers every night. He also said he had found a sense of peace and that he had also been sent a copy of the *Footprints in the Sand* story by a doctor friend of his. Hjördis told me that he kept it to the end of his life and read it almost every day. He also said that he had decided to take control of his life stating that he was not to be put on a life support machine at any time.

Among old friends who visited him was Richard Burton. When I was with Burton on the set of *1984*, which was the last time I saw Richard, he told me that he had been to see David shortly before he died and was amazed at how David was able to make jokes about his condition. 'He looked so terrible,' Rich said, 'and his voice was very slurred and I had trouble understanding him. He suddenly said, "My dear Richard, I am not deaf so please kindly stop shouting at me." I hadn't realised I was shouting.'

In July David was photographed and the picture, showing him looking very emaciated, appeared in the *Sun* newspaper. When he saw it he was distraught and believed he would have better privacy at Château d'Oex. He also felt that the clearer air up there would do him good. Hjördis remained at Lo Scoglietto and was later criticised for doing so, but in 1986 she told me, 'David insisted that I stay at Lo Scoglietto so that I could have a rest from him. I think he also needed to be away from me.'

He had, she claimed, asked her to commit suicide with him. She said, 'Before he left for the chalet, he said to me, "Let's jump hand in hand into the pool, go down three times but only come up twice." I was shocked.'

Fiona, then 19, came home to attend Geneva University and was often at Château d'Oex, and so was Hjördis's nephew, Michael Winstrad; he was fond of his uncle but Hjördis seemed to resent him being there and told him he needed to return to Sweden where his mother was dying – a blatant lie, apparently. She was never able to give a rational explanation why she did that.

Meanwhile, Kristina was in Geneva and David Jnr and Jamie were both in the States. Niven's sons were later critical of Hjördis for failing to give their father the love and care he needed in the last weeks of his life, but she was equally critical of them, telling me, 'He was their father and we all knew he was soon going to die. They should have dropped everything to be with him.' There was no love lost between Hjördis and her stepsons.

On 27 July, a Wednesday, Hjördis telephoned David and apparently berated him about no longer being a man and refusing to come to him when he asked her to. Hjördis was unable to recall that incident when I met her in 1986, although she conceded, 'I may have been so drunk and so full of pills that I could have done or said anything. I am very sorry for my behaviour.' And I believe she was. She cried often throughout the interview, and I believe she was sincere about her behaviour which she admitted was 'unforgivable'. She also admitted that she had taken a new lover, a painter called Andrew Vicari.

David still kept her photograph on his desk.

That night he had trouble getting to sleep and stayed up late talking to Katherine about Primmie. David Bolton came to see him in the morning and saw how desperately ill he looked so he sent for the local doctor. It was decided that David needed to be hospitalised and put on a respirator, but

Jamie and David Jnr, by telephone, confirmed that their father was not to be given any form of life support. David apparently made one concession to allow himself to be more comfortable; he wore an oxygen mask.

The next morning, Friday 29 July, David finally fell asleep around 3am. Katherine checked on him at 7am and when he gave her the thumbs up sign, she went downstairs to make coffee. Then she heard a noise from his bedroom and returned to find that he had taken off the oxygen mask. He smiled at her, held her hand, and passed away. He was 73.

Some years later I discussed with Sheridan Morley David's manner of dying. Sheridan said that from what he understood, it was as though David had simply decided the time had come, had removed his oxygen mask, and then quickly slipped away. 'I don't think he was going to wait any longer and actually stopped living rather than choosing to die, if that makes sense.' I said that it made perfect sense to me. I think he'd given up his life. He'd made his own decision.

As soon as Roger Moore heard the news, he drove from his home in St Paul de Vence with his daughter Deborah to help with the funeral arrangements. Fiona was also there, as well as David Bolton and a friend from David's war days, Alistair Forbes. Fiona, Bolton and Katherine decided what suit David should wear; it was a dark green which was his favourite colour.

Hjördis arrived the next day, Saturday. Roger Moore only ever mentioned her once to me, when he was filming A View to a Kill. 'When she arrived and saw me she said, "Are you here for the publicity?" so I quickly left and didn't stay for the funeral because I might have ended up killing her. I'm quite sure that if he had lived, he would have divorced her.' Moore regretted not being able to be at Niven's funeral.

David Jnr and Jamie arrived on Saturday night.

The funeral was set for Tuesday 2 August at 2.30pm at a small Anglican Church, St Peters, in the main street of Château d'Oex. Hjördis arrived drunk, hanging on the arm of Prince Rainier.

'I hadn't wanted to go,' she told me. 'I couldn't accept that David was dead. I couldn't accept that he had been so ill. When the news came I broke down. I know everybody hated me, and I suddenly found I couldn't face any of them – even my own daughters, and David's sons. Roger Moore despised me – he has never spoken to me again. I was agoraphobic and the very thought of going to the funeral terrified me. It's a crippling illness of the mind. Rainier was very sweet and also very strong, telling me I *must* go. He *made* me go, and if it hadn't been for him, I wouldn't have been there.'

Audrey Hepburn was among the mourners, so was Capucine, and just about everyone in the village turned up. 'The people of the village loved

David,' Hjördis said. 'He always had time for them and he loved to chat to them. He was the perfect English gentleman at all times. I think Kristina's real mother was at the church.'

I asked her what made her think that. She said, 'It was just a moment of recognition in the eyes. Just a second when I saw clearly. The rest of the time I was drunk and in tears.'

She sat in the front row next to Prince Rainer, her girls and David's lawyer, but she refused to allow David Jnr or Jamie and his family to sit with them.

Yehudi Menuhin and several of his students from his music school in Gstaad played Mendelssohn's *Andante*. There were readings from Paul's epistle to the Corinthians, and the hymns sung included *The Lord is My Shepherd* and *To Be a Pilgrim*.

David didn't expect Hjördis to outlive him by much. She would have surprised him – as she did everyone. At first, immediately following his death, she remained lost in a world of depression, panic attacks, sedatives and alcohol, and became a recluse at Lo Scoglietto. But in 1984 she took everyone by surprise when she was persuaded by her doctor friend/lover to check into a French clinic where she was treated for her alcoholism and underwent therapy and made a remarkable recovery.

She became involved with an AIDS charity and began going out a lot more, especially with Andrew Vicari. Their relationship didn't last, but it certainly had a beneficial effect upon her.

David had thought that I would never be able to interview Hjördis. I did, in 1986. She had been sober for two years, and when she came to London, she went through David's former PR to arrange for an interview with me. We also dined out and talked about many things in general. I was, at that time, becoming disillusioned with the Mormon Church and all religion, and she told me, 'Whatever you believe now, what you believed then [in 1982] got David through a difficult time.'

I don't think her stepsons ever got to know her as I did. She was sober, cohesive, confident and very personable. She accepted responsibility for her own shortcomings. But within a few years she slipped back into her old ways. She became completely estranged from her stepsons, and they became estranged from their stepsisters. While David was alive he was able to hold the family together. After his death, the family unit splintered. Even at her best, in 1986, Hjördis was barely able to keep the family together but after she slid irrevocably into alcoholism, the family had no chance of survival. That, I think, is the most tragic part of it all.

Hjördis died from a stroke on Christmas Eve 1997. She was 78. She had asked not to be buried next to David but to be cremated and her ashes scattered from Lo Scoglietto over the Mediterranean.

After David died, Doubleday and Hamish Hamilton found themselves with an unfinished book by him. They decided that not to publish it would be a greater favour to Niven than to try and edit it into something that might have made them back some of their huge advance but would have disappointed readers. That was a generous act by publishers who could have cashed in on David's death.

At his funeral, among the flowers and wreaths that adorned the church, was a huge wreath from the porters at Heathrow Airport with a card that read, 'To the finest gentleman who ever walked through these halls. He made a porter feel like a king.'

I would say that pretty well summed up David Niven. He was a fine gentleman and a very English one at that, which is no bad thing in this day and age. He wasn't perfect, of course, but he was a decent man to those who came into contact with him – it didn't matter what class you were. You could be a hotel porter, a member of royalty or just a mere messenger boy as I was when I first met him in 1970.

A Brief Afterword

Why didn't I write this book after David died? The reason is very simple. I was not an established author, I had no agent and the publishers I was then dealing with – neither of which exist any longer – didn't feel that a biography of David Niven was possible because of *The Moon's a Balloon*. Sheridan Morley proved them wrong when his excellent *The Other Side of the Moon* was published in 1985. Several years ago, on one of my regular rounds of radio studios to promote one of my books, I talked to Sheridan about the things Niven had told to me, and he said, 'You *have* to write your book.' But then Graham Lord's biography *Niv* was published. Even shortly before Sheridan died on 16 February 2007, he continued to urge, encourage and generally enthuse me to write this book. So here it is.

Michael Munn

The Films and Television
Work of David Niven

The Films

Without Regret (1935, Paramount). Elissa Landi, Robert Cavanagh, Frances Drake, Kent Taylor, Gilbert Emery, David Niven. *Producer* B.P. Finemann. *Director* Harold Young. Trivia: Elissa Landi retired from acting in 1943 and wrote poetry and six novels before dying of cancer in 1948 aged only 43.

Barbary Coast (1935, Goldwyn). Miriam Hopkins, Edward G. Robinson, Joel McCrea, Walter Brennan, David Niven (billed 9th). *Producer* Samuel Goldwyn. *Director* Howard Hawks. Trivia: The film received an Oscar nomination for its photography.

A Feather in Her Hat (1935, Columbia). Pauline Lord, Basil Rathbone, Louis Hayward, Billie Burke, Wendy Barrie, David Niven (billed 12th). *Producer* Everett Riskin. *Director* Alfred Santell. Trivia: Ruth Chatterton was originally cast in Pauline Lord's role but decided to take a break from acting for a year.

Splendour (1935, Goldwyn). Miriam Hopkins, Joel McCrea, Paul Cavanagh, Helen Westley, Billie Burke, David Niven (billed 8th). *Producer* Samuel Goldwyn. *Director* Elliot Nugent. Trivia: The original title is actually *Splendor*, spelt without the 'u' for American prints.

Rose Marie (1936, MGM). Jeanette MacDonald, Nelson Eddy, Reginald Owen, Allan Jones, James Stewart, Alan Mowbray, David Niven. *Producer* Hunt Stromberg. *Director* W.S. Van Dyke. Trivia: Nelson Eddy didn't want to be upstaged by Allan Jones and insisted that Jones's only solo number, the aria 'E lucevan le stelle' from Puccini's *Tosca*, be cut.

Palm Springs (1936, Paramount). Frances Langford, Sir Guy Standing, Ernest Cossart, Smith Ballew, Spring Byington, David Niven. *Producer* Walter Wanger. *Director* Aubrey Scotto. (US title *Palm Springs Affair*) Trivia: In an eerie coincidence, the day Sir Guy Standing died from a rattlesnake bite in the Hollywood Hills in 1936, Humphrey Pearson, co-writer of *Palm Springs*, died in Palm Springs of a gunshot wound.

Thank You, Jeeves (1936, 20th Century-Fox). Arthur Treacher, Virginia Fields, David Niven, Lester Matthews. *Producer* Sol M. Wurtzel. *Director* Arthur Greville Collins. Trivia: A sequel, *Step Lively, Jeeves*, followed in 1937 with Arthur Treacher again as Jeeves, but without the character of Wooster.

The Charge of the Light Brigade (1936, Warner Brothers). Errol Flynn, Olivia de Havilland, Patric Knowles, Henry Stephenson, Nigel Bruce, Donald Crisp, David Niven. *Producer* Hal B. Wallis. *Director* Michael Curtiz. Trivia: Over 200 horses were reportedly killed during filming, resulting in the US Congress passing new laws to protect animals used in motion pictures.

Dodsworth (1936, Goldwyn). Walter Huston, Ruth Chatterton, Paul Lukas, Mary Astor, David Niven. *Producer* Samuel Goldwyn. *Director* William Wyler. Trivia: Walter Huston and Charles Halton repeated their roles from the Broadway play but all of Halton's footage was cut from the film.

Beloved Enemy (1937, Goldwyn). Merle Oberon, Brian Aherne, Karen Morely, Jerome Cowan, David Niven. *Producer* George Haight. *Director* H.C. Potter. Trivia: The retired film star Eve Southern loaned Goldwyn a rare Rolls-Royce to use in the film.

We Have Our Moments (1937, Universal). Sally Eilers, James Dunn, Mischa Auer, Thurston Hall, Warren Hymer, David Niven. *Producer* Edmund Grainger. *Director* Alfred L. Werker. Trivia: Mischa Auer, famous for playing mad Russians, was a quiet, scholarly gentleman who spoke Russian, English, Italian, French, German and Spanish.

The Prisoner of Zenda (1937, Selznick International). Ronald Colman, Madeleine Carroll, Douglas Fairbanks Jnr, Mary Astor, C. Aubrey Smith, Raymond Massey, David Niven. *Producer* David O. Selznick. *Directors* John Cromwell, W.S. Van Dyke. Trivia: Douglas Fairbanks Jnr tested for the double role and was devastated when it went to Ronald Colman.

Dinner at the Ritz (1937, New World). Annabella, David Niven, Paul Lukas, Romney Brent. *Producer* Robert T. Kane. *Director* Harold Schuster. Trivia: Annabella's real name was Suzanne Georgette Charpentier.

Bluebeard's Eighth Wife (1938, Paramount). Claudette Colbert, Gary Cooper, Edward Everett Horton, David Niven, Elizabeth Patterson. *Producer/director* Ernst Lubitsch. Trivia: This was the first collaboration of screenwriters Charles Brackett and Billy Wilder.

Four Men and a Prayer (1938, 20th Century-Fox). Loretta Young, Richard Greene, George Sanders, David Niven, C. Aubrey Smith. *Producer* Kenneth MacGowan. *Director* John Ford. Trivia: Niven often tried to include the names of friends and family in his films; in this, one of his lines was 'I knew a man named Trubshawe'.

Three Blind Mice (1938, 20th Century-Fox). Loretta Young, Joel McCrea, David Niven, Stuart Erwin. *Producer* Raymond Griffiths. *Director* William A. Seiter. 1938. Trivia: Remade as a musical, *Three Little Girls in Blue*, in 1946.

The Dawn Patrol (1938, Warner Brothers). Errol Flynn, David Niven, Basil Rathbone, Donald Crisp. *Producer* Hal B. Wallis. *Director* Edmund Goulding. Trivia: Seventeen vintage World War I aircraft, most of them Nieuports, were assembled. Flying them proved so hazardous, by the time filming ended, all but two of them had crashed.

Wuthering Heights (1939, Samuel Goldwyn). Merle Oberon, Laurence Olivier, David Niven, Flora Robson, Donald Crisp. *Producer* Samuel Goldwyn. *Director* William Wyler. Trivia: Niven called one of the dogs in the film 'Trubshawe' but Wyler cut the line out.

Bachelor Mother (1939, RKO). Ginger Rogers, David Niven, Charles Coburn, Frank Albertson. *Producer* B.G. DeSylva. *Director* Garson Kanin. Trivia: The screenplay by Felix Jackson was nominated for an Oscar as Best Original Screenplay.

Eternally Yours (1939, Walter Wanger). Loretta Young, David Niven, Hugh Herbert, Billie Burke. *Producer* Walter Wagner. *Director* Tay Garnett. Trivia: Tay Garnet became one of the regular directors of Four Star's TV dramas, and also directed most of Loretta Young's TV shows.

The Real Glory (1939, Samuel Goldwyn). Gary Cooper, Andrea Leeds, David Niven, Reginald Owen, Broderick Crawford. *Producer* Samuel Goldwyn. *Director* Henry Hathaway. Trivia: The film was re-issued in 1942 with the title *A Yank in the Philippines*, but the Office of War Information insisted it was withdrawn because the film's villains, the Philippine Moros, had become allies in World War II.

Raffles (1939, Samuel Goldwyn). David Niven, Olivia de Havilland, Dame May Whitty. *Producer* Samuel Golwyn. *Directors* Sam Wood, William Wyler. Trivia: Co-screenwriter Sydney Howard died before filming began. He won a posthumous Oscar for his screenplay of *Gone With the Wind*.

The First of the Few (1942, British Aviation Pictures). Leslie Howard, David Niven, Rosamund John, Roland Culver. *Producer/director* Leslie Howard. (US title *Spitfire*) Trivia: Leslie Howard's last screen appearance. He was in an aircraft shot down by the Luftwaffe over the Bay of Biscay in June 1943.

The Way Ahead (1944, Two Cities). David Niven, Raymond Huntley, William Hartnell, Stanley Holloway. *Producers* John Sutro, Norman Walker. *Director* Carol Reed. Trivia: This was a remake of an Army Kinematograph Service training film *The New Lot* written by Peter Ustinov and Eric Ambler which so upset the Army top brass with its frankness that they suppressed it.

A Matter of Life and Death (1945, J. Arthur Rank). David Niven, Roger Livesey, Raymond Massey, Kim Hunter, Marius Goring, Robert Coote. *Producers/directors* Michael Powell and Emeric Pressburger. (US title *Stairway to Heaven*) Trivia: Robert Coote played a character called Bob Trubshawe.

Magnificent Doll (1946, Universal). Ginger Rogers, David Niven, Burgess Meredith, Horace McNally. *Producers* Jack H. Skirball, Bruce Manning. *Director* Frank Borzage. Trivia: This was the least successful of all the films Ginger Rogers made without Fred Astaire.

The Perfect Marriage (1947, Paramount). Loretta Young, David Niven, Nona Griffith, Eddie Albert, Virginia Field. *Producer* Hal B. Wallis. *Director* Lewis Allen. Trivia: Lewis Allen went on to direct many successful Four Star TV productions including *The David Niven Show*, *The Rifleman* and *The Rogues*.

The Other Love (1947, Enterprise Production). Barbara Stanwyck, David Niven, Richard Conte, Gilbert Roland. *Producer* David Lewis. *Director* André de Toth. Trivia: The film was re-released in 1953 under the title *Man Killer*.

The Bishop's Wife (1947, Samuel Goldwyn). Cary Grant, Loretta Young, David Niven, Monty Woolley, James Gleason, Gladys Cooper. *Producer* Samuel Goldwyn. *Director* Henry Koster. Trivia: Niven made a slight change to a line he gives during a Christmas sermon. Instead of saying, 'You give me a tie. I give you a book,' he said, 'I give you a book, you give me a tie,' because he felt it sounded better.

Bonnie Prince Charlie (1948, London Films and British Lion). David Niven, Margaret Leighton, Judy Campbell, Jack Hawkins. *Producer* Edward Black. *Director* Anthony Kimmins. Trivia: The original running time of 138 minutes was cut by Goldwyn to 98 minutes for release in the US.

Enchantment (1948, Goldwyn). David Niven, Teresa Wright, Evelyn Keyes, Farley Granger, Jayne Meadows. *Producer* Samuel Goldwyn. *Director* Irving Reis. Trivia: Evelyn Keyes cohabitated with Niven in 1939 and later lived with Michael Todd at the time he made *Around the World in 80 Days*.

A Kiss in the Dark (1949, Warner Brothers). David Niven, Jane Wyman, Victor Moore, Wayne Morris, Broderick Crawford. *Producer* Jack L. Warner. *Director* Delmer Daves. Trivia: Jane Wyman converted to Roman Catholicism and regularly attended Mass with her good friend Loretta Young.

A Kiss for Corliss (1949, Strand Productions). Shirley Temple, David Niven, Tom Tully, Virginia Welles. *Producer* Colin Miller. *Director* Richard Wallace. Trivia: Shirley Temple's last film.

The Toast of New Orleans (1950, MGM). Kathryn Grayson, Mario Lanza, David Niven, J. Carrol Naish. *Producer* Joe Pasternak. *Director* Norman Taurog. Trivia: Mario Lanza's first film in a movie career cut short when he urinated on a piano in front of reporters.

Happy Go Lovely (1950, A.B.P.C.). David Niven, Vera-Ellen, Cesar Romero, Bobby Howes. *Producer* Marcel Helman. *Director* H. Bruce Humberstone. Trivia: H. Bruce Humberstone had, four years earlier, directed *Three Little Girls in Blue* which was the musical remake of Niven's 1938 film *Three Blind Mice*.

Soldiers Three (1951, MGM). Stewart Granger, Walter Pidgeon, David Niven, Robert Newton. *Producer* Pandro S. Berman. *Director* Tay Garnett. Trivia: Robert Newton, a drunkard and the screen's definitive Long John Silver in three films, was called by Niven 'Legless Silver'.

The Elusive Pimpernel (1951, London Films). David Niven, Margaret Leighton, Cyril Cusack, Jack Hawkins. *Producers/directors* Michael Powell and Emeric Pressburger. Trivia: Richard England loaned his schooner to the producers provided he played the schooner captain and operated it himself.

Appointment with Venus (1951, British Film Makers). David Niven, Glynis Johns, Barry Jones, Kenneth More. *Producer* Betty E. Box. *Director* Ralph Thomas. Trivia: Ralph Thomas is often wrongly credited as the director of the *Carry On* films. However, his brother, Gerald Thomas, was the producer of the *Carry Ons*.

The Lady Says No! (1952, Stillman). Joan Caulfield, David Niven, James Robertson Justice, Lenore Lonergan. *Producers* Frank Ross, John Stillman Jnr. *Director* Frank Ross. Trivia: Frank Ross's only attempt at directing. Its failure convinced him to stick to producing.

The Moon is Blue (1953, Preminger-Herbert). William Holden, David Niven, Maggie McNamara, Tom Tully, Dawn Addams. *Producers* Otto Preminger, F. Hugh Herbert. *Director* Otto Preminger. Trivia: The movie was used as part of a plot line in the *The Moon is Not Blue* episode of TV's *M*A*S*H*.

The Love Lottery (1953, Ealing Studios). David Niven, Peggy Cummins, Anne Vernon, Herbert Lom. *Producer* Monja Danischewsky. *Director* Charles Crichton. Trivia: Shortly after this picture, Charles Crichton stopped directing films and turned to TV but made a phenomenal comeback with his very last film, *A Fish Called Wanda*, in 1988.

Happy Ever After (1954, Mario Zampi for A.B.P.C.). David Niven, Yvonne de Carlo, Barry Fitzgerald, George Cole. *Producer/director* Mario Zampi.

Trivia: Mario Zampi was an Italian but made quintessentially British comedy films.

The King's Thief (1955, MGM). Ann Blyth, Edmund Purdom, David Niven, George Sanders, Roger Moore. *Producer* Edwin H. Knopf. *Director* Robert Z. Leonard. Trivia: Stewart Granger was originally cast in the lead role but after production was delayed he was unavailable and replaced by Edmund Purdom.

Carrington V.C. (1956, Romulus). David Niven, Margaret Leighton, Noelle Middleton, Laurence Naismith. *Producer* Teddy Baird. *Director* Anthony Asquith. Trivia: Margaret Leighton suffered from claustrophobia.

The Birds and the Bees (1956, Gomalco Prods). George Gobel, Mitzi Gaynor, David Niven, Reginald Gardiner. *Producer* Paul Jones. *Director* Norman Taurog. Trivia: The film was intended to launch TV star George Gobel's movie career – it failed.

Around the World in 80 Days (1956, London Films–Michael Todd Prods). David Niven, Cantinflas, Robert Newton, Shirley MacLaine, Charles Boyer, Ronald Colman. *Producer* Michael Todd. *Director* Michael Anderson. Trivia: The film reputedly features 140 purpose built sets, 68,894 extras, 74,685 costumes, 90 animal handlers, 3,800 sheep, 2,448 buffalo, 950 donkeys, 800 horses, 512 monkeys, 17 bulls, 15 elephants, 6 skunks and 4 ostriches.

The Silken Affair (1956, Dragon Films). David Niven, Genevieve Page, Ronald Squire, Beatrice Straight, Wilfred Hyde White. *Producers* Douglas Fairbanks Jnr, Fred Feldkamp. *Director* Roy Kellino. Trivia: The last film of Roy Kellino, a former cinematographer and special effects designer who died of a heart attack on 16 November 1956.

The Little Hut (1956, MGM). Ava Gardner, Stewart Granger, David Niven, Walter Chiari. *Producers* F. Hugh Herbert, Mark Robson. *Director* Mark Robson. Trivia: Was remade in Belgium in 1966 as *La Petite Hutte*, directed by the play's author Andre Roussin.

Oh Men! Oh Women! (1957, 20th Century-Fox). Dan Dailey, Ginger Rogers, David Niven, Barbara Rush, Tony Randall. *Producer/director* Nunnally Johnson. Trivia: The final film appearance by comedy character actor Franklin Pangborn, and the first by Tony Randall.

My Man Godfrey (1957, Universal). June Allyson, David Niven, Jessie Royce Landis, Robert Keith, Eva Gabor. *Producer* Ross Hunter. *Director* Henry Koster. Trivia: The film was intended to launch German star O.W. Fischer in American films but he suffered from memory loss and was replaced by Niven.

Bonjour Tristesse (1957, Wheel Productions/Columbia). Deborah Kerr, David Niven, Jean Seberg, Mylene Demongeot. *Producer/director* Otto Preminger. Trivia: Jean Seberg was Preminger's protégé but found success in Jean-Luc Godard's *À bout de souffle* in 1960 and thereafter in European films.

Separate Tables (1958, A Clifton Production/Hill-Hecht-Lancaster). Deborah Kerr, Rita Hayworth, David Niven, Wendy Hiller, Burt Lancaster. *Producer* Harold Hecht. *Director* Delbert Mann. Trivia: Originally Vivien Leigh and Laurence Olivier were to play the dual roles played by Kerr and Hayworth, Niven and Lancaster, and Olivier was to direct.

Ask Any Girl (1959, Euterpe Productions/MGM). David Niven, Shirley MacLaine, Gig Young, Rod Taylor, Jim Backus. *Producer* Joe Pasternak. *Director* Charles Walters. Trivia: Pasternak's mantra was, 'Never make an audience think. It always worked for me.'

Happy Anniversary (1959, Fields Productions Inc/United Artists). David Niven, Mitzi Gaynor, Carl Reiner, Loring Smith. *Producer* Ralph Fields. *Director* David Miller. Trivia: Gaynor's role was originally declined by Doris Day who feared it would damage her pure screen image.

Please Don't Eat the Daisies (1960, Euterpe Productions/MGM). Doris Day, David Niven, Janis Page, Spring Byington. *Producer* Joe Pasternak. *Director* Charles Walters. Trivia: Spring Byington began her feature film career playing Katharine Hepburn's mother in *Little Women* in 1933 and ended it playing Doris Day's mother in this picture.

The Guns of Navarone (1961, Open Road Films/Columbia). Gregory Peck, David Niven, Anthony Quinn, Stanley Baker, Anthony Quayle. *Producers* Carl Foreman, Cecil Parker. *Director* J. Lee Thompson. Trivia: David Niven wore a Highland Light Infantry cap badge on his beret.

The Best of Enemies (1962, Dino De Laurentiis Cinematografica/Columbia). David Niven, Alberto Sordi, Michael Wilding, Amedeo Nazzari, Harry

Andrews. *Producer* Dino De Laurentiis. *Director* Guy Hamilton. (Original Italian title *I Due Nemici*) Trivia: Rex Harrison's son Noel's film debut – he was billed 11th in the cast.

The Guns of Darkness (1962, Cavalcade/Concorde/A.B.P.C.). Leslie Caron, David Niven, James Robertson Justice, David Opatoshu, Derek Godfrey. *Producers* Ben Kadish, Thomas Clyde. *Director* Anthony Asquith. Trivia: Derek Godfrey was dubbed by Roger Delgado.

The Captive City (1962, Maxima Films/Lux Films/Galatea). David Niven, Ben Gazzara, Michael Craig, Martin Balsam. (US title *The Conquered City*; original Italian title *Le Citta Prigioniera*) Trivia: Cut from its original 108 minutes to 87 for release in the US.

55 Days at Peking (1963, Samuel Bronston). Charlton Heston, David Niven, Ava Gardner, Robert Helpmann, Fora Robson. *Producer* Samuel Bronston. *Director* Nicholas Ray (uncredited: Guy Green, Andrew Marton). Trivia: A Florentine family loaned out to the producer a number of authentic clothes for the Royal Chinese Court which had been rescued from the collapse of the dynasty right after the Boxer Rebellion.

The Pink Panther (1963, Mirisch Company/United Artists). David Niven, Peter Sellers, Robert Wagner, Capucine, Claudia Cardinale. *Producer* Martin Jurow. *Director* Blake Edwards. Trivia: Edwards thought that Claudia Cardinale's Italian accent was too difficult to understand so all her dialogue was dubbed by an anonymous actress.

Bedtime Story (1964, Lankershim/Pennebaker/Universal). Marlon Brando, David Niven, Shirley Jones, Dody Goodman. *Producer* Stanley Shapiro. *Director* Ralph Levy. Trivia: Brando's stand-in was a girl.

Where the Spies Are (1965, MGM). David Niven, Francoise Dorleac, Cyril Cusack, John Le Mesurier, Nigel Davenport. *Producers* Val Guest, Steven Pallos. *Director* Val Guest. Trivia: Niven was unable to master the idiosyncratic gearbox of the Cord 810 and subsequently drove it in bottom gear, resulting in its overheating. The scene was rewritten to work around the problem.

Lady L (1965, Concordia/Champion/MGM). Sophia Loren, Paul Newman, David Niven, Claud Daupin. *Producer* Carlo Ponti. *Director* Peter Ustinov. Trivia: The film was originally intended as a comedy vehicle for

Tony Curtis, Gina Lollobrigida and Sir Ralph Richardson, with George Cukor directing.

Eye of the Devil (1966, Filmways/MGM). Deborah Kerr, David Niven, Donald Pleasance, Edward Mulhare, Flora Robson. *Producers* Martin Ransohoff, John Calley. *Director* J. Lee Thompson. Trivia: Filming began with Kim Novak as the leading lady but when she was injured in a riding accident eight weeks into production she was replaced by Deborah Kerr.

Casino Royale (1967, Famous Artists/Columbia). Peter Sellers, Ursula Andress, David Niven, Orson Welles, Joanna Pettet, Daliah Lavi, Woody Allen, Deborah Kerr, William Holden, Charles Boyer, John Huston. *Producers* Charles K. Feldman, Jerry Bressler. *Directors* John Huston, Ken Hughes, Val Guest, Robert Parrish, Joe McGrath, Richard Talmadge, Anthony Squire. Trivia: For a brief uncredited cameo, Peter O'Toole was paid a case of champagne.

The Extraordinary Seaman (1968, MGM/Frankenheimer/Lewis). David Niven, Faye Dunaway, Alan Alda, Mickey Rooney. *Producer* Edward Lewis. *Director* John Frankenheimer. Trivia: While filming a scene in which Niven falls into the sea, he saw a dorsal fin, yelled, 'Shark!' and refused to get back into the sea for another take. Director Frankenheimer insisted it was a dolphin but Niven took no chances.

Prudence and the Pill (1968, 20th Century-Fox). Deborah Kerr, David Niven, Robert Coote, Irina Demick, Edith Evans. *Producers* Kenneth Harper, Ronald Kahn. *Directors* Fielder Cooks, Ronald Neame. Trivia: Niven wore a watch in the film given to him by Deborah Kerr.

The Impossible Years (1968, Marten Productions/MGM). David Niven, Lola Albright, Chad Everett, Ozzie Nelson, Christina Ferrare, Jeff Cooper. *Producer* Lawrence Weingarten. *Director* Michael Gordon. Trivia: Film debut of 18-year-old Christina Ferrare, later wife of disgraced auto executive John DeLorean. She later gave up acting and became a born-again Christian and TV personality.

Before Winter Comes (1969, Windward/Columbia). David Niven, Topol, Anna Karina, John Hurt, Anthony Quayle. *Producer* Robert Emmett Ginna. *Director* J. Lee Thompson. Trivia: Niven agreed to do the film without reading the script because of his unending gratitude to director J. Lee Thompson for *The Guns of Navarone*.

Le Cerveau (1969, Gaumont International/Dino De Laurentiis). David Niven, Jean-Paul Belmondo, Bourvil, Eli Wallach, Silva Monti. *Producer* Alain Poire. *Director* Gerard Oury. (US & UK title *The Brain*) Trivia: The film was shot in two languages, French and English.

The Statue (1971, Joseph Shaftel/Cinerama International Releasing). David Niven, Virna Lisi, Robert Vaughn, Ann Bell, John Cleese. *Producer* Anis Nohra. *Director* Rodney Amateau. Trivia: Only the head of the statue was modelled on David Niven.

King, Queen, Knave (1974, Maran/Wolper Pictures). Gina Lollobrigida, David Niven, John Moulder Brown, Mario Adorf. *Producer* David L. Wolper. *Director* Jerzy Skolimowski. Trivia: This was a West German/American co-production but was filmed in English only.

Vampira (1975, World Film Services). David Niven, Teresa Graves, Peter Bayliss, Jennie Linden, Nicky Henson, Linda Hayden. *Producer* Jack H. Weiner. *Director* Clive Donner. Trivia: Renamed *Old Dracula* for North American release to cash in on the success of *Young Frankenstein*.

Paper Tiger (1975, Euan Lloyd/MacLean & Co). David Niven, Toshiro Mifune, Hardy Kruger, Ando. *Producer* Euan Lloyd. *Director* Ken Annakin. Trivia: Toshiro Mifune was dubbed by David De Keyser.

The Remarkable Rocket (1975, Potterton/Reader's Digest Films). David Niven, Graham Stark. *Producers* Marvin Kane, Gerald Potterton. *Director* Gerald Potterton. Trivia: Niven recorded the narration in a single day.

No Deposit, No Return (1976, Walt Disney). David Niven, Darren McGavin, Don Knotts, Herschel Bernadi. *Producer* Ron Miller. *Director* Norman Tokar. Trivia: While filming at San Francisco Airport, Niven signed copies of *The Moon's a Balloon* for surprised passengers who had bought the book to read during their flights.

Murder by Death (1976, Columbia/Rastar Pictures). Eileen Brannan, Truman Capote, James Coco, Peter Falk, Alec Guinness, Elsa Lanchester, David Niven, Peter Sellers, Maggie Smith. *Producer* Ray Stark. *Director* Robert Moore. Trivia: The sound of the screaming doorbell was Fay Wray in *King Kong*.

Candleshoe (1977, Walt Disney). David Niven, Helen Hayes, Jodie Foster,

Leo McKern. *Producer* Ron Miller. *Director* Norman Tokar. Trivia: Laurence Olivier was originally sought for Niven's role but turned it down.

Death on the Nile (1978, G.W.Films/Mersham/EMI). Peter Ustinov, Bette Davis, Mia Farrow, Angela Lansbury, David Niven. *Producers* John Brabour, Richard Goodwin. *Director* John Guillermin. Trivia: Filmed aboard the *Memnon*, one of the few paddle steamers remaining on the Nile.

Escape to Athena (1979, ITC/Pimlico Films). Roger Moore, Telly Savalas, David Niven, Claudia Cardinale, Stefanie Powers, Richard Roundtree, Sonny Bono, Elliott Gould, Phillip Locke. *Producers* David Niven Jnr, Jack Wiener. *Director* George Pan Cosmatos. Trivia: Michael Sheard, best known to British TV audiences as Mr Bronson in the British TV series *Grange Hill*, dubbed Phillip Locke.

A Nightingale Sang in Berkeley Square (1979, S Benjamin Fisz Prods). Richard Jordan, Oliver Tobias, David Niven, Elke Sommer. *Producer* Benjamin Fisz. *Director* Ralph Thomas. Trivia: Jean Seberg was offered the female lead in this film but died before filming began.

Rough Cut (1980, David Merrick Prods/Paramount). Burt Reynolds, Lesley-Anne Down, David Niven, Timothy West, Patrick Magee. *Producer* David Merrick. *Director* Don Siegel. Trivia: The script was constantly being revised and for one hastily written scene Reynolds, Down and Niven had to read cue cards.

The Sea Wolves (1980, Lorimar Prods/Richmond Light Horse Prods/Varius Entertainment). Gregory Peck, Roger Moore, David Niven, Trevor Howard, Barbara Kellerman, Patrick Macnee, Patrick Allen. *Producer* Euan Lloyd. *Director* Andrew V. McLaglen. Trivia: Dedicated to Lord Louis Mountbatten who was assassinated by the IRA.

Trail of the Pink Panther (1982, Titan/United Artists/Amjo/Blake Edwards/Lakeline). Peter Sellers, David Niven, Herbert Lom, Richard Mulligan, Joanna Lumley, Capucine. *Producers* Tony Adams, Blake Edwards. *Director* Blake Edwards. Trivia: The author of this book was at the recording of some of the score and had a crash course from Henry Mancini in conducting the *Pink Panther Theme*.

Better Late Than Never (1983, Golden Harvest/Warner Brothers). David

Niven, Art Carney, Maggie Smith, Catherine Hicks, Lionel Jeffries. *Producers* Jack Haley Jnr, David Niven Jnr. *Director* Bryan Forbes. Trivia: Niven sang on screen for the first time, performing Noël Coward's 'I Went to a Marvellous Party'.

Curse of the Pink Panther (1983, Blake Edwards/Titan/Jewel/United Artists). David Niven, Robert Wagner, Herbert Lom, Capucine, Joanna Lumley, Ted Wass. *Producers* Tony Adams, Blake Edwards. *Director* Blake Edwards. Trivia: The film was intended to launch the character of Clifton Sleigh, played by Ted Wass, in a series of new Pink Panther movies, but it was a box office flop.

Television

Nash Airflyte Theatre, episode *Portrait of Lydia*, 1950 *Schlitz Playhouse of Stars*, episode *Not a Chance*, 1951

Celanese Theatre, episode *The Petrified Forest*, 1952

Chesterfield Presents, episode *A Moment of Memory*, 1952

Robert Montgomery Presents, episode *The Sheffield Story*, 1952

Hollywood Opening Night, episodes *Sword Play*, 1952; *Uncle Fred Flits By*, 1953

Four Star Playhouse, episodes *The Island*, 1952; *Man on a Train*, 1953; *No Identity*, 1953; *Night Ride*, 1953; *Finale*, 1953; *A Matter of Advice*, 1953; *For Arti's Sake*, 1953; *A Man of the World*, 1953; *The Bomb*, 1954; *Operation in Money*, 1954; *The Book*, 1954; *Village in the City*, 1954; *Never Explain*, 1954; *Vote of Confidence*, 1954; *Meet a Lonely Man*, 1954; *The Answer*, 1954; *Breakfast in Bed*, 1955; *Tusitala*, 1955; *Henry and the Psychopathic Horse*, 1955; *The Collar*, 1955; *Madeira! Madeira!*, 1955; *Uncle Fred Flits By*, 1955; *Broken Journey*, 1955; *The Firing Squad*, 1955; *Full Circle*, 1955; *Here Comes the Suit*, 1955; *The Thin Line*, 1955; *Tunnel of Fear*, 1956; *Safe Keeping*, 1956; *Red Wine*, 1956; *The Rites of Spring*, 1956; *Touch and Go*, 1956

Mr Adams and Eve, episode *Taming of the Shrew*, 1957

Goodyear Television Playhouse, episode *The Danger by Night*, 1957

Alcoa Theatre, episodes *Circumstantial*, 1957; *In the Dark*, 1958; *The Fatal Charm*, 1958; *Night Caller*, 1958; *My Wife's Next Husband*, 1958

Goodyear Theatre, episodes *The Tinhorn*, 1957; *The Danger by Night*, 1957; *Taps for Jeffrey*, 1958; *Decision by Terror*, 1958

Zane Grey Theatre, episodes *The Accuser*, 1958; *Village of Fear*, 1957

The David Niven Show. Niven introduced the dramas of this anthology but starred in only one of them, *The Last Room,* 1959

The DuPont Show with June Allyson, episode *The Trench Coat,* 1960

Burke's Law, episode *Who Killed Billy Jo?* 1963

The Rogues, episodes *The Personal Touch,* 1964; *The Project Man,* 1964; *Fringe Benefits,* 1964; *Gambit by the Golden Gate,* 1965; *Bless You, G. Carter Huntington,* 1965

The Canterville Ghost 1974

A Man Called Intrepid, mini-series, 1979

Bibliography

Berg, A. Scott, *Goldwyn*, Hamish Hamilton, 1989

Gardner, Ava, *Ava*, Bantam Books, 1990

Garrett, Gerard, *The Films of David Niven*, LSP Books, 1975

Granger, Stewart, *Sparks Fly Upward*, Granada Publishing (UK), 1981

Hawkins, Jack, *Anything for a Quiet Life*, Elm Tree Books, 1973

Herndon, Booton, *Mary Pickford and Douglas Fairbanks*, W.H. Allen, 1977

Higham, Charles, *Errol Flynn The Untold Story*, Granada Publishing, 1980

Korda, Michael, *Charmed Lives*, Random House (US), 1979

Lewis, Roger, *The Life and Death of Peter Sellers*, Century (UK), 1994

Lord, Graham, *Niv*, Orion, 2003

Mills, John, *Up in the Clouds, Gentlemen Please*, George Weidenfeld & Nicolson, 1980

More, Kenneth, *More or Less*, Hodder & Stoughton, 1978

Morley, Sheridan, *The Other Side of the Moon*, George Weidenfeld and Nicolson, 1985

Moseley, Roy, with Philip & Martin Mashetter, *Rex Harrison*, New English Library, 1987

Niven, David, *The Moon's a Balloon*, Hamish Hamilton (UK), 1971

Niven, David, *Bring on the Empty Horses*, Hamish Hamilton (UK), 1975

Norman, Barry, *The Film Greats*, Hodder & Stoughton/BBC, 1985

Siegel, Don, *A Siegel Film*, Faber and Faber, 1993

Ustinov, Peter, *Dear Me*, William Heinemann, 1977

Index